PLAYING CHICKEN
WITH THANATOS

Díre McCain

APOPHENIA

This book is a work of literature, written entirely from the author's point of view, using her preternatural powers of recall. All of the names have been changed, and most of the dates, places, and other identifying details have either been changed or left intentionally vague. Although the author has an exceptional memory, including the useless ability to recite TV commercials she saw at age three, creative license has been taken with some of the dialogue, while remaining true to the gist of each conversation, as well as the characters' personalities.

First published in the world in 2013 by Apophenia

ISBN: 978-0615903156

For the lost and forgotten...

Although it was a solitary journey, I was never alone. Heartfelt thanks and love to Rick Joel, Jim Coleman, Kim Dallesandro, Clive Goheen, Stewart Home, Percy Howard, Darius James, Richard Meade, Bernard Meisler and the rest of the crew at *Sensitive Skin Magazine*, D M Mitchell, Christopher Nosnibor, JG Thirlwell, Nick Tosches, Tony Visconti, Craig Woods, and every other being, deceased and living, who helped bring the book to life by inspiring, encouraging, supporting, and motivating.

PRELUDE

I misspent years struggling to forget an integral chapter of my life, a time I should have been able to reminisce upon with some degree of fondness. Instead, it was a wellspring of grief and self-inflicted shame. In an effort to cope, I renounced my true self, crammed the memories into the deepest, darkest recesses of my mind, and denied that any of it ever occurred. I did so believing it would lead to wellbeing, but it backfired and I became an invalid instead. I don't advocate dwelling on the past, but have learned the hard way that it can't be altered or erased, and attempting to do so can be disastrous. Each day is as essential as the next, and one's experiences – both good and bad – serve as the building blocks for one's character. By hindering the construction or worse yet, leveling the structure altogether, one runs the risk of feeling painfully incomplete.

My entire adolescence was a maelstrom of drug abuse, crime, and self-annihilative behavior. It was not a rebellious or experimental phase. I was an incurable junkie and habitual delinquent. Drugs had seduced and subjugated me before I'd hit puberty. Like an obsessive infatuation, they haunted my conscious and subconscious minds 86,400 seconds a day, dictating my every move. I abandoned my biological family and took up with an ever growing faction of like-minded, equally troubled souls who embraced an anarchistic and transgressive lifestyle. Like every individual, I'm the product of my upbringing, which in my opinion was exceptional in every sense of the word. Unfortunately, when I flew the coop, I left behind one of my most valuable belongings, an intangible that's just as essential for life as any of the vital organs. Although I survived without it, I ultimately fell into a prolonged coma.

On a spring day in 2004, I unexpectedly emerged from that deep state of unconsciousness with my true self restored. Rather than analyzing the how and why, I felt impelled to revisit and dissect the source of the affliction I'd given a chunk of my life to. It began as a form of therapy and soon evolved into a personal panacea, which led to the resurrection of the creative spirit I'd sacrificed years earlier. The upshot is the book you're about to read. Telling the whole tale would have resulted in a tome with a cast of hundreds, so I've limited it to the essential. While there is some degree of chronology, I've focused on substance and continuity instead.

Like all else in life, reading a book is an entirely subjective experience. I have no control over how the story will be perceived, I can only tell it. Having said that, it's not my intention to promote or glorify drug addiction. Having lived the hellish existence of a junkie, I wouldn't recommend it to *anyone*. Yet at the same time, I'm not out to dissuade. I firmly believe in freedom of choice. Human beings have the intrinsic right to make their own decisions, even if one of those decisions is to deliberately poison their bodies, knowing they may prematurely go west and lose all that is near and dear along the way. Bad decision? Arguably, but again, each person's to make.

On a trivial note, the word "normal" will only appear in quotation marks. I haven't the faintest idea what it means to be "normal," but for the purpose of our journey, "normal" will be used to describe what's considered "normal" by people who believe that they're "normal."

One final point before proceeding: I had a vulgar mouth as a kid, as did all of my comrades. In order to accurately portray the characters in the book, I found it necessary to use an abundance of expletives. I'm not apologizing, I'm simply warning you. If you're easily offended by profanity, I suggest you read no further. Otherwise, fasten your fucking seat belt and hold the fuck on…

ACHERON

SIX BUCK

I was born rootless and restless, the youngest child of six, three of each kind. I materialized in Raleigh, North Carolina, USA, and on the eighth day, found myself in Memphis, Tennessee.

The first phase of my life was spent in excruciating discomfort. Midway through the gestation period, my pill-popping mother was stricken with pleurisy and pericarditis. Due to her already delicate condition, she was hospitalized and infused with a cocktail of medications. I arrived late, and the birth itself was long and difficult, but she fought for both of our lives and prevailed. Between her addiction, the illnesses and related treatments, I was afflicted with a number of chronic ailments, including severe intestinal problems that affected my appetite and growth and caused me to scream in agony for months on end. I eventually developed into a healthy toddler, but it's been suggested that the early trauma permanently rewired the circuitry in my brain, and who knows, perhaps there's some validity to that theory.

By age three I was living in Harrisonburg, Virginia, and it was there that my inner hellion came to life. I was recalcitrant and mischievous by nature, and the quintessential tomboy. I truly disliked being female, it felt completely unnatural. And no, I wasn't suffering from Gender Identity Disorder, I simply couldn't relate to girls at all. Although there were some exceptions, I generally found them prissy and boring, and our dissimilar interests didn't help. While they were into dolls and tea sets, I was into Snoopy, mud, and frogs. I also enjoyed eating flowers, paper, crayons, Silly Putty, and Play-Doh. For obvious reasons, the little lambs thought I was weird, which made it difficult to make and keep friends. My mother enrolled me in a handful of girlish activities, hoping I'd find some playmates, but to no avail. The prospective companions wanted nothing to do with me, or I with them. I felt like the lone Socialist in a roomful of Birchers, and it wasn't long before I returned to my solitary existence. I wasn't entirely friendless, though. My brother, who was closest in age, was more than happy to be my pal. In fact, he was one of my best friends until I surrendered to the false gods. Then he was unceremoniously dumped, along with every other member of my biological family. Unless I needed something from them, that is.

As you can imagine, my asocial, insubordinate nature made it nearly impossible to function in most controlled environments, including school, which I hated intensely from day one. So deep was my hatred I routinely refused to attend. It began with preschool and continued for the duration of my compulsory education. Early on, my parents attempted to intervene, but it proved to be frustrating and futile. They ultimately gave in and let me play hooky whenever I chose. I didn't take to the authoritarian atmosphere of a classroom, and the daily dose of ridicule I received from the female students only exacerbated matters. I saw school as an indignity with no redeeming qualities, and was certain I could learn far more on my own. My keen instinct overpowered any sense of obligation, and thankfully, my mother enjoyed having me at home with her.

Conveniently, she was running a daycare center out of our house, while my father taught full-time at James Madison University and served one weekend per month as a Naval Reservist. By economic standards their combined income was decent, but in truth, it was barely sufficient. Children are expensive, and my parents should have stopped after four, because they were already strapped. I won't hyperbolize, we weren't poverty-stricken, starving, and living in a car, but definitely struggled to make ends meet. With the exception of Christmas and birthdays, my siblings and I went without nonessentials. New clothes were rarely in the budget either. Our wardrobes consisted mostly of hand-me-downs, bargain-basement duds, and homemade garments, some of which were shabby, stained, and downright hideous. In Harrisonburg no one thought much of it. It was an unassuming and idyllic place that suited our family perfectly, but our time there was to be short-lived.

It was on a spring day that my father received a promising job offer at California State University of Long Beach, which he eagerly accepted. After making all the arrangements, we pulled up stakes and headed west. Ten days and several stops later, we pulled into the driveway of our new residence.

Since a Southern California home was way out of my parents' price range, they'd settled for a modest, single-story, four-bedroom rental on the east side of Long Beach, the second largest city in Los Angeles County.

After eight months of living in cramped quarters, my mother happened upon an uncared-for, two-story, five-bedroom rental in an area about five miles away. The place was an eyesore, and on the cusp of being uninhabitable. It looked as though it hadn't been *cleaned* in years, let alone renovated. The paint was faded and peeling, the carpet soiled and threadbare, the tile and counters chipped and grimy, the asphalt driveway cracked and riddled with potholes, both yards were impenetrable jungles, and if that weren't enough, the property was teeming with rodents, inside and out. On the positive side, the house was large enough to accommodate us, the rent was affordable, and the neighborhood was safe. The stingy, negligent owners refused to spring for an exterminator, but did pay for new carpet, paint, and tile, except my parents were stuck doing the labor. Once the rattrap was relatively livable, my mother went back to work as a nurse, while my father began teaching part-time at three other schools, in addition to his full-time job and Naval Reserve obligations.

It wasn't long before my parents' already strained marriage began to rapidly deteriorate. The inevitable showdown occurred merely days before my birthday, and in my young mind I mistakenly believed I was somehow to blame. In reality, it was a desperate attempt by my father to save his mind before it was lost along with my mother's, and for my mother it was an equally desperate attempt to regain a semblance of control.

The five kids who were still at home remained with my mother while my father found an apartment in a nearby neighborhood. My parents had known each other since adolescence, and remained civil for the sake of their children, but it was clear they'd never reconcile. I think they both wanted to work it out, but my mother was incapable of even trying. She'd been plagued by chronic, debilitating depression, and unpredictable bouts of violent rage since arriving in California. When the blue devils hadn't confined to her bed, she'd unleash her fury by throwing around furniture and whatever else she could get her hands on, while shouting and sobbing for hours on end. Needless to say, it was horribly upsetting and at times frightening, but so routine my siblings and I became somewhat inured.

My mother also attempted suicide on three occasions, but unlike many attempters, who are merely "crying out for help," she was intent on dying and came dangerously close to succeeding, particularly on the final attempt when she flatlined. On the second and third attempts, some of her children and their friends were nearly taken along with her, when she swallowed a lethal amount of sleeping pills before getting behind the wheel of the family van. In addition to her undiagnosed mental disorder, she'd been addicted to prescription amphetamines and barbiturates for most of her adult life, and had finally reached a point where she wanted to get off the roller coaster once and for all. In her tormented mind she was already dead and nothing could resuscitate her, not even the love of her children. At the time I was too young and naïve to understand why she'd want to take her own life, I only knew that she couldn't die because I needed her. Even though her volatility was a major mindfuck that could be devastating at times, she was still my Mommy, and the thought of my world without her in it was terrifying. I can remember visiting her in the psychiatric ward and begging her to come home. I was afraid they'd lock her away forever and I'd never see her again. My fear intensified with each attempt, and by the third, I began to question her motives. I never doubted her love for my siblings and me, but couldn't help wondering if the responsibility was too much. I also wondered what would have happened if we'd stayed in Virginia. It seemed as though the whole world crumbled when we came to California. My mother was angry, despondent, and suicidal, my father was worried, frustrated, and stressed-out, both were overworked and exhausted, and when all was said and done, our once endearingly dysfunctional family was now shattered beyond repair. I felt helpless, frightened, and lost, as though I'd been parachuted into the depths of a dense, shadowy forest with only the clothes on my back. I wasn't equipped with the skills to find my way out, so I curled up into a ball and buried my face in my arms, hoping someone would come along and save me, but it never happened. It wasn't anyone's fault.

Perhaps if I'd stood up and screamed for help, someone would have heard, but I was petrified. I eventually learned to deal with the situation by pretending it wasn't real. I also barricaded myself behind a thick wall of artificial stoicism, where I'd remain for many years. I found that denial and detachment were by far the most effective coping mechanisms, but each carried a hefty price tag.

My father was diligent about paying child support and had full visitation rights, but his busy work schedule ate most of his time. I typically saw him once a week, if that, and even though I was living with her, I rarely saw my mother either. Again, kids aren't cheap, and the cost of living in Southern California has always been astronomical. We probably had no business moving there in the first place, but it was too late to retreat. Survival was the only option, which meant my parents had to work as much as they could. When they were around, the older kids looked after my brother and me, but for the most part, he and I were left to fend for ourselves. We fed ourselves, did our own laundry, got ourselves to and from school, etc. It was a considerable amount of responsibility, but we didn't mind, because it made us feel grown-up. The lack of supervision also allowed us to indulge in a favorite pastime with minimal interference. Both of us had a seemingly inborn craving for danger, and dreamed of becoming stunt performers. Whether it was jumping off the roof onto a mattress, riding down the stairs in a sleeping bag, or catching a treacherously humungous wave, as long as the activity involved a high level of risk, we'd do it. In hindsight, I suspect we both suffered from a serious behavioral malady. Throughout it all, my brother only fractured his arm, but I was far less fortunate. By age eleven, I'd broken my nose, cracked open my head directly above my right eye, snapped my right clavicle in two, fractured my left arm in several places, damaged a growth plate in my left leg, broken two fingers on my left hand, sliced open my left cornea, nearly severed my left pinky toe, fractured my coccyx twice, and sprained both ankles a few times each. Not bad, for a girl.

I wasn't merely a hyperactive adrenaline junkie, though. I was also a voracious reader and prolific writer. Besides being one of my favorite hobbies, reading was a means of escapism that could extricate me from the brutally real and often complicated world in which I dwelled. The first book I ever read was *Fraidy Cat* by Sara Asheron, and I wrestled angrily with it for weeks. My father used to tell me to relax, that reading was supposed to be fun, not exasperating, and in time I'd be outreading every kid in Harrisonburg. But I was impatient, compulsive, and stubbornly determined. I took that damn book wherever I went, and once I did get the hang of it, I embarked on an endless binge. When I didn't have my nose planted in a book, I was busy creating my own literary masterworks, many of which I still have. The first was a novella called *Black* that told the "lachrymose" tale of a black cat named Henry who was ostracized by the feline community because of his color. Writing had an incredibly therapeutic effect. It not only gave me a sense of wellbeing, but also made me feel productive, so I set aside time every week to work on my projects. Having no parental discipline was a blessing in that I had plenty of free time to explore my interests.

It's difficult to believe, but apparently, my mother was once quite strict. It wasn't until my brother and I came along that her attitude toward child rearing changed. I'm not sure if she was sick and tired of being a parent, or in the throes of a midlife crisis, but by the time the family landed in California, she'd become more of a buddy than an authority figure. Although it was certainly detrimental in some ways, it was also beneficial, particularly for the older four. While the girls were nonentities at school, the boys were both big men on campus with an army of friends who, much to my mother's delight, frequented our home, as though it were a tavern, or better yet, a frat house, complete with all the usual hedonistic activities. While it may sound like a horribly unhealthy environment for a child, my memories are only fond, probably because everyone seemed happy, including my mother.

Amid the debauchery, I developed an addiction to music and cinema, both of which played a vital role in my upbringing. My father was a musician, and my mother a music lover. I was exposed to an eclectic variety from the moment I was conceived. The same went for cinema, and aside from the feature-length Disney cartoons, I saw no more than a handful of family-oriented films as a child, which was fine with me. After tasting the other varieties, the kiddy flicks seemed bland in comparison. The small-screen fare was equally "mature," for lack of a better word. While most girls my age were watching *National Velvet*, I was immersed in Russ Meyer's *Harry, Cherry, & Raquel!* Like literature, I found temporary escape in cinema, and when the weekends rolled around, I'd affix myself to the boob tube for hours at a time, soaking up pictures from nearly every genre and era, as well as a variety of syndicated television shows. Thanks to the tutelage of my oldest sister, I was also an Alfred Hitchcock aficionado. My first Hitch flick was *Psycho*, and it's still my favorite, with *Rear Window* coming in a close second. I was barely seven when I made the acquaintance of Norman Bates. While the film scared the hell out of me, I was left utterly intrigued and hungry for more. In the years that followed I watched every feature that was aired on television, and when a portion of Hitchcock's oeuvre was rereleased into theaters, my sister took me to see the whole lot. On the opposite end of the spectrum was Elvis Presley. I've been a devout fan since birth. Even when it was not "cool" to like him, my loyalty remained unwavering. I've never been one of those rabid nutcases who view him as the second coming of Christ. In fact, I have to yet to visit Graceland. I simply respect him as a performer, and as dreadful as most of them are, I've always dug his movies, they make me feel good, which was precisely what I needed as a kid. Throughout my childhood, there were two enduring fantasies that never failed to pull my sometimes dejected mind out of the abyss:

running away with the Marx Brothers and being adopted by Elvis Presley.

I had one other interest that was peculiar for a little girl: I was fascinated with boxing. I watched my first fight at age seven. Since I was viewing it through a child's eyes, the technicalities of the sport went right over my head. I had no idea why these men were clobbering each other, and was even more perplexed by the audience's enthusiasm. After seeing more bouts, I not only caught on, but became so obsessed with the sport I began making references to it in my elementary school writing assignments, which went over fabulously with the teachers.

As you can see, I was not a "normal" child. I'm not implying that I was better or worse, I simply marched to a different drummer, and that drummer happened to take after Keith Moon.

I was in fifth grade when my unusual predilections led to some trouble. The class was assigned a book report, and the students were instructed to read a biography on someone they admired. My classmates opted for the usual suspects: George Washington, Walt Disney, Helen Keller, and the like. Fully believing that I was following the instructions as given, I chose *No One Here Gets Out Alive*, which I'd received as a gift from my sister. My teacher, who I'll call Mrs. McGillicutty, was not pleased. She left a note on my desk that read: *"Re your book report: See me after class."*

I hadn't the faintest idea what I'd done, and wasn't too anxious to find out. When the bell rang, I tried to sneak out, but she caught me at the door.

"We have a serious problem, young lady" she said, leading me over to her desk. "I want you to sit down right now."

"What?" I asked, plopping down onto the chair and crossing my arms. "I did the assignment right, didn't I?"

"Yes, you did," she replied, "but there was nothing admirable about Jim Morrison. He was a horrible, horrible man."

"Says who?" I asked smartly.

"Do not give me any lip, or I will send you directly to the principal's office," she said, tossing my report into the garbage can. "I want you to choose a more appropriate person and redo the assignment."

"Why?"

"Because I said so."

"But that's not fair!" I protested. "I like Jim Morrison, and the book report is supposed to be about someone I like!"

"I do not wish to discuss it any further," she said curtly.

"How about Montgomery Clift?" I asked, after stewing in silence for a moment. "I just finished reading his biography the other day."

"Montgomery Clift was an alcoholic and a homosexual," she replied in a condescending tone.

"So what?" I retorted. "Your husband is a crossdresser."

Yes, I actually said that, and it was tame when compared to some of the other utterances I spit out impulsively and liberally.

"That is quite enough, young lady!" she gasped. "That sort of talk may be allowed in your home, but I will not tolerate it in my classroom!"

I stuck my tongue out at her.

"Stop that right now," she said sternly. "This behavior cannot go on any longer. No matter how many times I discipline you, you continue to act up. I do not know if you are starving for attention or in need of psychiatric help, but I intend to find out." She removed a note pad from the top drawer and wrote a letter of summons. "You are to give this to your mother as soon as you see her," she said, shoving the paper into my hand. "You can go now."

Two days later, when my mother and I met with McGillicutty, the first words out of the schoolmarm's mouth were: "There is something seriously wrong with your daughter. I strongly recommend that you seek counseling for her before it is too late."

"There's not a thing wrong with her," my mother said, after taking a moment to analyze the allegation, "and I'm offended by the implication, you make it sound as though she's retarded."

McGillicutty was shocked, and so was I. My mother had never argued with any of my teachers before.

"I know all about the book report, and I don't see what the problem is. She was told to choose someone she admired, and that's exactly what she did."

"Yes, I understand that," McGillicutty argued, "but it is inappropriate for a fifth-grader to admire someone such as Jim Morrison."

"I disagree," my mother said, "and I also disagree with your pedantic teaching methods."

Pardon the interruption, but I have to agree. I've always viewed our nations' primary and secondary schools as indoctrination factories that discourage independent thought, and drain youngsters of their individuality. In my opinion, children should be taught to explore and express themselves rather than assimilate and conform.

"I will have you know that I follow the standard curriculum for fifth-grade students to the letter," McGillicutty said in an offended tone, "the same curriculum I have been following for many years now."

"Maybe that's the problem," I interjected. "It's the 1980s, not the 1880s."

My mother ordered me to be quiet.

"I have not had any complaints thus far," McGillicutty argued.

"Well, she's not going to redo the assignment," my mother said firmly. "She worked very hard on that report, and I think she should be commended, not punished." Then she paused for a moment and continued, "Besides, she can't help it if she's brighter than her peers. You need to learn to accept it."

Bright? Hardly. Restless, bored, preoccupied, desperate for attention, and heavily influenced by my erratic home life and rich cinematic diet would be more accurate. I was continually penalized for tardiness, excessive absences, truancy, disrupting the class, using foul language, talking out of turn, disobeying orders, and nearly every other violation in the book. I was a holy terror if there ever was one, and spent a good deal of time sitting in the corner and at the principal's office. I didn't realize how bad it was until I revisited my school records, which thankfully, my mother saved. It's miraculous I made it through kindergarten, never mind high school.

I detested school for a number of reasons, including the incessant teasing I endured from day one, which worsened significantly when I entered the Southern California system. In Harrisonburg the girls had picked on me because I was odd, but never because of my physical appearance. In the Wicked West, it was a different and more venomous story. I was told day after day that I was an ugly, grody, weird, white trash loser. The malicious snobs made fun of my cheap outdated clothes, my unkempt hair, my lingering hick twang, my curved pinky fingers, my banana-seated, whitewall-tired, metallic grape bicycle, my fascination with cemeteries, my obsession with Led Zeppelin, the "abnormal" way I held my pencil and wrote my capital Ts... the list went on and on. I always fought back both verbally and physically, but the bitches outnumbered me tenfold, leaving me no choice but to retreat. I was familiar with the old adage, *Sticks and stones may break my bones, but words will never hurt me,"* but thought it was a false platitude. Let's face it, words do indeed hurt, just as much if not more, and I think anyone who's been subjected to incessant teasing would agree. It's not only painful at the time, but can also scar you for life. I'm not sure if I was permanently scarred, but my trust in the female gender was definitely impaired. I couldn't understand why those girls despised me so. I never did them any wrong. Or so I thought. Apparently, being a broke, unfashionable misfit was criminally offensive and merited punishment.

DUMBERT KUMBERT

The maliciousness continued when I entered middle school, as I knew it would, except the number of tormentors had multiplied significantly, which can be expected when you move from a fishbowl into a pond. Even though my feelings toward school hadn't changed, I began attending more regularly when I reached seventh grade. My reason was quite simple: I had a new best friend named Sydney, who'd recently moved to the area. On her first day, I'd volunteered to show her around campus, and before long, we were doing everything together, including things we shouldn't have been doing. I'd finally found a partner in crime, so to speak. You see, up until this point, the handful of girl pals I did have were fairly innocent and sensible. I, however, craved action, which typically meant trouble for whoever was with me. While my other girlfriends wanted no part of it, Sydney was game for just about anything. It was on a Sunday afternoon, at the local bowling alley, that I broached the subject of smoking – giving it a whirl, more specifically.

"Do you ever think about trying cigarettes?" I asked casually, as she attempted to beat my Galaga score.

"Sometimes," she replied, concentrating intently on her game. "Why, do you?"

"All the time."

"How come you don't then?"

"I just haven't gotten around to it yet."

One of my all-time favorite answers, by the way.

"Do you want to try them right now?" I asked, glancing over at the unattended vending machine. "Because I can get some from the machine. No one's watching it."

"I guess so," she replied hesitantly. "I mean, if you want to."

That was all I needed to hear. I sauntered on over, dropped five quarters into the slot, and selected a pack of Benson and Hedges Menthol 100s. Sydney was now standing next to me.

"How come you bought the mint ones?" she asked with a confused look on her face.

"They're supposed to taste better," I said confidently, "and they're easier on the throat too."

I don't know where the hell I got that idea, but it sounded logical, and sure enough, Sydney agreed. "Oh, okay," she said, smiling and nodding, "that makes sense."

After grabbing a book of matches from the snack bar, we slipped out to the back parking lot, and chain smoked until the pack was half empty. As expected, violent coughing fits ensued that gradually subsided with each subsequent puff.

"Do you feel like ice cream?" I asked, extinguishing cigarette number ten in the sand-top ash receptacle.

"Sure," she replied, pointing toward the bicycle racks with her thumb. "Should we walk or ride our bikes?"

Thrifty Drug Store was on the other side of the shopping center, and when it came to ice cream, I required instant gratification.

"I'm pretty hungry," I said, yawning and scratching my head, "and bikes are faster."

As we pedaled along, Sydney asked a question that seemed reasonable in light of our latest transgression. "Have you ever been drunk?"

"No," I replied, glancing over at her, "but I've had booze before."

"You have?" she asked, glancing back at me.

"Yeah, my mom used to give me margaritas, before she quit drinking."

"She did?"

"Uh-huh, but they were really small, and barely had any tequila in them."

"Didn't they taste yucky, though?"

"No, they were yummy, actually."

"They were?"

"Yeah, she used to blend strawberries and whipped cream into the mix, like a Julius."

"Mmmmm, that does sound yummy."

After wolfing down triple-scoop cones on the bench outside the store, we returned to the bowling alley parking lot and finished off the cigarettes.

Two weeks and a hundred coffin nails later, I was officially hooked on nicotine, smoking up to a pack a day. My addiction would eventually be brought to an abrupt and permanent halt by a nasty case of tonsillitis, but I'm getting ahead of myself.

My friendship with Sydney continued to blossom, until the day came when it was put to the ultimate test. It was a mild Sunday afternoon. As was common, I'd been invited over to her place for a swim. She lived in a townhouse complex with a community pool, which we took full advantage of, no matter what the weather.

When I arrived, her father, Dave, answered the door. Out of all my girlfriends' fathers, Dave was easily my favorite. He was considerably less strict and far more approachable. I always felt comfortable in his presence, and the fact that he bore a striking resemblance to Frank Zappa made him even cooler.

"Hey, kiddo," he said, smiling warmly. "Syd's in her bedroom, she's been waiting for you."

"What are you up to?" I asked, walking in and letting the screen door slam behind me.

"Not much," he replied, cracking open the can of beer he was holding, "just enjoying the day off."

"Cool," I said, following him into the kitchen.

"I'm waiting for Elvira to start," he laughed, placing his beer on the counter, and tearing open a bag of potato chips. "I sure get a kick out of her."

"She's pretty cool, isn't she?"

"Easy on the eyes too."

"Got any root beer?" I asked, opening the refrigerator.

"I picked up a six-pack just for you," he said, dumping the chips into a plastic bowl. "Help yourself."

I did just that, then walked out of the kitchen and over to Sydney's bedroom.

"It's me," I yelled, knocking on the door.

"Come on in," she yelled back.

When I entered the room, she was leaning over the bed, placing some items into a tote sack.

"Do you have any smokes?" she asked, looking up at me.

I removed a fresh pack from the right pocket of my zip-up hoodie and tossed it onto the bed.

"Cool," she said, throwing it in with the other paraphernalia. "Are you ready then?"

"Yeah, just let me go pee real quick."

"Okay, I'll meet you out back," she said, pointing toward the dresser. "Can you grab the boom box?"

"Yeah, I got it. Be there in a sec."

We splashed around in the pool for a while, then gathered up our gear and headed back to her place for a warm shower. As we walked through the front door Dave called out to us from the kitchen.

"Is that you, girls?"

"Yeah, Dad," Sydney replied.

"Hope you're hungry. I'm making tuna melts and tomato soup."

"We're famished," I said. "I hope you're making them with cheddar."

"Yeah," Sydney added, "are you, Dad?"

"Of course," he laughed, "you girls have trained me well. None of that grody processed American shit around here."

He only swore in front of us when he was drunk. Sydney and I looked at each other and started to giggle.

"Why don't you go ahead and get cleaned up. The chow'll be ready in twenty or less."

"Thanks, Dad! I love you!"

"Love you too, Pumpkin!"

Being partial to the shower in Sydney's bathroom, I made a mad dash for it, forcing her to use the master bathroom, which was located upstairs. Yes, it was a bit selfish on my part, but I viewed showering as a sacred act that's done out of ardent love, not necessity, and the hotter the water, the better. Incidentally, my feelings haven't changed.

Approximately twenty minutes later, I emerged from the fiberglass temple, dried myself off, and wrapped the damp towel around my body, like a sarong. The windowless room was now permeated with blinding steam, a common occurrence due to the temperature and length of my showers. I opened the hatch to release the humid mist, and lo and behold, there was Dave teetering over the threshold, looking slightly disheveled. At first I thought he'd gotten into a scrap with one of the neighbors, until I got a solid whiff of him. His entire body reeked of beer, as though he'd been bathing in it rather than drinking it, and his breath was so pungent I had to turn my face to keep from gagging.

"Hi there," he slurred.

I did not like his countenance, it was terribly unsettling. I was practically naked, and he was eyeing me carnivorously, as though I were a juicy slab of prime rib. I tried to close the door, but he wedged his elongated foot in between it and the jamb, leaving it ajar.

"What are you doing?" I asked confusedly, looking up at him.

"Nothing," he replied, leaning forward and smiling. "Just wanted to tell you the chow's ready."

"Okay," I said, hiding behind the door, which was now more than ajar. "Can you move your foot? I'm not decent."

"Now why do you say that?" he asked in a suggestive tone. "You're more than decent."

I was instantly overcome by a wave of acute consternation that ebbed as quickly as it had risen. I knew deep down what he was insinuating, but it was too implausible to be true.

"What do you mean?" I asked.

Nothing would ever prepare me for what happened next.

He pushed open the door and stumbled into the bathroom, nearly knocking me down in the process.

"You're so pretty," he sighed, placing his hand on my face, "I have to touch you."

It was so unimaginably sickening and surreally shocking I couldn't react, verbally or otherwise.

He mistook my temporary paralysis for compliance, and moved in on me.

"Is it okay if I hold you?" he asked, grabbing my arms and pulling me toward him.

Reality kicked in the moment he touched me, and I immediately shifted into fight-or-flight mode.

"No, it's not okay!" I yelled, trying vainly to push him away. "Get your hands off me!"

"Shhhh," he whispered, "it's okay. I just want to hold you for a little while. Promise I won't hurt you."

"No, it's not okay!" I reiterated, still trying to push him away.

I continued to shove him, but he wouldn't budge, so I stomped on his foot.

He took a step back, and moved in on me again. Only this time, he started tugging at my towel.

"Leave me alone!" I yelled, securing the towel with one hand and fending him off with the other.

"Shhhh, shhhh," he said calmly. "You don't have to be afraid."

"I'm not afraid!" I growled, hiding behind a façade of courage. "Just get your fucking hands off me! Now!"

I'd never been more frightened, but knew damn well that admission would only lead to defeat. Unfortunately, he saw right through my brave posturing, and started snickering, as though he were mocking me. I wanted to cry, but glared at him instead, hoping it would intimidate him, which it didn't. In fact, it only seemed to encourage him.

He cupped my warm face in his clammy hands, and gazed into my eyes lecherously, as though I were a runaway junkie prostitute he'd picked up along Beach Boulevard and planned to sodomize.

"You're different than Syd's other friends," he whispered with a wicked smile. "So grown-up and pretty, and you have the body of a woman, not a girl. I've always liked you, I thought you knew?"

I looked up at the ceiling.

He let out a deep sigh, then placed his hands on my hips and continued, "Just let me hold you for a little while, and I promise I'll let you go."

I impulsively dug my fingernails into his filthy paws as hard as I could.

"Ouch!" he yelped, pulling them away and recoiling. "If I didn't know better, I'd think you were trying to hurt me!"

"I am!" I screamed. "And if you don't stop touching me, I'll fucking kill you!"

He began to cachinnate sinisterly.

I hoped that Sydney would hear the racket, but the whistling sound of the water pipes was echoing through the walls around me, clearly indicating that she was still showering.

Panic set in, and swallowed me whole. I could feel my heart throbbing behind my sternum as my lungs struggled to respire.

Dave sensed that I was terror-stricken, and began shaking his head in what appeared to be amusement. Then he placed his hand under my mandible, gently lifted my chin, and looked deep into my fearful eyes. "What's the matter?" he asked, grinning lewdly. "Don't you like me anymore? I thought you liked me too?"

I closed my eyes and didn't respond.

"I've seen the way you look at me. "You're a dirty little nymph. I bet you've already had sex with lots of boys."

I knew exactly what he was implying, and it rattled me to the point of nausea. Even more disturbing, he said it with such conviction I almost believed it myself. I opened my eyes and glared at him, but remained silent, which annoyed him tremendously.

"You think I'm stupid?" he snapped. "I know all about girls like you! You send out all kinds of signals, and then act surprised when a guy picks up on them! Well, I've had it with your little games!"

I was now at a total loss as to what I should do. He was bigger, stronger, and far more aggressive. I feared that he'd seriously harm me if I didn't cooperate. As impossible as it was to accept, I was completely at his mercy. I had no choice but to resign myself to the nightmarish reality that my best friend's father was going to molest me. I wondered how far he would take it. Would he merely fondle me? Or brutally rape me? The very thought of the latter possibility nearly caused me to faint.

Then, right at that moment, the following words came spilling out of my quivering mouth: "You'd better let me go or I'll call the cops on you."

Why I didn't think of it sooner, I'll never know, and I suppose it doesn't matter. All that mattered was that it worked. Animals are inherently terrified of cages, and this animal was no exception. His countenance changed instantly from that of an aggressive predator to that of a spineless coward.

"Oh no, oh no, don't, don't, don't, there's no need to do that," he stammered, stepping aside, "here, here, go ahead, I was only playing around."

I bolted out of the room, and scrambled up the stairs, nearly losing my towel along the way.

Once inside the master bedroom, I slammed the door closed and locked it.

Seconds later, Sydney emerged from the bathroom in her underwear, with her hair turbaned in a towel. Looking at her, I wondered how I could possibly say what I was about to say. For a moment,

I contemplated not saying anything at all. But what if he did it again? Tomorrow, the next day, or a month from now? I also contemplated disappearing until it all blew over, but had a strong suspicion that it would *never* blow over. How on earth could it?

"Your dad just made a pass at me," I blurted out with my head down, far too ashamed to look her in the face.

"What?" she asked incredulously.

"Your dad just made a pass at me," I repeated.

"Are you sure?"

"Positive."

"What did he do?" she asked dubiously, as though she were hoping it was merely a misunderstanding or perhaps a figment of my vivid imagination.

"He tried to pull off my towel," I said bluntly, "and he..."

She interjected before I could finish, which was fine. Elaboration wasn't necessary, it was already horrific enough.

"Oh my god!" she gasped.

A choking lump swelled up in my throat. I forced it down into my gut, and struggled to ignore the feelings of fear, anguish, and humiliation that were overrunning my limbic system.

"I have to get out of here," I mumbled.

Sydney didn't react.

"I have to get out of here," I repeated, in a more audible tone.

"I'll come with you," she said, staring blankly at the wall in front of her, "lemme comb my hair."

She began working out the tangles methodically, appearing to be in a daze, while I sat on the edge of her parents' bed, so overwhelmed with confused anxiety I was trembling. I couldn't fathom why Dave would have done something so atrocious, and couldn't help wondering whether his actions were premeditated or spur-of-the-moment. I also wondered if I *had* tempted him in some way. Had I been too outgoing with him? Maybe he thought I was coming on to him. I'd noticed that he was constantly looking at me, but had assumed that it was perfectly innocent. After all, he was Sydney's middle-aged father, I was her prepubescent friend – he couldn't possibly be attracted to me, could he?

"Okay," Sydney said, interrupting my distressing train of thought, "let's go."

We tiptoed down the stairs and into her bedroom, then got dressed, and crept past Dave, who was now snoring on the couch.

In hindsight, it boggles my mind that he was able to fall asleep so easily merely minutes after attempting to molest a child, which to me, indicates a complete lack of conscience. It also makes me wonder whether I was his first and only victim, or if there were others. It hadn't occurred to me until now, but perhaps that was why the family had left New England and come to California.

Sydney and I rode our bikes over to the local park, sat down under a sprawling, thick-trunked tree, and began discussing our possible courses of action. As expected, she was mortified, and didn't want anyone to know what her father had done.

Whether or not she actually believed it, she'd convinced herself that it was a harmless little misstep, an isolated incident that would never be repeated if we kept our lips buttoned.

"I don't think we should tell anyone!" she pleaded. "He only did it because he was drunk! He won't do it again!"

I sympathized with her deeply, but her dear old dad was obviously a sick fuck who needed therapy, or castration, or perhaps euthanasia.

"But he really scared me!" I argued. "I'm not saying that we should tell the cops, but we have to tell our moms!"

"We can't!" she begged, tugging on my sleeve. "Please!"

"We have to! I don't ever want him touching me like that again! And what if he does it to someone else?"

"He won't!"

"How do you know?"

She buried her face in her hands, and began to weep. "I don't want my dad to get in trouble!" she sobbed. "And I don't want anyone to know what he did!"

"But it was wrong!" I said, fighting off the tears that were welling up in my eyes. "We have to tell our moms!"

"We can't!" she repeated over and over again.

It was hands down one of the most stressful, agonizing moments of my entire life. Sydney and I were just little girls, who hadn't even begun to menstruate yet, and here we were arguing about her depraved father's (secret?) pedophiliac compulsion. We sat there under that tree for two interminable hours, but never reached an agreement. Sydney was adamantly against the idea of telling anyone, while I was bound and determined to tell as many people as I could, starting with my mother.

As the sun completed its descent, my best friend and I parted ways. She returned home to face god knows what, while I raced back to my dump, now in tears, hoping someone would be there to console me. My mother was working until eleven, but surely one of my sisters would be around.

By the time I arrived at my house, I was sobbing convulsively. I abandoned my bicycle on the front lawn, rammed the key into the hole, and tore open the door, only to discover an empty house. I was all alone, horribly confused, and scared to death. In the back of my highly imaginative and often paranoid mind, I feared that Dave might show up to finish what he'd started.

I picked up the telephone, and began dialing my mother's work, but Sydney's desperate plea kept reverberating in my spinning head. When I'd left the park I was resolved to tell my mother right away, but was now having second thoughts. After all, it was a major decision to make. Once the cat was out of the bag there was no turning back, and I had to be able to live with whatever ensued. I placed the telephone back on the receiver, then picked it up and called my friend Linda.

Linda was one of my closest pals throughout sixth and seventh grade. She came from a strong and stable Mexican family that was remarkably functional. They even ate dinner together every night, which was unheard of in my household. Her parents were extraordinarily kind, and treated me as though I were their fourth child. They cooked for me, entertained me, bought me gifts, and even took me to my first live show, at the now-defunct Dancing Waters in San Pedro, which would eventually become an occasional haunt. Their casa was my haven, my home away from home. I'd spend hours, sometimes days there, fantasizing about them adopting me all the while.

The instant I heard Linda's voice I broke down.

"What's wrong?" she asked. "Are you okay?"

I mumbled a couple of incoherent sentences.

"I can't understand you," she said. "Hold on, I'm gonna get my mom."

"No, wait!" I sobbed. "Let me tell you what happened."

I was having serious doubts about incriminating Dave – all fueled by the possible aftermath – but needed to unload on someone before I cracked. After regaining my composure, I related an explicit account, making certain not to omit one detail, no matter how awkward or appalling. I knew Dave could be criminally charged, and possibly end up behind bars. Therefore, I needed to be positive that I hadn't misinterpreted his actions, and if I hadn't, that I wasn't overreacting.

Linda's reaction confirmed what I already knew.

"Oh my god!" she yelled, dropping the phone. "Don't hang up!"

After hearing the story, her mother insisted that I come over at once, and offered to pick me up. I didn't object.

My mother arrived at Linda's door within the hour, took me home, and wasted no time in calling Sydney's mother. After a lengthy telephone conversation, which I was not privy to, my mother agreed to keep the police out of it. Apparently, Sydney's mother begged for leniency, and promised she'd take the appropriate action. She kept her word, but her idea of "appropriate" was quite different from mine.

She kicked her execrable spouse to the curb that night, and filed for separation shortly thereafter, but the "reparative punishment" did nothing to mend the gaping, raw, gangrenous wound that had been left. At the time, and for many months to follow, I felt guilty. Not only about the incident itself, but the breakup as well, and whenever I saw Sydney, I was asphyxiated with self-reproach. Because of me, her family was now a statistic. If I hadn't been there that day, her parents would still be together. I truly believed that, and it ripped out my last scintilla of innocence. To add insult to injury, Linda was forbidden to see me, and I was barred from the one place I found serenity. I'm sure her parents were only trying to protect her, but I was convinced that they blamed me entirely, and was left feeling like a leper, or worse yet, a home-wrecking Lolita.

I've never been one to feel sorry for myself. Some people seem to get off on it, but in my opinion, self-pity is a weak, contemptible emotion, and wallowing in it only impedes the healing process. That said, I think it's fair to say that the two-ton load of unsolicited shame and guilt would be an incredibly onerous burden for *any* child to shoulder.

As expected, my friendship with Sydney was irreparably damaged, and within weeks, kaput, as though it had never existed. Linda's parents eventually lifted the ban, but my relationship with their daughter would never be the same. We became increasingly more distant, and ultimately stopped speaking altogether.

This entire ordeal – both the inexcusable crime and torturous aftermath – psychologically mangled me, and I never attempted to heal the wound. I simply poured antiseptic on it, bandaged it up, and ignored it for years. This is the first time I've recounted the nightmare in such painstaking detail, and by doing so, I've realized that I'm still furious with this motherfucker. I've managed to release most of the pain, but cannot, and *will not* shake off the justifiable indignation. Yes, I know that harboring anger can be counterproductive, but it's been my experience that granting someone undeserved absolution has no curative effect whatsoever, and I take great umbrage at being told otherwise. It's easy to be an armchair adviser, and just as easy to have a change of heart once you've been directly or indirectly subjected to whatever it is you're opining about. There is an *immense* difference between forgiving and forgetting. For the most part, I've chosen to forget, simply because this maggot is not worthy of renting space in my overcrowded cerebrum. However, I can say with absolute certainty that I will *never* forgive him. With one heinous act, he emotionally maimed half a dozen people, including his three young children, and caused an incalculable amount of irreversible damage. In my penal code book, that's a capital offense.

If anyone *ever* did this to my kid, I'd hang him by his balls from a rusty meat hook, skin him alive with a dull butter knife, and pour salt onto his exposed flesh. And Dave, I still have a score to settle with you, you vile piece of shit. Thanks to the miracle of modern technology, I also know where to find you, you fucking pedophile. If you're a religious man, you'd better pray that our paths never cross.

TWIG

Shortly before the attempted molestation, I'd made the acquaintance of a girl named Minnie, who would be the catalyst for the next phase of my life. She was a year older and when compared to me, financially well-off. It was her innovative sense of style that first caught my eye. While her clothing was obviously expensive, she'd rejected the trendy "uniforms" that had pervaded our school. She had a distinct air of elegance, and her face was always made up impeccably. I knew zilch about cosmetics, and had always viewed clothing as a necessity, along with food and shelter. When I stood next to her, I looked like an asexual backwoods ragamuffin, it was pathetic. We were in the same drama class, and had been paired up to do a scene from *The Odd Couple*, appropriately. Otherwise, she never would have spat on me, let alone been kind. Perhaps it was an act of charity, but Minnie took a liking to me, and I reluctantly became her life-size dress-up doll. Apparently, she saw something no other girl had seen before.

"You're wasting your potential!" she'd say enthusiastically, at least once a day. "You could be so pretty if you tried! It wouldn't take much, just a little makeup and some cool clothes!"

She must have had astigmatism. I was not pretty by any stretch of the imagination, and no amount of makeup would ever change that. No matter how much I protested, she insisted on teaching me how to apply the gunk, and also began lending me her clothes. Both were itchy and suffocating, but she'd invested so much time and faith in me, I had no choice but to comply. She seemed to derive great pleasure from making me over, and to be honest, I appreciated the attention, even though I felt like a clown-faced poseur.

After being excommunicated from Linda's, Minnie's place became my new sanctuary. She lived with her absentee mother in a spacious two-story beach house that would be the starting point of a life changing sequence of events.

It was a Saturday afternoon. My sophisticated mentor and I were trying on the latest additions to her already limitless wardrobe, when the telephone rang. She answered the call, and after a brief conversation, joined me by the vanity, where I was treating my olfactory system to her perfume collection.

"That was Adam," she said, tossing the cordless phone onto the bed. "You know, the punker I told you about?"

How could I forget? She'd been telling me about him since I'd met her. He was an older guy who lived down the street, in a beachfront apartment.

"Yeah," I replied, dabbing Chanel No. 5 onto my neck. "What did he say?"

"He wants us to come over and hang out with him and this other guy, Sam. You met Sam's sister at the pier last weekend, remember?"

"I did?"

"Yeah, Helen, remember?"

"Oh, yeah! She was cool, and I liked her hair."

"I know, isn't it rad?" she said, looking in the mirror and running her fingers through her hair. "I wish I could wear mine that short. I guess I could if I had her beautiful face."

I smiled at her reflection.

She smiled back.

"So, do you wanna go over there for a while?"

"What are we going to do over there?"

"Listen to music, smoke, drink some beer."

I looked at her as though I were waiting to hear more, even though she hadn't steered me wrong yet.

"It'll be fun," she added. "These guys are totally cool. You'll like them, I promise."

"Okay," I replied, shrugging my shoulders, "why the hell not?"

Upon arriving, Minnie rang the bell repeatedly, but it was being drowned out by blaring, unintelligible music.

"Fuck!" she said in a frustrated tone.

"Why don't you bang on the window?" I suggested.

"Good idea," she said, doing just that.

Seconds later, the music abruptly stopped, and the door flew open.

When I landed in Southern California, the first real friend I made was a pigtailed, rosy-cheeked Mädchen who quickly became my closest ally. In her long-lashed, liquid blue eyes, I was not the least bit strange, and she was not at all bothered by my secondhand duds or unkempt hair. She was a fellow precocious freak, struggling to stay afloat in a choppy sea of conventionality. Her older brother was a musician, and the first punk rocker I ever saw in the flesh. At first I simply viewed him as a tall guy with weird clothes and bad hair, but after learning more about punk via magazines and whatever music I could find, my perception changed dramatically. As expected, the antiauthoritarian aspect struck a deep chord, and I was utterly intrigued by the blatant defiance toward societal standards. Granted, it wasn't the first counterculture to emerge from the underground, but it was certainly the most radical in terms of appearance. And Adam, the young man who stood before me now, was a prime specimen.

I impulsively reached up and touched his hair, which was standing on end, as though he'd jammed his finger into an electrical socket and dunked his head in a bucket of glue.

"This is Adam," Minnie said, laughing.

I introduced myself, and apologized for pawing his head.

"Don't worry about it," he said, smiling, "happens all the time. Come on in."

As I entered the cramped quarters, I saw another young man sitting on the loft bed. Sam, presumably. He looked like an older, larger, male version of his sister, right down to the hair.

After making the necessary introductions, Minnie and I joined Sam on the loft bed while Adam sat down on the floor Indian style.

"So, what's your favorite band?" Adam asked, offering me a can of beer.

"Zeppelin," I replied, cracking it open.

"Do you ever listen to any punk?" Sam asked, also cracking open a can of beer.

"Yeah, sometimes," I replied, after taking a hearty swig.

"Like what?" Sam asked.

"The Ramones, the Clash, the Buzzcocks, the Sex Pistols, Generation X, stuff like that."

"How 'bout X?" Adam asked, smiling. "Chicks always dig X."

"Yeah, they're cool," I replied. "My sister saw them live, her boyfriend took her."

"Seen 'em loads of times," Adam said, lighting a cigarette and taking a long drag. "They kicked fuckin' ass!"

"One of the best bands I've ever seen," Sam added. "They never disappointed."

"I turned the only Barbie I ever had into Billy Zoom," I said without thinking.

They both looked at me oddly, and for a split second I regretted saying it.

"How the fuck did you do that?" Sam laughed.

"I chopped off her hair, melted her boobs with a lighter, and dressed her in some of Ken's clothes."

"You had a Ken doll too?" he said teasingly.

"Yeah," I replied, rolling my eyes. "Some prissy girl from my neighborhood gave me the stupid dolls for my birthday one year. I wanted to stuff them into the garbage disposal and flip the switch, but my mom wouldn't let me."

"So, I guess you don't like Barbie, huh?" Sam said with a wide grin.

"Fuck no!" I exclaimed. "She's an evil, stuck-up bitch! I wish she'd die and burn in hell!"

Incidentally, my feelings toward Barbie have changed. At the time, she reminded me of my tormentors, presumably the reason for the barbaric gender reassignment surgery.

Both Sam and Adam doubled over in laughter, while Minnie giggled quietly in the corner.

"Is it just me," Adam said, still laughing, "or does Ken seem a little light on his feet?"

Sam started to roar.

"No, dude!" Adam argued. "I'm serious as shit! I always thought he was a queer!"

"I never really thought about it before," Minnie said musingly. "I guess Ken could be a queer."

"That's what Kinko the Clown thinks," I said confidently.

"Did you just say Kinko the Clown?" Adam asked, doing a double take. "Who the fuck's Kinko the Clown?"

"Dude, I was just gonna ask the same thing myself!" Sam laughed, clapping his hands together.

"He's one of my brother's best friends," I said, even more confidently. "He's a queer, and his alter ego is a clown."

"Your brother's a gay clown?" Adam exclaimed, laughing.

"No, dummy!" I said, pushing him playfully. "Kinko is!"

"No shit?" Sam asked. "Like, a real clown?"

"Oh, okay, I get it," Adam said jokingly. "What, is he like John Wayne Gacy or somethin'?"

"No," I replied smartly, "he's not like John Wayne Gacy or something. Kinko's really cool. Before my brother moved out, he used to stay over at our house all the time."

"You mean he slept there?" Sam asked, cracking open another beer and taking a swig.

"Yeah, all the time. And he used to buy me ice cream and take me skating and to the movies, I even saw Rocky Horror with him."

"And how did your brother know this Mr. Kinko?" Adam asked, smiling.

"It's not *Mr.* Kinko," I replied, in an even smarter tone, "just Kinko."

His smile turned into a wide grin.

"Oh, *excuse me*," he said, crossing his eyes at me.

"They went to high school together," I replied, crossing my eyes back at him. "He's like family, all of my siblings' friends are."

"Your parents must be really fuckin' cool."

"They're okay, but I don't live with my dad, just my mom, my two sisters, and my brother. My oldest brother moved to Santa Cruz a couple of years ago, and the other just moved to Santa Barbara last year."

"Her parents are divorced too," Minnie interjected.

"Shit," Adam said, placing his hand on his forehead. "Sorry, I didn't know."

"It's no big deal," I replied, lighting a clove cigarette and taking a drag, "everybody's parents are divorced nowadays."

"Ain't that the truth," Sam chuckled.

A moment of awkward silence ensued.

Then Adam cracked open a can of beer and said contemplatively, "Billy Zoom. He's a killer guitarist, but he smiles waaay too much."

"No shit!" Sam laughed, lighting a cigarette. "Fuckin' weird, isn't it?"

"It *is* weird," Minnie agreed. "Creepy even!"

"What's wrong with smiling?" I asked in his defense. "Maybe he's happy."

"Yeah, maybe," Sam laughed, exhaling. "Either that or he's fuckin' fryin' all the time."

"He's a fuckin' alien, dude!" Adam exclaimed.

"Get the fuck outta here!" Sam said, dismissing him with his hand.

"I'm tellin' you, man, I've been rackin' my brain for years, and that's the only logical explanation. Shit, that's probably why he's such a virtuoso too. He's like one of those extraterrestrial motherfuckers from Close Encounters or somethin'."

Okay, I was having a difficult time relaxing. Adam and Sam were amusing and surprisingly affable, but wouldn't stop *staring*. I was a paranoid, self-conscious mental case who couldn't stand being stared at. No matter who was doing the staring, I was convinced they were thinking the worst. I typically responded by flipping the bird or flinging the nearest object with intent to injure, but since these two were so friendly I refrained. I couldn't help wondering what they were staring at, though. It had to be the hat. I was wearing a Greek fisherman's cap, which they obviously found repulsive. Why else would they stare so intently? I'd later learn that their motives were boyishly prurient, but at the time I assumed they were passing judgment. How was I supposed to know? When you've been told repeatedly by the privileged girls that you're "an ugly rag," you begin to believe it.

What happened next was expected, but that didn't make it any easier to deal with. Sam removed a joint from his pocket, lit it, took a drag, and passed it to me. I'd first learned about marijuana from Pedro De Pacas and Anthony 'Man' Stoner. My siblings and their friends idolized Cheech & Chong, and thought *Up in Smoke* was the *Lawrence of Arabia* of the 70s. I'd seen the film a number of times, and could even recite the script from start to finish, along with every album the duo produced. Of course I'd never smoked pot before, and knew it was probably a bad idea, but didn't want to appear uncool, so...

I didn't realize it at the time, but that beer and marijuana klatsch was one of the most pivotal moments in my life. Minnie and I began spending every weekend with Adam and Sam, drinking, smoking dope, and listening to records. I was also introduced to a gang of unbridled young men who I'll call the Locals. They lived their lives exactly as they chose, *no one* told them what to do. Having come into the world a recalcitrant hellion who despised all forms of authority, these guys spoke my language. After searching fruitlessly since arriving on Planet Earth, it felt as though I'd finally found my own kind, and the age difference was irrelevant. These guys epitomized cool, and more important, made me feel as though I mattered. In their bloodshot eyes, I was not that ugly, grody, weird, white trash loser, and they didn't give a shit if I was wearing a pair of $100.00 jeans from Nordstrom or a pair of $1.00 jeans from the Goodwill store. I'd spent my entire life feeling out of place and being spurned by my so-called "peers." Now, without even trying, I'd found acceptance and camaraderie among the most unlikely group of people – people who'd been labeled as good-for-naught malefactors by the "normal" and supposedly superior sector of society. How ludicrous. The most evil, worthless lot I'd come across were those superficial, elitist clones who'd derided and excluded me simply because my shell didn't suit their dogma.

PRYSKYRNÍKOVITÉ

By the time the fall semester had commenced I'd changed my appearance drastically. Sporting a brush cut, several self-inflicted piercings, and clothing that flew in the face of the dress code established by the school district and society at large. As expected, the wardrobe was mostly black, but not for the reason you'd think. I'd finally located myself, and was "mourning" – as in *celebrating* – my identity crisis' death.

Sadly, Minnie and I had drifted apart, although it was completely amicable. She'd moved on to high school, and I'd since become tight with a couple of girls who lived in my neighborhood: Kiki, who my sisters used to babysit, and Amy, a transfer student from the local Catholic school. The latter lived under the draconian rule of her oppressively puritanical British mother, who would make Amy's presence in my life short-lived.

It was another Sunday. I didn't particularly care for Sunday. You'd think I would have savored the day, since it accounted for fifty percent of the fleeting hours that made up the weekend. Instead, I viewed it as the last day of freedom before surrendering for execution of sentence. I always wondered who the genius was that came up with the five-day school week. Three days would have been more than enough. Amy, Kiki, and I had plans to hit the mall for a shoplifting spree. It was no secret that Amy was an undiagnosed kleptomaniac who couldn't walk out of a store empty-handed. Oddly, she didn't appear to derive any pleasure from stealing, almost as if it were a rote chore, like doing laundry. Kiki and I, on the other hand, found the rush titillating.

Our list for the day consisted of three items: music, jewelry, and cosmetics. The first two stops were a breeze, but the last would be our demise. Sears department store was notorious for its tight security. Moments after wandering back out into the mall, we were intercepted by two security guards.

"Stop right there, ladies," the pudgy one said, blocking our path with his arm. "I'm going to have to ask you to come with us."

"What do you mean?" Amy asked innocently. "Come with you where?"

"Back to the store."

"Why?" Kiki asked, also feigning innocence.

"Because you just broke the law," the lanky one replied.

"How so?" I asked, in an annoyed tone.

"Let's not play this game," Pudgy said gruffly. "You know exactly what you did."

"Honestly, we don't," Amy argued.

"And I suppose lumpy pants pockets are the latest thing in women's fashion, eh?" he said sarcastically.

"Yeah," Amy snapped back, "maybe they are. What's it to you?"

"I've had a long day," he said, grabbing her arm, "and I'm due to go home in an hour, so let's just get this over with."

"Get your fat little hands off me, you fuckin' wanker," she yelled, pulling away from him, "or I'll scream bloody murder!"

Her loot-filled handbag fell off her shoulder and onto the ground. She looked down at the incriminating evidence, then glanced up at Pudgy and grinned.

He returned the grin and grabbed her again.

"Okay! Okay!" she exclaimed, pulling away from him. "Let me go!"

"Are you gonna do what I say?"

"Yeah, yeah, you got us," Amy sighed.

"All right," he said, glancing over at his partner, "I'm gonna release my hold now, and when I do, you'd better not run, because all it's gonna do is make me mad."

"The same goes for you," Lanky added, grabbing hold of Kiki and me, "and we *will* catch you, so don't even think about takin' off."

Right at that moment I was wishing Lanky had been on the same diet and exercise regimen as Pudgy. While the latter surely would have suffered a coronary in front of Spencer's, the former could have chased us all the way to the Mexican border without even breaking a sweat.

Minutes later, the girls and I found ourselves locked in a pantry-sized room with a fold-up table and chairs.

"Fuck!" Amy yelled, trying to open the door. "This sucks!"

"You may as well sit down," I yawned. "I don't think we're going anywhere for a while."

She plopped down on the chair across from me, and crossed her arms angrily.

"Anyone have a deck of cards?" Kiki chuckled.

Amy and I looked at her and laughed.

"I am so fuckin' busted!" Amy cried. "My mom's gonna kill me!"

"*You're* busted!" Kiki exclaimed. "If I'm lucky, my mom will only ground me for a month!"

They both looked at me enviously, as though I'd already been granted immunity, and it was highly probable that I would be.

Suddenly, the door flew open.

"How's it goin' in here?" Pudgy asked, stuffing his enormous noggin into the room.

We didn't respond.

"I can't believe you girls are only thirteen! What the hell are you doin'? If you keep this kinda behavior up, you're gonna end up behind bars before you know it!"

"Are we free to go now?" Amy asked, ignoring his admonition.

"Nope, I'm afraid not."

"Why the fuck not?" I asked, glaring at him.

"Hey!" he snapped, pointing his forefinger at me. "Watch your mouth!"

I flipped him off under the table.

"What's the deal?" Kiki said, yawning. "You can't call the cops 'cause we're juveniles, and you can't keep us locked up in here forever."

"You girls think you're *so* smart," he replied smugly. "I can call the cops all right, and I probably should, but I'm not gonna."

"So can we go then, or what?" Amy asked impatiently.

"Only after your parents get here. You're not goin' anywhere until then, so just make yourselves comfy."

"Shit!" Amy yelled, slamming her hands on the table. "You called our parents?"

"Who did you think I was gonna call, *Ghostbusters*?" With that, he broke into a raucous belly laugh and slammed the door shut.

Kiki and I flipped him off, while Amy ejaculated a stream of vitriol. "Fat bastard motherfuckin' cocksucker wanker piece of shit cunt! I fuckin' hate you! I hope you drop dead!"

Of course he couldn't see or hear any of it, but it was gratifying to vent anyway.

Our mothers soon came rolling in one after another, with mine being the last to arrive. As was common, she'd picked up an extra shift at the hospital, and didn't get off until three, so I was trapped in that cubbyhole, all alone, for thirty minutes. I occupied myself by mulling over the day's events, but not in a repentant manner. Instead, I was pissed off that we'd been busted, and even more pissed off that my new L'Oreal Sandstone lipstick had been confiscated. I'd had my eye on it for weeks, and now I'd be forced to either swipe another tube, or god forbid, purchase one.

Amy, Kiki, and I were equally guilty, but our respective sentences couldn't have been more disparate. After being briefly lectured, I was acquitted, as predicted. Kiki was reprimanded by her father and grounded for a week. Poor Amy received the harshest punishment of all. Rather than issuing a standard penalty, which would have been more than sufficient, her mother opted for deportation back to the UK. Which brings us to the purpose for Amy's inclusion in the book...

Shortly before her exile, Amy had introduced Kiki and me to Mia, a classmate at her former school. I'd never encountered *anything* quite like her: animal, vegetable, or mineral. We harmonized effortlessly right off the bat, as though we'd been derived from the same zygote, and she would ultimately become the closest female friend I've ever had.

Mia came from an insanely large family that I'd heard tragic tales about, including the suicide of her brother and the recent death of her mother. Her father, who I'll call Whitman, was the personification of eccentricity. Although he was a devout Catholic, who attended mass and confession religiously, he was a heretic through and through. The family was viewed as a clan of oddballs by many of the neighbors, primarily because they dwelled in the biggest dump on their street. Whitman had a penchant for collecting police auction clunkers, which he'd drive mercilessly until they went kaput. Rather than having them repaired or towed to the junkyard, he'd simply park them in the driveway or on the lawn, and pick up another at the next auction. While our neighborhood was considered inferior to the larger and more expensive one on the west side of the main drag, it was still an unusual sight. The meddlesome neighbors filed numerous complaints with the city, but nothing ever came of it. They should have minded their own damn business. Whitman had just lost his wife, for crying out loud, and still had three young daughters to bring up on his own.

Immediately after Amy's departure, three fellow students signed on as full-time comrades. Damita and Nola were former members of an exclusive clique they'd recently outgrown. Both were heavy dope smokers with a propensity for fast living. Then there was Lisa, who'd only dabbled with marijuana and booze, but her strong rebellious streak compensated for her lack of experience. All three came from broken homes, and lived with their mothers who were grossly negligent. Granted, the women had to work, but that only accounted for a meager portion of their absence. So why did they leave their teenage daughters unsupervised for days at a time? The answer is simple: they were in relationships, and like many divorcées, hoping to remarry. Believing their daughters would frighten away the potential husbands, they simply abandoned them. I've often wondered if they're aware of the life-altering effect it had on their children. Their desire for companionship was perfectly understandable, but it didn't excuse their behavior. The way I see it, if you decide to bring a child into the world, you'd better be prepared to do whatever's required of you, even if it means sacrificing your own wants and needs. My mother was also negligent, although her lack of parental involvement was somewhat justified, as she frequently worked double shifts at the hospital to offset the family's expenses. She attempted to delegate parental authority to my sisters, but to no avail. I was being beckoned by an insidious force. Even if I'd been locked in a closet, I would have chewed my way through the walls to answer the call. Miraculously, Kiki's parents were still married, and her mother made a conscious effort to be involved in her daughter's life, including issuing a curfew. The rest of us were left to our own devices.

And what would a pack of precocious juvenile delinquents do with such freedom? Raise hell and party, naturally. In addition to smoking marijuana on a daily basis and quaffing gallons of booze on the weekends, our hobbies included larceny, taking in live shows, piddling peddling, and lounging around on the beach with the Locals. At thirteen, we could pass for at least eighteen, and behaved as though we were in our twenties, staying out until all hours of the night. We obeyed no one, and if we wanted something, whether it was a candy bar, wallet, or bike (even if someone was on it) we took it.

We also had a knack for locating people who were willing to feed our drug habits. One of our first marks was a trio of disturbingly puerile twentyish men, who we called Larry, Darryl, and Darryl, a la the *Newhart* woodsmen. They only cared for five "pleasures" in life: Marijuana, Beer, Pizza, Porn, and Professional Wrestling. None of them were named Larry, and only one was named Darryl, but naturally, we called him Larry. We seemed to irritate the hell out of them, but they kept inviting us over to watch wrestling and skin flicks, and while we weren't particularly fond of either, it was a fabulous place to get free drugs. The arrangement continued until we wore out our welcome by dropping in, unannounced, at all hours of the night, to raid their kitchen. Needless to say, they weren't too pleased, especially after Damita accidentally blew up their toaster oven, nearly burning the place to the ground. It eventually reached a point where they'd try barring us at the door, but we'd plow right through their human bulwark, flattening all three of them in the process. Sometimes they'd turn out the lights and pretend they weren't home, but one of us would climb through an open window, and let the others in through the back door. The harassment surely would have continued indefinitely if they hadn't threatened to call the police.

After figuring out that drunken men could be easily fleeced, we took up panhandling as well. We'd plant our bikini-clad pubescent bodies outside of the beach pubs, and catch the fools as they came stumbling out. It was a quick and painless way to make a few bucks here and there, as well as a source of amusement.

Then there were the drugs, naturally. Our thoughts on the matter were: "If pot's so fucking killer, imagine what the stronger shit must be like?"

Cocaine would be the first endeavor beyond marijuana and alcohol. One weeknight, Mia, Damita, Nola, and I acquired a gram through a middleman, then headed over to the local pizzeria, slid into one of the back booths, and snorted it up. All I can remember is feeling restless and mildly paranoid, which were traits I already possessed, they were merely accentuated. A couple of nights later, I gave cocaine another whirl, and the sensation was *sheer rapture*. I fell head over heels, embarking on what would turn out to be a long-term, love-hate romance with the drug.

Before long, methamphetamine came into the mix. Then LSD, PCP, mushrooms, heroin, nitrous oxide, opium, Valium, a variety of uppers, downers, all arounders... Are you getting the picture? I was an equal-opportunity junkie. I'd smoke, snort, or swallow whatever I could get my hands on. By age fourteen, I'd tried nearly every drug, and was hooked on a handful.

In hindsight, what I find most absurd is my own flagrant hypocrisy. While I was busy preaching the tenets of "independence" and "liberty," I was a thrall who was ruled by controlling substances.

56E 478

If drug addiction were matrimony, the police would be the meddlesome in-laws one gets stuck dealing with from time to time. It was unavoidable, but being a minor certainly came in handy. Not only were the cops more lenient, but whenever my girlfriends and I did find ourselves locked in a cage, "bail" was met with a simple phone call to our parents. Being female was a mixed blessing, depending on the arresting officer, as I'd find out a bit down the road. I experienced a hint of what was to come on what should have been a typical summer night. Kiki and I were in a filthy Taco Bell restroom, limbering up en route to a party, when there was a gentle rap at the door.

"Is everything all right in there?" a female voice asked timidly.

"Fuck off!" I yelled, after taking a hearty swig of vodka.

"I beg your pardon?" the voice said, in a less timid tone.

I tore open the door to find a Taco Bell employee standing there. "F-U-C-K O-F-F," I reiterated slowly, before slamming the door in her face.

"Who is it?" Kiki asked, exhaling and passing me the pipe.

"Some chick who works here," I replied, taking the pipe and passing her the bottle.

There was another gentle rap at the door.

"Fuck, she's a nuisance!" I laughed. "Can't she catch a hint?"

"Excuse me," the voice asked, "is that marijuana I smell? Did you know that marijuana is illegal?"

Kiki and I started to roar.

"No shit, Sherlock!" Kiki yelled. "Fuck off!"

"Smoking marijuana is illegal!" the voice squealed. "I'm going to call the police!"

"Go ahead, narc bitch!" Kiki laughed.

Assuming that the voice was merely talking through her Taco Bell visor cap, we resumed our warm-up session. Five minutes later, there was a louder, more authoritative knock at the door. Clearly that of a cop.

"Oh, shit!" Kiki whispered, giggling. "I can't believe that bitch called the pigs!"

She dumped the blazing bud into the toilet and flushed it, while I began fanning my hands through the air in an effort to get rid of the pungent odor. We locked eyes for a split second then burst out laughing.

"I know you're in there," the cop said sternly. "Now open the door."

"Shhhh," I whispered, struggling to stifle my laughter. "Don't move. Just pretend there's no one in here, maybe he'll go away."

"He *knows* we're in here," Kiki giggled, shoving the pipe and bottle into her handbag. "I wish there was a fuckin' window, so we could sneak out."

"All right," the cop said, knocking once more, "you have exactly ten seconds to open the door." Then he began counting.

When he reached nine, Kiki and I came stumbling out. Much to our surprise, there were two uniformed policemen, standing akimbo with scowls painted on their faces. One looked uncannily familiar, but I couldn't place him. While he did bear a close resemblance to a certain television private eye, there was no doubt in my mind that I'd actually met him before.

"Good evening, girls," he said, removing his sunglasses and clipping them onto his shirt. "I'm glad you decided to come out. It makes my job a whole lot easier."

"We didn't have anywhere else to go!" Kiki giggled, attempting to hide her handbag under her arm. "There's no fuckin' window in there."

"Yes, I'm well aware of that. Would you mind watching your language, please?"

"Shit, sorry," she said, covering her mouth.

"Why are you smoking marijuana in a public restroom? Do you have more marijuana, or any other drugs in your possession?"

Being an incurable wiseass, my gut reaction was to respond with: "Would it be okay if we were smoking marijuana in a *private* restroom?" But I somehow managed to restrain myself.

"Marijuana?" I lied, feigning innocence and batting my eyelashes. "What makes you think we've been smoking marijuana, officer?"

"I can smell it on you," he replied bluntly. Then he pointed to Kiki's handbag and asked, "Do you mind if my partner has a look inside your purse, young lady?"

"Hell yeah, I mind!" Kiki exclaimed with a loopy expression on her face.

Both cops glared at her.

"I know my rights," she continued flippantly, "and you guys can't search my purse unless I let you, which I'm not gonna do."

"All right," the cop said in an extremely annoyed tone, "turn around and place your hands behind your back."

Kiki reluctantly obeyed his orders, while his partner proceeded to frisk and handcuff her.

"That goes for you too, young lady," the cop said, looking at me. "Turn around and place your hands behind your back."

For a split second I considered fleeing, but knew I wouldn't get far. I had no choice but to obey.

After I was frisked and handcuffed, the cop ordered Kiki and me to sit down on the curb next to the dumpster, while his partner searched Kiki's bag.

"Well, look what we have here," the partner said, displaying the incriminating evidence with a smug look on his face, as though he'd just uncovered a kilo of heroin.

"Okay, girls," the boss sighed. "Stand up. You have the right to remain silent. If you give up that right, anything you say can and will be used against you in a court of law. You have the right to an attorney and to have an attorney present during questioning. If you cannot afford an attorney, one will be provided to you at no cost..." And so on.

Kiki and I were taken to the station and booked on a handful of drug and alcohol related charges, then tossed into a cell. After filling out the necessary paperwork, the cop came over and sparked up a conversation through the bars.

"So, you girls must be excited about starting high school next year, huh?" he said through a phony smile.

"What's there to be excited about?" I scoffed. "Except that it'll be easier to cut class."

"That's a very negative way of looking at it," he said in a lightly admonishing tone. "You're one step closer to being an adult. Isn't that what you want?"

I didn't respond.

"What makes you think that?" Kiki laughed, standing up and stretching her legs.

"Well, you certainly behave as though you're adults… drinking, taking drugs… and I think it's safe to assume that you don't heed orders at home either."

"And you'd be right to assume that," I said smartly. "In fact, they're not even given in my home, never have been."

"And I wouldn't be the least bit surprised if you were sexually active," he added with a cocky grin.

Then it hit me. I *knew* I'd met him before. A few years prior, he'd dated a close friend of my sister's, *before* she was of legal age. And that wasn't all. He'd also dated an acquaintance of mine, who was only fourteen at the time. Both had claimed that he supported his own habit by confiscating drugs from arrestees. The pig was police corruption personified. I couldn't believe he had the gall to lecture us about *anything*, especially vices.

"Hey, I know where I know you from," I said, smiling slyly and pointing at him.

"I beg your pardon?" he said, running his fingers across his mustache.

"You used to go out with Cathy Simpson. She's a friend of my sister's. You came over to my house with her one day, remember?"

"No," he said, nervously, "I can't say that I do."

"But you do know Cathy, right?" I asked, standing up and walking toward him.

"Yes, I know Cathy."

His countenance was that of a guilty man. He clearly had regrets about answering in the affirmative, and now that I had him cornered I saw no reason to stop.

"Didn't you go out with Vicky Parsons too?"

His face turned ashen for a moment, as though the blood supply to his head had been cut off. Being the seasoned criminal he was, he quickly collected himself and replied calmly, "No, I don't know anyone by that name."

"Are you sure?" I pried, with my hands on the bars. "Because she told me that she used to know you *really* well."

"No," he reiterated in an even calmer tone, "I don't know anyone by that name. Now if you'll excuse me, I have paperwork to catch up on."

"He's so full of shit," Kiki laughed, as soon as he was out of range.

"Tell me about it," I agreed, sitting back down.

"I *thought* he looked familiar," she said, yawning, "but I couldn't place him."

"Me neither," I said, catching her yawn, "but that line about us being sexually active jogged my memory. He's a fucking pig."

"In more ways than one," she laughed, sitting down next to me.

"You do realize he pocketed that weed, right?"

"You think so?"

"I *know* so."

"Fucker."

Our parents weren't called until well past midnight, which was a bit distressing. I was worried I may have gone too far with my little game. Kiki and I were at the cop's mercy. If he'd wanted to, he could have pinned a litany of trumped-up charges on us. I was tremendously relieved when our parents showed up. I was even able to overlook the usual upbraiding from Kiki's father. As for the charges, I can only conjecture as to why, but they vanished. I'm not even sure if there's a record anywhere.

Throughout my criminal adolescence, I had numerous run-ins with the law, and often found myself sitting on the undesirable side of the bars, sometimes until the following day. I'll never know how I pulled it off, but throughout it all, I was only booked that one time.

FUNGUS KU

Jamie and Tai were living proof that drug addicts are incapable of functioning in relationships, and shouldn't bother trying. It's simply impossible for two fragmented souls to co-exist in one fragmented world. No matter how blissful the relationship may be *at first*, one or both parties will inevitably sabotage it, blighting at least one innocent bystander in the process, often a child.

I first collided with Jamie during the spring semester of eighth grade, amid a PCP induced rampage. She was a student at the rival middle school, who I knew by reputation only. Nola, Damita, and I chased her down one afternoon, fully intending to beat the shit out of her, but had a change of heart when she begged for mercy. Less than a week later, she was one of the gang.

Tai was one of the Locals. He was a remarkably understanding soul, who I trusted implicitly. He was not only a patient listener and thoughtful adviser, but also had an avuncular nature that made me feel safe. As long as they weren't trying to molest me, I preferred the company of older men, and not merely because they were feeding my drug habit. They were far more attentive than guys my age, far more dependable and less moody than most of the girls, and considerably more stimulating than both.

When I cut class throughout my freshman year I spent hours with Tai, building an intimate platonic friendship that would last nearly five years. I learned right away that he loved music, but unlike most of the Locals – who lived and breathed "punk fucking rock" – his taste was refreshingly eclectic. He believed that by limiting your musical diet to one particular genre, you were not only depriving yourself of essential nutrients, but also submitting to the same conformist creed you were adamantly claiming to despise.

Besides our like-mindedness and common interests, Tai knew how to deal with me, and went out of his way to bolster my sunken self-esteem. I was always painfully insecure about my appearance, and sincerely believed that I was an ugly blimp. Yes, I know, every girl says that, and some truly mean it, while others are merely fishing for compliments. Well, this neurotic freak was convinced, and I'd clobber myself ad nauseam, ad infinitum. I had dangerous, borderline lethal body image issues, and would rattle on about my grotesqueness on a regular basis. No matter how many times he'd heard it before, Tai would counter my self-flagellations and assure me that I was a lovely person on both the outside and inside. Of course, I never believed him, and often belted him and told him to "shut the fuck up" in return, but he continued to inspirit me anyway.

My paranoid self-consciousness drove him up the wall and through the roof. He once told me that he feared I'd commit suicide if I had a zit. Well, I don't know if I'd take it *that* far. That may be a bit histrionic, and it wouldn't get rid of the pimple either, I'd just be a corpse with a zit. But I've been known to cancel appointments, rearrange my schedule, and hide under a blanket until the zit is gone. I've been known to do the same when my weight surpasses a certain number on the scale. No, I'm not joking, and I assure you, it's not vanity. Along with every other neurosis in existence, many of which I've possessed at one time or another, the shrinks have given it a fancy, new-fangled label, but I prefer calling it by its proper name: Crippling Racking Lunacy. I'm pleased to report that it no longer dominates my life, but as a kid, it was so overpowering I plunged headfirst into a bout of anorexia, which was facilitated significantly by Uncle Charlie. Tai was gravely concerned, and confronted me about it, without mincing words. On one occasion, he threatened to weight me down with bricks and throw me off the end of the pier if I didn't seek help. Mind you, his seemingly insensitive words were delivered through a sly yet caring smile that never failed to have an uplifting effect. He was a wise and wonderful soul, who generously nourished my young mind with invaluable knowledge that I've retained to this day.

The following conversation took place on an autumn afternoon, when I was supposed to be in class. As was common, Tai had joined the girls and me for lunch at the grease pit across from the high school. As was also common, when it came time to return to the yard, I simply couldn't justify doing so. I thought it was a terrible waste of my precious time, especially when the sun was shining so gloriously.

Tai was heading to the beach, and I saw no reason why I shouldn't join him.

"I want you to listen carefully now," he said, extinguishing the Cocoa Puff we'd just smoked, and tucking the roach into his wallet, "'cause I'm about to give you some of the most valuable advice you'll ever get. Hardly any women know this, so consider yourself lucky."

"Okay, Confucius," I said, putting my hands together and bowing, "enlighten me."

"I'm not fuckin' around!" he yelled, slapping my hands. "If you don't wanna hear it, just tell me, and I won't waste my breath!"

"Go ahead," I said smartly, "you big baby."

"Are you listenin'? 'Cause I'm only gonna say it one time."

"I'm all ears."

He took a deep breath and uttered the following words: "A chick can always get laid."

After taking a moment to digest his coarse proverb, I burst out laughing. "That's it? *A chick can always get laid?* What the fuck is that supposed to mean?"

"Shut the fuck up and I'll explain," he replied, also laughing.

"Please do," I said sarcastically, "because that may be the deepest shit I've ever heard."

"It's not meant to be deep, and it's no big secret either, but most women are too ignorant and brainwashed to figure it out. They just keep believin' all that female written bullshit they read in those stupid fuckin' magazines of theirs."

"Figure *what* out?"

"Two things, but they go hand in hand. Numero uno: no matter how fat and ugly a chick is, she'll always be able to rope some horny dickhead into humpin' her. The same can't be said for guys. They'll never admit it, but most guys know they're fuckin' losers when it comes to pickin' up chicks. A lotta what you see is bravado bullshit, especially when they're wasted. The truth is they're scared shitless of rejection, even guys who score all the time. Are you followin' me?"

I nodded and gave him a look that indicated he should proceed.

"They make it look so fuckin' easy in movies and TV shows. Like a dude has a chance with any chick he wants, no matter how fine she is. It's a joke! The average Joe's lucky if he can get a *five* into bed, never mind a perfect ten."

"Yeah, but not every girl has her choice of guys either, and I bet there are loads out there who have a hard time finding dates at all."

"True," he agreed, lighting a cigarette. "Some chicks might have a hard time findin' guys who'll go *out* with 'em, but take my word for it, they'll never have a hard time findin' guys who'll go *to bed* with 'em. Maxi Pad is a primo example. She's the skankiest, nastiest mutt I've ever forced myself to look at. That wet brain La Grange keeps tellin' me that she fucks like a champion, but I wouldn't fuck her if my life depended on it, I wouldn't fuck her if she was the last chick on Earth, I wouldn't fuck her with my worst enemy's dick, I wouldn't fuck her..."

"Okay, I get your point," I interrupted in an irritated tone. "She's a friend of mine, lay off, or I'll be forced to give you a backchop."

"I know she is, but I can't stand her."

"She's not too crazy about you either, San Te."

"She hates my fuckin' guts!" he exclaimed. "She looks at me like she wants me dead!"

"That's because she *does* want you dead," I said matter-of-factly, "and I'm sure she'll be very happy to know that you get the message. Can we move on now?"

He grinned puckishly, then grabbed a chunk of my hair and yanked it.

"Let go, fucker!" I laughed, smacking him in the head.

He continued to tug, so I grabbed his nipple and began twisting it mercilessly.

"Owwwww!" he shrieked, tossing his cigarette onto the sand. "Let go of my tit!"

"Not until you let go of my hair!"

I clearly had the upper hand. Unlike most people, I've always enjoyed having my hair pulled, and if my neck weren't being wrenched to one side, I wouldn't have felt any discomfort at all. Tai, however, was in severe pain. If you've ever been on the receiving end of a purple nurple you know exactly how painful it can be. He lasted two minutes before releasing his grip. I gave his nipple one final twist. Then he cleared his throat, and picked up where he'd left off.

"What I was sayin' is that Maxi Pad gets laid whenever the fuck she wants and it doesn't cost her shit. The fuckin' losers are linin' up at her door. This would *not* be happenin' if she was a guy, unless he had somethin' to offer in return, which brings us to numero dos. You still with me?"

"Yeah, go on."

"Most women have no fuckin' clue how much power they have over men. It's not like we think about sex twenty-three hours a day, but we do think about it a helluva lot more than we should." He paused for a moment, then looked directly into my eyes and said emphatically, "No matter how bad you want somethin', or how tough things get, don't you *ever* whore yourself out for *nothing, EVER.*"

I wasn't used to him being so serious, and didn't know how to react.

"It's totally unnecessary," he continued. "If a guy so much as *thinks* that he can score with a chick, he'll do whatever it takes to make it happen, and you'd be very surprised at how long he'll stick to it, even if she shoots him down a thousand times. It's like the more she resists him, the more he wants her. Make sense?"

I nodded.

"It's a pitiful statement about men, but one of the best things about bein' a chick, especially a hot chick. But even an okay-lookin' chick can get whatever she needs without compromisin' herself, and if she does have to compromise herself for somethin', it's not worth havin'. You get it, Blondie?"

"Yeah," I said in an uncertain tone, "I think so."

I understood what he meant, but a couple of months would pass before it would fully register.

While words can certainly be influential, experiences tend to drive the point home. Incidentally, it was indeed some of the most valuable advice I ever received, particularly the latter portion of the previous passage, which was permanently etched into my brain. Of course, the interpretation of the term "compromising oneself" varies with each individual, and god knows I'm in no place to judge.

"Are you sure?" he asked, looking right at me.

"Yeah, I'm sure," I lied, looking back at him.

"Good. And don't you ever forget it. Besides, one day you're gonna wanna boyfriend, and take it from me, most guys want nothin' to do with a chick that's been passed around like the fuckin' Stanley Cup, even if she looks like Bo Derek."

He was brimming with malodorous shit, and when I finished laughing at his brilliant simile, I called his bluff.

"Are you saying that you wouldn't fuck a chick who looks like Bo Derek just because she's a slut?"

"I didn't say that," he said, grinning. "Of course I'd fuck her, I'm not stupid."

"That's what I thought, you big fat hypocrite."

"But I *definitely* wouldn't get serious with her. Maybe some guys wouldn't give a shit if their girlfriends fucked every Tom, Dick, and Harry before hookin' up with 'em, but I couldn't deal with that. It'd be like stickin' a wad of gum in your mouth after a buncha other guys already chewed it."

"What about guys who fuck anything with tits and a hole?" I asked in an annoyed tone. "Are they judged by different criteria?"

"I *knew* you were gonna ask that!" he laughed, smacking my back.

"Well, are they?"

"What's good for the goose is good for the gander. I don't think *anyone* should sleep around, especially with this AIDS shit out there."

"Yeah, it's pretty fucking scary."

"It's *really* fuckin' scary. Before, you only had to worry about catchin' herpes or the clap, but this motherfucker is a death sentence, and it's a long, miserable death."

We fell silent for a spell, while staring out at the pitifully small waves as they broke on the shore. I hadn't a clue what was running through Tai's mind, but I was thinking about how beautiful Rock Hudson looked as Taza, Son of Cochise, bad wig and all.

"I've got the worst case of the munchies," he said, breaking the silence.

"Me too."

"You wanna hit the usual spot?"

"Are you buying?"

"Why do you bother askin'? We both know you're a broke mooch. Hangin' out with you is like havin' a fuckin' kid."

"Can we go for ice cream sundaes too?" I asked, after sticking my tongue out at him.

"Only if you eat your vegetables," he replied, grinning.

I gave him the finger.

He reciprocated, then stood up and extended his hand. "Okay, Blondie," he said, pulling me up, "let's blow this taco stand."

PING WING WO

At the onset of summer, Mia, Damita, Nola, and I had made a pact to drop acid together. It was now autumn, and the time had come to fulfill that pact. Earlier in the day, I'd been given four hits by a rambling, agoraphobic punker who was infamous for having the most potent poison in town. After dosing at Damita's around five, the girls and I walked up the street to the liquor store for our weekly Ms. Pac-Man tournament. A couple of rounds into it, two local skateboarders/future sociopaths walked in. I looked up and was shocked by what I saw. Not only were their faces grotesquely distorted, but their pimples had floated off and were flitting about, like a fleet of miniature, flesh-colored flying saucers. I quickly averted my gaze and fled to the candy aisle, which was located on the opposite side of the store. Damita followed.

"Did you see that crazy shit?" she laughed with her hand over her mouth.

"Fuck," I sighed in relief, "I thought I was the only one."

"I'm fuckin' trippin'!" she exclaimed, waving her hand in front of my face. "And look at *this* crazy shit!"

Trails: The LSD-induced perception that moving objects leave multiple images or trails behind them.

The drug had definitely taken effect, and in a furtive manner.

"What time is it?" I asked, surveying the store.

"Just after six," she replied, looking at her watch.

"Fuck, this shit creeps up on you, and hits you like a ton of bricks."

"I know," she giggled, "and we're not even close to peaking yet!"

Mia came over, leaving Nola alone amid the swarm of unidentified flying pustules. "Whoa, trippy!" she said, staring into my eyes through a pair or conspicuously dilated pupils. "You look possessed! Your irises have been swallowed by your pupils!"

"I think we should split," I said, glancing out the window at a passing patrol car.

"I was thinking the same thing," she agreed, also glancing out the window. "It's fucking sketchy around here, man."

"Let's head back to my place," Damita said, motioning toward the skateboarders with her head, "and ditch these clowns."

By the time we reached Damita's, the drug had completely inhabited my being, resulting in the most contradictory sensation. I was ridiculously disoriented, and rapidly vacillating between spells of serene euphoria and paranoid agitation, as though I were suffering from an aberrant form of bipolar disorder. Every sound that poured into my ears – music, voices, birds, cars driving by, planes flying overhead – had a bewildering reverb effect. It was as if my sensory faculties had developed a mind of their own, and it was a warped, jumbled mind. At times, I felt as though I wanted to stop the Earth, and just *breathe*. I was well on my way down a road I'd never traveled, and wondered what would happen if I couldn't find my way back. All of the sudden, I began to feel breathless, as though the apartment had been filled with a heavy, noxious gas. I looked at the clock, and noticed that another hour had passed.

The girls were lying on the carpet in a meditative state, with images of *Top Secret* flickering on the television, while *L.A. Woman* played on the turntable. "L'America" – which sounded more carnivalesque than usual – had just ended, and "Hyacinth House" was about to begin. In a desperate effort to reassemble my disconnected mind, I began alphabetizing Damita's record collection. I hoped that concentrating on a methodical task would get my mind off the fact that I was frantic and suffocating for air. I couldn't believe I was the only one snapping her crackle.

"I have to get the fuck out of this box!" Nola exclaimed, jumping up.

"Me too!" Mia gasped, springing to her feet.

Apparently, I wasn't the only one after all.

"Wait," Damita said, squinting and swaying her head back and forth to the music like Stevie Wonder. "Let's listen to this tune, maybe it'll calm us down."

Nola and Mia glared at her, as if to say, *"Are you fucking kidding?"*

"Here," Damita said, patting her hand on the floor, "just sit down, close your eyes, and chill."

They sat down on either side of her and closed their eyes.

Less than a minute later, Damita stood up and yelled, "FUCK IT! Let's get the hell outta here!"

I looked at them, then at my handy work – which I'd barely put a dent in – then back at them. As a rule, my OCD-like streak would have forbidden me to leave the task unfinished, even if the building was engulfed in flames, but in this instance, I was able to override it with relative ease.

After wandering aimlessly for an hour we stumbled into an area known as Tecate Flats, a dilapidated, almost uninhabitable shanty complex filled with gangbangers and illegal immigrants. Supposedly, it was a drug trafficking hotbed, but we'd never bothered to explore.

While passing through someone whistled, prompting us to stop and turn around. Standing near the main gate was a guy with enough hair on his head for five men. He flashed a toothy grin, and yelled something to the effect of, "Aychicasup?"

I wondered what language he was speaking. His head was encircled by a warm gold nimbus. At least, that's what I saw. The girls must have seen it too, for without exchanging a single word, we made a bee line for him, like a flock of geese running toward a pile of freshly dropped bread crumbs.

"Sup? Wareugoeeng?" he asked, still grinning.

"Don't know," Nola replied, gazing into his eyes, as though she were hypnotized.

"Wannagithiiii?" he asked, widening his grin.

I soon realized that he was speaking English at a highly accelerated speed. His thick accent was making it unintelligible, and the fact that every sound entering my ears had a nebulous "Wall of Sound" quality made it even more garbled.

"Whatcha got?" Damita asked, also grinning.

"Ohhpeeuum," he replied, pointing toward one of the houses, and suddenly sounding clearer. "I'm Flaco. C'mon, let's go. I live right over there."

Upon entering the yard, we were greeted by a circle of hombres, who were drinking cerveza and smoking cigarillos. "Buenas noches, Senoritas!" they yelled cheerfully in unison.

After making the necessary introductions, Flaco handed the girls and I chilled bottles of Dos Equis. Then he removed a pipe from his jacket pocket, and proceeded to load it repeatedly for the next couple of hours. Only one of the other hombres spoke fluent English, which more or less limited the conversation to two subjects: the refreshing beer and blessed opium. Damita did have a firm grasp of the Spanish language, but for reasons unknown, played down her ability, making it seem as though she only spoke it brokenly.

Two of the hombres stood out from the others, and for different reasons. Rico was a slick character, who appeared to be in his early thirties. Decked out in designer duds and lavishly adorned with gold jewelry, his English was impeccable, and his vocabulary vast. The others addressed him deferentially, as though he were a monarch. Then there was Ramon, who spoke minimal English and had shifty, convex ojos, like a black moor goldfish. In stark contrast to Rico, he looked as though he'd been rolling around in a soggy cow pasture for a week.

His hair and clothing were filthy, and he smelled like a crate of rancid, manure-coated red onions. I rarely made snap judgments, but the guy was downright fishy. He would have aroused my suspicion even if I hadn't been under the influence of a powerful hallucinogen. He kept goggling and licking his lips like a licentious retard. I made repeated attempts to move out of his sight, but those bulging eyes were equipped with a homing device. What ensued was an exhaustingly annoying game of cat and mouse that I hadn't asked to be a part of in the first place. As is human nature, my evasiveness only encouraged him. I finally planted myself right next to him, and while he continued ogling, it wasn't quite as bothersome from a peripheral view.

As the night progressed, my high remained the same, no matter how many bottles of beer I guzzled or how much opium I inhaled. The agoraphobe had warned me about the phenomenon, and had given explicit orders to use discretion when ingesting other drugs. He claimed to have known a girl who'd unintentionally overdosed because she couldn't properly gauge her state of intoxication. I'd written it off as bunk, pure exaggeration flowing from the yap of a nutcase, but perhaps there was some validity to it after all. Before I knew it, I was lost in a reverie, wondering what would happen if I snorted a mountain of blow or popped a handful of Valium.

I snapped out of it when Ramon – who'd been ogling without blinking for three hours straight – tapped my shoulder with his grimy forefinger.

I forced myself to acknowledge him.

"I wanna show you something," he said, motioning for me to come with him.

Yeah, I bet, I thought.

I ignored him.

He tapped my shoulder again.

I forced myself to acknowledge him again.

He placed his hand in front of my face and opened it, revealing a pile of pills that appeared to be Quaaludes lying peacefully on his soiled palm. "Do you want?" he asked, pointing at the pills with his other hand.

I seriously considered grabbing and devouring them, but tapped Damita on the shoulder instead. "I'm not sure," I whispered into her ear, "but I think this fucker has some ludes, take a look."

As she leaned over to have a gander, he quickly closed his palm.

"No, no, no," he said, shaking his head. "Not you, only Rubia."

I glared at him. I wanted those fucking pills, but there was no way in hell I was going anywhere with him alone. "Tell him I'm not going unless you can come too," I whispered into her ear.

She relayed the message en Español, and after taking a moment to think about it, he agreed.

Once inside the house, Damita and I plopped down on a moth-eaten, pea green sofa that reeked of beer, cigarettes, and urine. Ramon planted himself on the coffee table opposite, and handed us two pills apiece. *What a tightass*, I thought. Damita and I glared at him. He smiled sheepishly and coughed up two more, which we immediately swallowed.

"I gotta take a piss," Damita announced, tucking the remaining pills into her shirt pocket.

Before I could object, she disappeared down the hallway, leaving me alone with El Pervertido, who was now drooling in my lap.

He smiled lecherously.

I curled my lip in disgust.

There was a brief, silent pause. Then, without any warning, he sprang at me tongue first and grabbed my crotch. I was *homicidally enraged*. If I'd been holding a shiv, I would have sliced him from ear to ear without giving it a single thought. I dug my fingernails into his chest and pushed him off, but he rebounded instantly, like a blow-up Weeble Doll.

"Get the fuck off me!" I yelled, shoving and clawing at him.

When I was first moved to California, one of the neighborhood boys (another piece of shit on my "To Kill If I Can Get Away With It" list) was molesting me on a regular basis. He'd sneak up, tackle me to the ground, and rape me with his forefinger. It must have happened a hundred times before his mother finally caught him in the act. Needless to say, it was horribly traumatic, especially the tortuous feeling of utter helplessness, as though I were sitting atop a Judas Chair. Ramon had successfully evoked that feeling for the first time since the last assault.

I drove my knee into his balls repeatedly until he fell to the floor, squealing and writhing in pain. Then I spat on him.

"What the fuck happened?" Damita asked, rushing back into the room.

"Motherfucker attacked me!"

"Are you fuckin' serious?" she said, looking down at him.

"As shit!"

"Are you okay?"

"Yeah," I said, straightening my disheveled clothes, "just a little freaked out."

"Chingate tu madre, Cabrón!" Damita yelled, giving him a swift, hard kick in the gut. "You're lucky I'm in a good mood."

I spat on him once more.

"Let's go tell on him," Damita said, linking her arm in mine.

The hombres appeared to be embarrassed by Ramon's behavior, but not surprised, which meant it probably wasn't an isolated incident.

Rico was not only embarrassed, but upset as well. "I am so sorry, mi amor," he said, putting his hands together, as if praying. "Please accept my deepest apologies."

"It's not your fault that your friend's a fucking pig," I replied gruffly.

"But I am your host. It is my responsibility to ensure that you enjoy yourself while you are here." Then he removed a money clip from his pocket. "Here," he said, handing me two Grants, "go buy yourself something special."

I thanked him twice – once for each bill – then shoved the dinero into my bra before he changed his mind.

Seconds later, Ramon sauntered into the yard, wearing a mask of innocence. Rico grabbed him by the shirt, threw him up against the fence, and lambasted him in Spanish. Although I couldn't understand what was said, Ramon's reaction spoke volumes. He was visibly terrified of Rico. After apologizing profusely, he never so much as glanced at me, ever again.

FAT WALLET

As luck would have it, Tecate Flats turned out to be a goldmine. Throughout the duration of my addiction, I had a fortuitous knack for attracting people – more specifically, men – who not only facilitated my habit, but subsidized it. I've often wondered how long my junkie career would have lasted if I'd been forced to work at it.

It was a Saturday night. Mia, Tits, and I headed over to Tecate Flats in search of stimulation. When we arrived, Flaco and Rico were sitting in the main yard, listening to Dire Straits, which was odd, since I'd only ever heard Tejano playing on that boom box. They looked ridiculously happy, almost *too* happy.

"Que onda!" they yelled, grinning ecstatically.

"What the fuck are you guys on?" Mia asked, smiling and motioning with her hand. "And where's mine?"

"No shit!" Tits laughed. "You guys are flyin'!"

Tits was an interesting character. Her most remarkable asset was a mixed blessing. At thirteen she had the biggest knockers I'd *ever* seen, hence the nickname. But unlike most overly endowed women, she was quite svelte, which made her a real freak of nature. On this particular night, the mammoth bosom was stuffed into a low-cut postman's vest she'd swiped from a mail truck earlier in the day. Rico – who had a Pablo Escobaresque penchant for pubescent girls – took one look and was smitten.

"You are in for a real treat tonight, mis amores," he said, rubbing his hands together. "Come on, hop in the Caddy."

"Where are we goin'?" Tits asked with an angelic look on her face.

"*That*, mi amor, is a secret," he said, smiling slyly.

"Well, when are we gonna be back?" she asked, putting a cigarette into her mouth. "My dad wants me home by midnight."

"Then we shall get you home by midnight, Cinderella," he said, lighting the cigarette.

Since Mia and I had no curfew to speak of, it didn't matter where we were going or how long we'd be there. It could have been a weeklong cruise to the Mexican Riviera for all we cared. Our parents would have flipped and contacted the authorities after a few days, but that was beside the point.

After bidding Flaco adios, we piled into the tricked out Barritz and were on our way. A half hour later, we pulled into the driveway of what appeared to be an auto body shop.

"I have been wanting to bring you here," Rico said, driving around to the rear of the building, "but needed to be certain I could trust you."

My curiosity was piqued and running at full tilt. The first thought that popped into my head was CHOP SHOP, but I couldn't figure out why he'd brought us there.

"Okay," he said, quickly surveying the area. "Vamos! Rápido!"

We jumped out of the car and made a dash for

the door, where we were greeted by two men, both decked out in garb similar to Rico's.

"Buenas noches, Jefe," one of them said, kissing Rico on the cheek.

The other followed suit.

After conversing in Spanish for a moment, Rico made the necessary introductions. Then he clapped his hands together and said, "Okay, mis amores, are you ready to party?"

"What do you mean?" Tits asked naively, batting her eyelashes.

The coy and innocent act had been going on since she'd shaken Rico's hand, and was all part of a well-calculated scheme. Biologically speaking, Tits was merely thirteen, but in Siren years, she was pushing thirty. The girl was a ruthlessly skillful operator who was only interested in what a man had to offer, and this man clearly had *much* to offer.

"Allow me to show you what I mean," Rico laughed, wrapping his arm around her waist.

Without further ado, our hosts escorted us into a spacious cement-lined room that was strategically hidden on the opposite side of the building. As I walked in, I nearly croaked from shock. Inside that bunker was a mother lode of cocaine, bag after bag after bag, from floor to ceiling. It was *breathtaking*.

The girls and I let out a collective gasp, which caused our hosts to burst out laughing.

"Omigod! Omigod! Omigod!" Tits exclaimed.

"Someone fucking pinch me," I said, gaping at the magnificent vision that sat before my eyes.

"Woooo hoooo!" Mia yelled, pinching my ass.

"Let's party, man!"

Which is precisely what we did. Unfortunately, my vivid, often paranoid imagination was lurking the entire time. The fact that Rico was obviously a major league drug trafficker, while certainly thrilling, was a bit unnerving. I was coked-up out of my gourd, and in my mind's eye, kept seeing graphic images of my own murder preceded by hours of rape and torture. Of course, it was only delusional nonsense fueled by the drugs, but as I'd find out later, it wasn't entirely illogical.

Around midnight, we piled into the Caddy and headed home. Planning to make a move on Tits, Rico insisted that Mia and I be dropped off first. Much to our surprise, he gave us a fat bindle as a parting gift. And if that weren't enough, *he asked if it were enough.* The guy gave new meaning to the words "chivalry" and more important, "munificence" – as we'd soon learn, when he began feeding our habits regularly and liberally, seemingly out of the goodness of his heart. It seemed too easy, too perfect, which it was, of course, but I'm getting ahead of myself again...

As Mia and I stood on the stoop of her father's house, waving goodbye to our new benefactor, a head popped out of the front door.

"And where have you two been?" the head asked, staring into our vastly dilated pupils.

It was Mia's brother Heath, a fellow junkie who was ten years our senior. He knew we were soaring, but wasn't sure how we'd gotten off the ground.

Mia answered with a wide grin and two words: "Fat Wallet."

Heath's eyes lit up like asteriated sapphires.

Fat Wallet was code for cocaine. Whitman was a diehard jazz fan, with an extensive vinyl collection that had to be worth a fortune. Whether records were spinning or the pianola was playing, the joint was always jumpin' whenever he was around. Amid it all, Mia and I had discovered that Fats Waller was a hoot and a half when you're high. One night, while searching for a flat surface on which to mince cocaine, Fats beckoned from the phonograph. From that moment on, whenever cocaine was snorted under that roof, he joined in. Mia dubbed the ritual "Fat Wallet." She had a knack for paronomasia, and was also a skilled parodist. She could have given Weird Al a run for his money any day of the week.

After snorting through the eightball in record time, the three of us hopped into Heath's truck and set out on what would prove to be a near-disastrous cocaine search.

"Okay, guys," Heath said, pulling into a 7-11 parking lot in Garden Grove, "I'm not sure if it's cool to bring you along, so just hang out here for a while."

Mia and I got out of the truck, and walked around to the driver's side window.

"How long are you going to be?" she asked.

"Ten minutes max." And he was gone.

She and I went into the store to buy some water, and after chatting with the cashier for a spell, went back out. Seconds later, a police car pulled into the lot, and merely seconds after that, Heath's truck appeared. The instant he caught sight of the black and white, he gunned it, leaving Mia and me in the lurch. My initial feeling was anger, but his reaction was perfectly understandable. He was wired to the hilt, and unlike us, if he were busted he'd go straight to County.

We watched as he sped off into the night.

"Let's get the fuck out of here," Mia whispered, glancing over at the cops, "before they spot us."

"I'm right behind you," I whispered back. "Whatever you do, don't turn around."

We sauntered aimlessly along the eerily quiet boulevard until reaching a Jack in the Box restaurant.

"Detour," she said, grabbing my arm, "we'll lie low in here until Heath comes back."

"How the hell is he supposed to see us if we're sitting in Jack in the Crack?" I asked, in a slightly annoyed tone.

"It's Itch in the Crotch," she laughed, "and we'll just have to be on the lookout for him."

Once inside, we planted ourselves in a rear booth. Within seconds, a police car pulled into the parking lot. Seconds later, two patrolmen got out.

"Are those the same fucking cops from 7-11?" I said, peering out the window.

"Sure as hell looks like it," Mia replied, glancing over at them as they walked in. "Malloy and Reed."

"Shit," I whispered, "they're coming over here."

"No they're not," she argued.

"Yes they are."

They were now standing right over us and oddly, did bear a resemblance to Malloy and Reed, with an extra thirty pounds of adipose tissue apiece.

"Hello, girls," Malloy said, looking at his watch.

"Kinda late for you to be out, isn't it?"

When you enlist as a juvenile delinquent, it's imperative that you learn how to deal with the police. Number one rule: never, ever, under any circumstances, volunteer unsolicited information. While you should remain cooperative throughout the entire interrogation, being overly forthcoming will only make you guilty in the eyes of the law.

"We're waiting for our ride," Mia replied politely.

"And who's coming to get you?" Reed asked.

"My brother."

"When's he supposed to be here?"

"Any minute now."

"Alright," Malloy said sternly. "Just stay put till he arrives. It's not safe for you to be wandering these streets at night."

"We're not going anywhere," Mia said, smiling. "Thanks."

They nodded and walked away.

Ten minutes later, there was still no sign of Heath.

"Maybe we should ask the cops for a ride," Mia said, chomping on some ice.

"What if they figure out that we're high?" I asked, obviously.

"They won't," she said, trying to convince not only me, but herself as well.

"How can you be so sure?"

"I can't, but if I have to sit here for one more second, I'm going to fucking snap. I need a fix… another line… another something… *anything*."

"I hear you loud and fucking clear," I sighed. "What the hell, let's give it a go."

We slid out of the booth, and approached them.

"Excuse me, officers," Mia said, after clearing her throat. "Do you think you might be able to give us a ride home?"

"Where do you live?" Malloy asked.

"About ten miles from here."

"Out of our jurisdiction," he said, shoving a handful of fries into his mouth, "can't do it."

Unbelievable, I thought. When you actually *want* them to lock you up in the back of their car, they refuse.

"Are you sure you can't make an exception just this once?" Mia asked, smiling flirtatiously.

"Nope," he replied gruffly, shoving more fries into his mouth, "call a cab."

I was livid. I felt like shoving those fries up his fat ass, and couldn't help glaring. Luckily, he couldn't pry his piggish eyes away from the grease feast that lay before him.

"Okay," Mia mumbled, "maybe we will."

"Good luck," Reed mumbled back, through a mouthful of milkshake.

"Isn't it bizarre that they're not harassing us?" Mia whispered, as we walked outside, entirely directionless.

"They're too busy stuffing their fat pig faces," I said, loud enough for them to hear. "We'd better get the hell out of here. I bet you a billion bucks that once they're done, they'll be on us like white on rice."

Besides hitching a ride – which was unwise, given the area and time of night – the only option was to head back to 7-11, and hope that Heath would return at some point.

Five minutes later, there he was.

"I'm so sorry, you guys," he said, leaning out of the window. "Those cops freaked me out."

Mia and I got in and fastened our seat belts.

"Don't sweat it," she said, smiling, "I would have done the same thing myself. So, did you get the goods or what?"

"Uh-uh," he said, shaking his head, "he's tapped out till tomorrow."

"Aww, man!" she exclaimed. "That's a bad fucking trip!"

"What the fuck are we going to do?" I asked, thinking about the inevitable crash that was waiting in the wings.

"We'll figure it out when we get home," he said, retrieving a joint from the ashtray and handing it to me. "In the meantime, spark this baby up."

Once back inside the safe confines of the house, we discussed our quandary at length, but couldn't reach a solution. Until Heath broached a precariously interesting idea, that is.

"I have some Morphine left over," he said contemplatively, "but I'm not so sure I want to give it to you guys, it might kill you."

Earlier in the year, he'd broken both of his legs in an accident. It was a prolonged recovery, and the pain was excruciating at times, prompting his doctor to prescribe liquid Morphine.

"What the fuck are we waiting for," Mia said, motioning with her hand, "let's do it."

"Uh-uh," he said emphatically, "I couldn't live with myself if you croaked."

"Yeah, but if *you croak too*, "she said, smiling slyly, "you won't have to live with yourself."

It was a morbid line of reasoning, but she did have a point.

I can't tell you with any certainty what happened next, although it was strikingly similar to the phenomenon that occurs when you're put under for surgery.

The following afternoon, I was jarred awake by a blaring clock radio. Bobby Darin's "Splish Splash" was pervading the room at full volume. I found myself lying face-up on the top bunk of a child-sized bunk bed, with Mia sawing wood in my face. I was unusually drowsy and hadn't the slightest recollection of how I'd gotten there. It was extremely disconcerting. During my seven years of chemical servitude, it was the only time, no matter what I'd ingested, that I *ever* blacked out.

I rolled Mia aside, stumbled down the miniature wooden ladder, and switched off Bobby D. Then I shook my snoring bedmate until she was conscious.

"What the fuck happened?" she asked sluggishly, rubbing her eyes.

"Your guess is as good as mine," I yawned. "I'm going home. Don't forget, you have to read *The Great Gatsby* by tomorrow morning."

"Fuck!" she exclaimed. "I haven't even opened it yet! What day is it?"

"Sunday."

"Are you sure?"

"Positive."

"Motherfucker! There's no way I can read that fucking book by tomorrow morning!" She paused for a moment and pursed her lips, which meant she was scheming. "Hey, I just thought of something."

"And what's that?" I asked, yawning again.

"Didn't *you* read it?"

I knew exactly what she was hinting at, but I was in no storytelling mood.

"Yeah, but I'm in a fucking coma at the moment. I can't even remember my name, never mind a book I read when I was ten."

"Just give me a brief synopsis," she begged, tugging on my shirt. "Come on, please? I'll be your best friend?"

"You *are* my best friend," I said, heading for the door. "Go buy the Cliffs, or better yet, rent the film, the one with Alan Ladd, if you can find it."

She looked at me with helpless doe eyes and an adorably tragic pout. Many a sap fell victim to this little ploy, but it never worked on me, for I knew her too well. What's more, I'd been known to use the same ploy myself.

"I need more sleep," I said, yawning once more and walking out. "I'll call you later."

She mumbled some words in French, then rolled over and resumed sawing wood.

The instant I stepped out into the blinding sunlight, I saw a trio of beaming faces waving from the garage across the street.

"Good morning, Sunshine!" one of them yelled cheerfully.

It was Ganja Ron, Green Bud, and Burnout Jackson, neighborhood denizens and buddies of Heath's. Each was invariably stocked with the most potent marijuana around, which they thoroughly enjoyed sharing with the girls and me. Running into one of them was a real score, but all three at once? A hat trick, although I wasn't so sure about the timing.

I forced a smile and waved back.

"You look like shit!" Ganja Ron yelled, holding up a hefty bag of weed. "Come on over, I've got just what the doctor ordered!"

I was already gorked, but like an idiot, I dragged my carcass across the street.

When I entered the garage, I heard Tangerine Dream's *Phaedra* playing softly on the stereo. Ganja Ron was not only hooked on drugs, but also Kraut and Prog Rock, which according to him "facilitated the journey." Exactly where he was headed, I never knew. I doubt he knew either.

"What the hell happened to you?" he laughed. "You look like you just went fifteen rounds with Marvin Hagler!"

Green and Burnout were also laughing.

"It's a looooooong story," I replied, shaking my head. "Do yourself a huge favor… unless you're in a hospital, don't fuck with Sister Morphine."

"Ahhhhhhhhhh" they said in unison, nodding their heads.

"So," Ganja Ron said, smiling, "do you wanna get high or what?"

"Why the hell not," I yawned. "If I'm lucky, maybe it'll finish me off."

"I scored a half-pound of that Golden Thai I smoked with you last month," Burnout said, raising his bushy, overgrown eyebrows and grinning. "Remember that shit?"

"How could I forget?" I scoffed.

He was referring to a premium breed of seemingly magical, opium-laced marijuana, which had caused me to believe that the half-gallon of Vanilla ice cream I was devouring was changing flavors with every bite. First it was Butter Pecan, then Peach, then Pistachio, then Chocolate Malted Crunch, then Pecan Praline, etc...

"Should we use Dr. Phibes?" Green Bud asked, pointing toward the work bench.

Dr. Phibes was a bong that Ganja Ron had built from scratch. What set it apart from other bongs was the respiratory mask attached to its body via a plastic hose. Can you see where this is going?

They took several turns apiece loading Dr. Phibes. After three rounds, I could barely stand, but continued to inhale the pungent fumes anyway. The rest is a blur. All I can remember is asking Ganja Ron for the time, and his answer verbatim: "A heckle past a frair."

I often wonder why I remember this useless crap. My head is abounding with it. I looked at him confusedly, then staggered out of the garage, crawled across the street, climbed back into the bunkbed – the bottom bunk this time – and fell into a deep slumber until the following morning.

The girls and I soon learned that Rico was a high-ranking member of a syndicate that shall remain anonymous, while Flaco and crew were members of an affiliated gang. The element of danger only intensified the appeal. Rico's generosity continued for weeks on end, until he attempted to employ us as mules, offering a handsome salary in addition to the existing drug stipend. After seriously considering his offer, we declined, which resulted in him cutting us off. Although it came as a blow, he did us a tremendous favor. Peddling dope locally was a risk we'd been willing to take, but smuggling it across international borders was another matter altogether. I'm certain it would have landed us behind bars, possibly in another country, and for a very long time.

Tecate Flats was eventually razed to make room for a new strip mall, forcing the gang to relocate to another area where they already had ties. Damita soon followed. Without any explanation, she just dropped out of school and stopped calling.

LICK THE SPOON

By now the girls and I had undergone a group makeover. After discovering that men of nearly every persuasion went for wholesome yet naughty filles, we remodeled ourselves into provocatively clad girls next door. Our motives were purely devious, self-serving, and opportunistic: we wanted free drugs, and women weren't going to provide them.

It was a weeknight. Mia, Nola, and I were at a party, where we made the acquaintance of an interesting gentleman named Kirk. What made him so interesting was his potential utility. Exploitation was the name of the game. What could we get and who could we get it from. This guy was an easy mark: self-conscious, desperate, and above all, manipulable.

He clung to us all night, expressing his deep reverence for cocaine, and bragging about the girth of his wallet. When considered separately, either would have been an absolute turnoff. As you've undoubtedly noticed, I was also immoderately fond of cocaine, but praising the drug as though it were a deity, was beyond creepy. And listening to some insecure gasbag boast about the depth of his pockets was as repellent as listening to some insecure gasbag boast about the scores of women who were supposedly lusting after him. When you added the cocaine worship and pecuniary resources together, however, the creepy, repellent blowhard became instantly appealing.

When the clock struck one, he said goodbye and headed for the door. My first instinct was to ask for his telephone number, but my defective ego refused to cooperate. I hoped that one of the girls would intercept before he got away, but no such luck.

"Fuck," I grumbled under my breath, watching him escape.

Suddenly, he turned around and walked back over. "I almost forgot," he said, smiling nervously, "I'm having a small party on Saturday night, and would love it if you came."

I breathed an internal sigh of relief, or perhaps *victory* would be a better word.

"I'll make it worth your while," he added. "I'll even provide shuttle service as long as you're all at one location. Can that be arranged?"

"You can pick us up at my place," Nola replied, retrieving a pen from her purse and grabbing his hand. "Gimme your palm."

Sixty-seven hours later, we found ourselves in the foyer of Kirk's elegant townhouse. It turned out to be a much more intimate gathering than I'd expected – a baker's dozen of guests, all men in their mid to late twenties. I wondered if they assumed that the girls and I were of legal age, and came to the conclusion that they probably didn't give a shit. I had yet to come across a benefactor who wasn't an ephebophile, either openly or latently.

After making the necessary introductions, Kirk directed everyone into the spacious living room, where a case of Dom Pérignon and a smorgasbord of mouthwatering hors d'oeuvres were begging to be devoured. I was famished, and itching to gulp down some of that exorbitantly priced bubbly, but naturally, one of Kirk's friends had to deliver an affected, platitudinous five-minute toast that ran on for five minutes too long. When the last scoop of buttery corn came gushing out of his yap, I knocked back three glasses of champagne and inhaled a plateful of food, while Kirk slapped the B-52s *Wild Planet* on the turntable and cranked it.

"All right, everyone," he yelled, raising his hands in the air, "let's party!"

Midway through "Quiche Lorraine," the phone rang. Kirk picked up the cordless and slipped into the kitchen for a spell, then emerged with an exultant expression painted on his face. "That was the connect!" he announced triumphantly. "The package is ready for pick-up!"

His friends clanged their glasses together and let out a collective cheer.

"I'll be back in less than an hour," he laughed, stuffing a thick number ten envelope into his back pocket, "and if I'm not, call my attorney!"

His friends clanged their glasses together again and let out another collective cheer.

He then came over to the couch, where the girls and I were enjoying a humungous spliff.

"Has anybody seen a dog dyed dark green?" Mia said, handing him the blimp with a smile.

He thanked her, then took two deep tokes and passed it to Nola. "So," he said in a slightly nervous tone while looking directly at me, "would you like to come along for the ride?"

I didn't want to offend the man, but it sounded like a terrible idea. What if he *did* get busted?

"Maybe," I replied hesitantly. "Where are we going?"

"Chuck E. Cheese's."

Not exactly a hot spot for cops, I thought. "Okay," I said, shrugging my shoulders, "why the fuck not."

When we arrived at our destination, Kirk parked in the lot behind the restaurant, then switched off the lights and stereo, but kept the motor running. I glanced over at him, and noticed that he was conspicuously ill at ease, so much so he couldn't even look at me. Contrary to my initial thought, his condition was not caused by the potential ambush we'd willingly walked into. Apparently, Kirk suffered from an episodic form of Social Anxiety Disorder that struck when he was alone, in dead silence, with a member of the opposite sex. While not an uncommon malady, it was the first time, to my knowledge, that *I* was the causative agent. Despite my best efforts to keep it in check, my meddlesome conscience began to rear its guilt-inducing head, and refused to get back into the steel vault where it was kept under lock and key. I felt pity for Kirk, the kind of pity one would feel for a social outcast. I suspected he was a nerd in another life, which was perfectly fine. There's certainly no shame in being intelligent and well-read, and judging from his financial situation, nerdiness had served Kirk well. I wanted him to know that I was not one of those stuck-up, hypercritical bitches who'd snubbed him throughout high school. More important, I didn't want to be a source of discomfort, it made me uncomfortable. I did what I could to allay his palpable anxiety by cracking jokes and patting him on the arm. Humor and physical contact can unwind even the tightest bundle of nerves. Of course I was nervous too, but for a different reason. As usual, my inordinately vivid and often paranoid imagination began to wander, and before long, I'd convinced myself that we were unwitting players in an elaborate sting operation. I was counting the seconds before the fuzz emerged from the bushes and surrounded the car.

All of a sudden, a hippie woman appeared at my window, causing me to jump in my seat. "Roll down the fuckin' window, man!" she whispered loudly, with frantic eyes bulging out of her head. "Hurry up!"

Kirk opened his window and motioned for her to come around to the other side. As she leaned into the car, I noticed that she was trembling and sweating profusely. When I saw the hefty package she gave Kirk, and the obscenely fat wad of dough he gave her in exchange, I knew why. She'd just peddled enough cocaine to earn her five plus in CIW. It was going to be an eventful night indeed.

If the girls and I had any doubts about our decision to attend this soiree, they were quickly entombed. The blow was being dispensed so rapidly and generously we could barely keep up. These guys definitely knew how to have a good time, but unlike us, they weren't your run-of-the-mill coke Hoovers. They were hardcore junkies, shooting up rhythmically and relentlessly. While not terribly unusual in itself, there was a catch: they insisted on being watched. I just assumed that it was idiotic machismo posturing intended to impress, but in reality, it was a sexual stimulus, a bizarre form of exhibitionism that Kirk seemed to be proud of.

"THERE IS *NOTHING*, DO YOU HEAR ME, *NOTHING* MORE AROUSING THAN HAVING AN AUDIENCE OF BEAUTIFUL GIRLS!" he yelled maniacally, slamming the needle into his arm. "*AAAND*, IT ENHANCES THE HIGH TENFOLD!"

It's safe to say that the man had issues – besides the obvious, that is – and as the night progressed, his demeanor changed drastically. By midnight, the nervous, awkward geek was nowhere in sight, and had been replaced by an aggressive, fast-talking gadfly, who was fixated on the idea of me shooting up. He began hounding me, like a desperate pitchman who stood to lose his left hand if he failed to make the sale.

"Come on!" he pleaded forcefully, getting right up into my face. "You have to try it! Come on! You don't know what you're missing! Come on! I swear to god it's better than an orgasm! Come on! You'll never go back to the straw or pipe again! Come on! Just try it once! Come on! For me! Come on! I'll do it for you! Come on! You won't feel a thing! Come on! Just a little prick! Come on! I promise! Come on! Come on! Come on! Come on! Come on! Come on!

Come on! Come on! Come on! Come on! Come on! Come on! Come on! Come on!"

I wanted to deck him. He wouldn't shut the hell up, and it was a major buzzkill. Besides, he wasn't revealing some highly coveted esoteric secret. People who have never even tried cocaine know that the high achieved from mainlining is the most rewarding. But I was not going to succumb to his exasperating spiel, no matter what, even if he *did* stand to lose his left hand. At least he'd still have the right one.

By now I'd come to terms with the fact that I was an incurable addict, who was not only playing with fire, but recklessly provoking it. But I was having such an infernal blast I saw no reason to quit, despite the ever-impending danger. I did, however, establish a couple of rules for myself. Number one: I'd never, ever inject any drug. I certainly had no aversion to pain, it was an intimate friend. And the seventeen self-inflicted piercings I was sporting at the time clearly indicated that I was not remotely belonephobic. In fact, I've always had a penchant for *watching* whenever I've been given a shot or had blood drawn. I simply believed that mainlining was synonymous with weakness, and that junkies who couldn't refrain from shooting their dope were utterly hopeless. What a shameless fucking hypocrite! I know exactly what you're thinking: "the pot calling the kettle black." I have no legitimate defense, and won't even attempt to offer one.

I articulated my position to Kirk the best I could without insulting him. In other words, I fed him a subtle line of bullshit about my supposed fear of needles, which he eagerly swallowed, and thankfully that was that.

Cocaine is an insidious siren that entices, enchains, and tyrannizes its minions. The initial sensation is indescribably euphoric, but mercilessly short-lived, forcing you to ingest dose after dose after dose after dose after dose in a futile attempt to recapture that orgasmic buzz. For me, the high never lasted longer than twenty minutes, if that, and each subsequent line or puff provided a significantly weaker result. There are also unbearable side effects to contend with, such as jaw clenching, twitching, cold sweats, palpitations, tachycardia, spontaneous nosebleeds, and the sudden urge to defecate. I once knew a dealer who claimed that the mere sight of the drug made him "want to take a big fat shit." In my opinion, the most intolerable side effect by far is the all-consuming, almost maddening restlessness. You feel as though you should be doing something remarkable and unprecedented, such as finishing the Ironman Triathlon in less than seven hours. When the bitter truth is, there's not a thing to do, except devour more and more and more and more and more and more and more while jabbering aimlessly with *anything* that has ears and a mouth.

By the crack of dawn I was a deliriously wired magpie, who would have struck up a conversation with *a cop* if no one else were around. Kirk and I were standing in the dining room, chattering frantically about the uncanny color coordination between his kitchen wallpaper and dish towels, when I honed in on his mouth, only to find that he seemed to be speaking Mandarin.

"Qīng qīng shān shàng yī gēn téng, qīng téng de xià guà tóng ling, fēng chuī téng dòng tóng líng dòng! Chī pútao bù tǔ pútao pí, bù chī pútao dáo tǔ pútao pí! Sì shí sì, shí shì shí, shísì shí shísì, sìshí shí sìshí, sìshísì zhi bùshízǐ zhi shíshīzǐ shì sǐ de! Jiào jǐngchá! Wǒ de qìdiànchuán zhuāngmǎn le shànyú!"

I hadn't the faintest idea what he was saying. All I could think about was how ludicrously odd the situation was. I glanced over at Mia and Nola, who were wrapped up in equally engrossing conversation with some of the others, then focused my attention back on Kirk and began to cogitate. We were three pubescent girls partying in a swank pad with thirteen grown men who were obsequiously catering to our every wish. What were they getting out of it? Sure, they had our company, but what else?

As I studied this pitiful, strung-out fool – who was showering me with gifts in the form of cocaine and absurdly overpriced champagne, even though he had no guarantee that his munificence would pay off – I experienced a jimdandy of an epiphany. It was the precise moment I became aware of the infinite power a woman can have over a man when he thinks there's a glimmer of a chance she's going to sleep with him. She doesn't even have to be a raving beauty, and depending upon how badly he wants her, she can persuade him to do nearly anything she desires. Although I'd discussed the matter with Tai on more than one occasion, it hadn't fully registered until now.

That second rule I'd established for myself? I'd never, ever sell my ass for a fix. Not merely because I didn't want to, I was literally incapable. It was a combination of my intractable pride and the psychological disfigurement I'd suffered at the hands of Dave. The attempted molestation had not only birthed an ineradicable ferocious rage toward unwanted advances, but had also left me with intimacy issues, making it impossible to engage in meaningless sex. Moreover, I knew that putting out wasn't necessary. Tai had assured me that the possibility was a far more effective tool than the act itself, at least in the short term, and I took him at his word. After all, he was a man, and who would know better than a man?

Fortunately – or unfortunately, depending on how you look at it, I suppose – there was never a shortage of suckers I could string along for a while before they figured out they were getting nowhere fast. If given the choice, I would have killed the fuckers and nicked their stashes before even considering allowing them to defile me. Unsurprisingly, my mother once confessed that she thought my girlfriends and I were teenage prostitutes. Our risqué clothing, irregular hours, unexplained income, and numerous "gentleman companions" had aroused her suspicions, and when she discovered my little black book and business card collection while snooping in my room one day, she became convinced. Well, I've said it myriad times, and will continue to say it whenever necessary: I came across a plethora of Kirks while trapped in the jaws of addiction, and the gospel truth is I *never* bartered my body for *anything*, not once.

Coincidentally, Nola hooked up with one of the guests that night, and embarked on what would turn out to be a long-term relationship. Like Damita before her, she eventually vanished from my life altogether.

After a month of freeloading, Kirk realized that Mia and I were never going to sleep with him, and abruptly gave us the boot. It was no skin off our noses, though. During our brief "fling" we'd milked thousands of dollars worth of cocaine from him, not to mention several meals. In our one-track minds, the grift was a smashing success.

LIME RANT

I learned of His existence from an acquaintance, who gushed about Him as though He were a divine being. After considering her atrocious taste in men, I'd all but written Him off, except she kept mentioning Him over and over again, propelling my curiosity into overdrive. I wasted no time in squeezing her for details, including the whereabouts of the alleged Adonis, so I could judge for myself.

As luck would have it, He was an avid surfer who hit the same beach at the same time every day. I decided to spy on him one afternoon, dragging Kiki along for moral support. We set up camp near the shore and waited impatiently for Him to emerge from the waves. When He did, I was *awestruck*. I wondered where on Earth He had been hiding. Not wanting Him to think that I was mentally disturbed, I quickly turned my head. Kiki, however, was unable to avert her stunned gaze, prompting Him to stop and say hello.

"Hey, how's it going?" he asked, smiling.

"Good," she replied, still goggling. "The waves look pretty shitty today, huh?"

"They're always shitty," He laughed, pointing toward the houses above the beach. "I just surf here because it's convenient. I live right there."

Neither Kiki nor I said a word. She kept staring while I tried my best to do the opposite.

"Well, I'd better get going," He said, checking His watch. "I have to be at work in an hour. See ya."

And He was gone, leaving His indelible mark on both my mind and heart.

Thirteen days would pass before I'd speak to Him, and in the meantime, a strange phenomenon began to occur. He kept popping up everywhere, and not merely in corporeal form. It seemed as though His name or initials were plastered everywhere I looked... license plates, billboards, menus, etc. Was it possible He'd always been there, and I'd somehow failed to notice? Or could it be attributed to infatuation-induced psychosis?

The decisive encounter took place on a tranquil yet sultry night. Kiki and I were loitering at the pier with some of the Locals, when He approached with a friend.

"Hey," He said, flashing that heavenly smile, "what's up?"

"Not much," Kiki replied, taking a drag on her cigarette, "just hanging out."

"Do you want to walk down to the beach with us?" He asked, revealing a fat joint encased in His palm. "I don't have anyone to share this with."

"What about him?" Kiki asked, pointing her thumb at the friend.

"You two are much nicer to look at," He laughed, looking at me.

I tried to turn my head, but it was stuck.

"Thanks a lot, you fuckin' prick!" the friend laughed.

"So, what do you say?" He asked, still staring.

I tried to respond, but my latent shrinking violet had reached up my esophagus and tied my tongue in a bowline knot. All I could do was gape at Him in reverence. I'd never been intimidated by *any* man, but this celestial creature made me swoon. I was officially in lust.

"Yeah, sure," Kiki replied, yanking me off the railing I was perched upon, "let's go."

As we walked down to the beach, the others engaged in small talk, while I fell deeper into my aphonic state. I couldn't make the slightest sound, and could only look at Him when He wasn't looking at me. He must have thought I was a mute imbecile. I *had* to get a grip if I was ever going to stand a chance with Him.

Sensing I was a complete mess, Kiki removed a pint of Jack Daniels from her purse, and handed it to me. I ripped off the cap and took a couple of healthy swigs, hoping it would boost my confidence, or at the very least, kick start my larynx. It did neither. Instead, it only intensified my incapacitating desire, which was already aggravated by the aphrodisiac effects of the crepuscular beach. I wasn't the only one who was aroused either. Before the joint had reached roach status, Kiki and the friend were sucking face, which put me in a rather precarious position. I could no longer focus my attention on them, but couldn't so much as glance at the object of my obsession, so I stared at the glistening black ocean and tuned out. The silence was painfully awkward, but I didn't know else what to do. I was so intimidated by His presence I nearly vomited.

Just when I thought it couldn't get any worse, Kiki and the friend stood up and walked away, hand in hand. I wondered where the hell they were going, and it was all I could do to keep from screaming, "COME BACK!!!!!"

Before I knew it, His arm was coiled tightly around my waist, leaving me no choice but to look at Him.

"Would you mind if I kissed you?" He asked, gazing into my luststruck eyes.

Would I mind? Was He kidding?

"No," I quavered.

He wrapped his hand around my nape, pulled me toward Him, and kissed me tenderly. The instant His lips touched mine, the crippling bashfulness vanished, and I metamorphosed into a wildcat in heat. I pushed Him back on the sand and attacked.

What ensued was a make-out session that was too sublime to be sublunary. Our mouths fit together perfectly, as though they'd been custom-made for each other, and He tasted ambrosial. I was helplessly spellbound, and at that moment, would have massacred an entire family if He'd asked – parents, children, and pets.

He and I quickly established a "relationship" that was far from conventional. Sometimes we'd hang out as platonic friends, and other times engage in prolonged make-out sessions. It was terribly confusing, but I didn't care, as long as I was with Him. My emotions were raging and vacillating between ecstasy and despair. Infatuation can be both blissful and excruciating. If you believe that the object of your desire may requite your feelings, blind obsession can take over, which was precisely what happened here. He sent out mixed signals, making it impossible to accurately analyze the situation. All I knew for certain was that He ruled me. My feelings for Him were overwhelming and uncontrollable, especially on a sexual level. All He had to do was *look* at me, and I'd be struck with a compulsion to tackle Him, tear off His clothes with my teeth, and lick every inch of His naked body. Despite my overpowering urge to jump His bones, a full year would pass before we would consummate our (non)relationship.

It happened on a weeknight at a local park, where Kiki and I had rendezvoused with Him and the friend on many occasions. The four of us were sitting on the jungle gym, polishing off our second case of beer, when Kiki and the friend started to kiss. Naturally, He and I followed suit.

As with every make out session that had preceded, I couldn't help wondering why He didn't at least make a run for third base. Believe it or not, His hands had never found their way down my pants or up my shirt. Any and all groping had been done through my clothing. While some girls may have found it gentlemanly, I was on the cusp of a nervous breakdown. *Why the hell didn't He want me? Was I that repulsive? Was it my face? Was it my body? Or was it the entirety of my grotesque physical deformities that were supposedly nonexistent and only visible to me? What the hell was it?* My young mind was overrun with these torturous thoughts. It wasn't His fault, but

He had a way of turning me into a self-doubting basket case. I read into whatever He said and did, misconstrued it, and took it personally. What a neurotic freak. I was so damn insecure I honestly believed that He didn't find me attractive enough to screw. Remember the advice Tai had given me on the beach that day? Well, whenever the object of my obsession was within range, I'd suffer a case of amnesia. *That* was the power He possessed.

In any event, I was legally drunk, illicitly horny, and tired of pussyfooting around. My maidenhead was still intact, and He was going to rupture it, whether He liked it or not. If that meant that I had to take the initiative, then so be it. After kissing passionately for a while, I came up for air and looked deep into His entrancing eyes.

"Let's do it," I whispered, smiling, "before I change my mind."

"Are you sure?" He asked, looking deep into my entranced eyes.

I responded with a long and lustful kiss.

His next question nearly spoiled the rapturous moment, although it was a reasonable one to ask.

"I don't have any condoms, do you?"

STDs didn't even enter my mind. I was willing to catch whatever He had, but the very thought of pregnancy was horrifying. Conveniently, my mother was terrified that some lascivious beast was going to fertilize me with his demon seed, and had forced me to go on the Pill a couple of months prior. Yes, I was a bit young, but I think it was a wise decision on my mother's part.

"Don't sweat it," I said, smiling confidently, "I'm on the Pill."

And off we went to His car…

What ensued was *transcendentally divine*. Actually, I'm romanticizing it. In truth, it was incredibly awkward and extremely uncomfortable. Every girl who undergoes this rite of passage suffers some degree of physical discomfort, but the fact that He and I were doing it in a confined space while half-dressed only exacerbated matters. There was also an unidentified hard object pressing into the center of my spine the entire time. And needless to say, achieving an orgasm was out of the question. *But* I was so ecstatic about *the idea* of losing my virginity to Him that it masked most of the pain, and when He climaxed, my infatuation skyrocketed to new heights. He now *owned* me. I swore right then and there that no other man would ever touch me again, for as long as I lived, only Him.

At fifteen, my knowledge regarding matters of the heart was scant, and when you want to believe something badly enough, the mind has a way of convincing you that it's true. It's called optimism, and while it can be deeply inspiring, it can also be dangerously deceptive, because it renders you blind. Even the most conspicuous truth becomes imperceptible because your visual acuity is being clouded by a pair of rose-colored trifocals. I wanted desperately to believe that He shared my feelings, and gave myself to Him *knowing* that our sexual friendship would progress into an intensely beautiful monogamous relationship. But it didn't and I was devastated. I'd learned early on not to have any exceptions in life, and more important, not to take stock in most human beings. I know that sounds dreadfully pessimistic, but when you're a kid, and feel as though you've been bombarded with disappointment, it's easy to become disillusioned. In an effort to survive, I also became detached, a defense mechanism that had never failed. As long as I remained stoic, I wouldn't get hurt. But the heart is self-governing. No matter how hard you try, it cannot be controlled.

A month later, I slept with Him again, and it was an utter fiasco. Even though we were naked and on a California King, it didn't help. I was doped up on a cocktail of drugs, and He was so tanked it was a miracle He was able to function at all. I went into the bedroom expecting tender, ineffable lovemaking, only to suffer through hurried, mechanical sex.

As horrible as it was, it didn't change the way I felt about Him. I simply wrote it off as an ill-timed mistake, and told myself it would be better next time. But there would never be a next time, for shortly after that second roll in the hay, He entered into a monogamous relationship with another. You'd think I would have wanted to decapitate and dismember the bitch then feed her into a wood chipper, but I didn't. She was a lovely girl who didn't have one unlikable bone in her willowy frame. She was the kind of girl who would make a fine "wife" one day: innocent, virtuous, domesticated, accommodating, and above all, "normal." The antipode of yours truly. She'd made Him fall in love with her, and destroyed me in the process, but she was so damn sweet I couldn't help liking her. Of course I'd be lying if I said it wasn't heart-wrenching to see them together. Sometimes I felt as though a thick corkscrew were being twisted through the center of my soul, and other times, as though I'd been disemboweled. It was *agonizing*, but what could I do? After contemplating suicide for a week, I drugged myself into oblivion, and forced myself to march on.

He and I remained amicable, but our relationship never returned to its previous state, even after He'd broken up with the girlfriend. A few years later, I saw him for the last time, and what a telling encounter that was. As I interacted with him, I couldn't help noticing the discernible changes. At first I thought it was my imagination, but as the night progressed, the sad truth was revealed. He was no longer that radiant god whose heart I would have murdered for. He was now a bitter mortal, who was clearly headed toward a dismal place. I can recall the exact moment when I realized I was over him. I was sitting on a couch with Mia, when he squeezed in between us, put his arm around me, and slurred the following words into my ear: "You're looking pretty fine. Should we see if the third time's a charm?"

Not only did I find his line disgustingly crass, but for the first time since I'd known him, his touch made me recoil. It was inconceivable, but I didn't want him anywhere near me. Not because I found him physically repulsive, he looked as delicious as ever. He simply wasn't the same person, and the person he'd become wasn't someone I wanted to know. It was difficult to imagine I'd ever had *any* feelings for him, let alone that he'd possessed me for what seemed like an eternity. It was troubling, yet cathartic, and above all, *liberating*. The manacles had finally been removed. I was free, and would *never* allow myself to become enslaved again.

THE BH AND THE BS

A month had passed since the second and final romp with the object of my obsession, who still owned my heart, despite the fact that His belonged to another. I desperately wanted to make Him mine, but hadn't the faintest idea how. My dealings with members of the opposite sex were limited to platonic friendships with those I loved or the necessary exploitation of those who could feed my habit. What's more, I was absent when the headgame microchips were being installed, which were obviously essential for functioning in the field of romance. I thought feigning disinterest in order to win someone's affection was absurdly dysfunctional, not to mention a complete waste of time and energy, but it seemed to be the way of the world. Then again, perhaps *I* was the maladapted one, since I'd rarely been physically attracted to *anyone*, and when I had, it was always instant and at times, inexplicable. Such was the case with a charming creature I encountered on a torrid summer night.

Kiki and I were at Carl's Jr., slurping down milkshakes, when in walked two men who had to be pushing thirty. Both were tall and moderately inked. The brawny bull had his head cleanly shaven, but it was the rawboned cat who caught my dexter and sinister. He had a perfectly pronounced jaw line and cheekbones, and tangerine hair that stood up on end like a crown of dancing flames, complemented by a pair of strikingly beautiful cerulean eyes. Although the coif bore a disturbing resemblance to Heat Miser's, he was attractive, in an ominous way. They swaggered over to our booth and sat down.

"Guten Abend," the skinhead said, with a crooked smile. "I'm Kyle, this is Jake."

Kiki and I introduced ourselves.

"We're on our way to a raging block party," he continued, "you gotta come along."

Kiki and I had spent the entire day at the beach, drugging with the Locals, and were completely played out.

"Sounds like a blast," Kiki yawned, "but we've been partying all day, we're gonna have to pass."

It was clearly not what they wanted to hear. Jake was now practically sitting in my lap, cooing honeyed words into my ears. "You're me" was his line. How crudely romantic. It reminded me of Tarzan. And isn't that what Ann Dvorak said to Paul Muni in the original *Scarface*, right before they took on the coppers?

"I'm flattered," I said sarcastically, scooting away, "but frazzled."

"Yeah, we're done," Kiki added, placing a cigarette in her mouth, "maybe some other time."

"That's too bad," Kyle said, lighting her cigarette, "'cause we got a shitload of blow."

"Damn!" she laughed, throwing her arm over his shoulder. "You just had to say the magic word, didn't you?!"

While walking to their van Kiki called shotgun, forcing me to ride in back with Jake, who was becoming increasingly more attractive. There was no denying it, the man exuded sex appeal, but my heart belonged to the object of my obsession, who'd busted my precious cherry, ripped out my ticker and entrails, and tossed them all into a multi-bladed Cuisinart. I couldn't even *think* about another man. Or so I thought.

En route to the party we stopped at the beach to limber up with Jack and Coke – Daniels and Caine, that is. It wasn't long before Kyle and Kiki were all over each other. While I ignored them, Jake stared and laughed out loud, as though he were watching a pornographic sitcom.

"Fuck off, dick!" Kyle yelled, flinging a lighter at him. "It's too crowded in here," he said to Kiki, "let's go for a walk."

And off they went. As expected, Jake wasted no time in launching a full-scale assault with his meat hooks. After trying in vain to rebuff the lecherous fusillade, I took refuge in the suicide seat. He followed and planted his repellently magnetic self in the driver's seat.

"Keep those fucking paws to yourself," I threatened, with my back pressed against the window, like a defensive cat, "or you'll be sorry."

"Why?" he laughed. "What are you gonna do?"

"Touch me and find out."

Realizing that he was getting nowhere fast, he let up a bit, and we began to chat in a "mature" manner. I noticed right away that he wasn't as shallow or one-dimensional as I'd thought. It turned out he was a musician, which was what I'd pegged him as. We discussed music, film, literature, drugs, and politics, and much to my amazement, jibed all the way. At first, I thought he was bullshitting to win me over, but his knowledge was far too extensive and his opinions far too explicit.

"Have you ever made it all the way through *Cut the Crap*?" he asked, placing his hand on my thigh.

"Once," I replied, removing the hand.

"And?"

"It was like eating a Reese's Peanut Butter Cup without the peanut butter."

"That's the right answer, but I've never heard anyone put it like *that* before. You're wacky."

I stuck my tongue out at him.

"It's weird that you used a food analogy though, 'cause I do that all the time."

"Wow, and I figured you for a sex analogy guy," I said smartly.

"It's just another sign that you and I are destined to be together, baby," he sighed, ignoring my remark and placing his hand back on my thigh.

"The only reason I used a food analogy is because I'm fucking famished," I said, removing the hand again. "I haven't had a solid bite since breakfast. My stomach feels like it's eating itself from the inside out. Is there anything to munch on in this piece of shit?"

He reached into the glove box and pulled out a three-pack of assorted fruit flavored Tums.

"Thanks," I said, grabbing them.

"You're not really gonna eat those, are you? It was meant to be a joke."

I tore open one of the packages and began popping them into my mouth like Sweet Tarts.

He started to roar. "You're a fuckin' freak! I can't believe you're actually eating those!"

"Why not?" I said, chewing on a chalky mouthful. "I'm on the verge of a hypoglycemic fit, and these fuckers are loaded with sucrose."

"I don't know if you should eat that many," he said, taking the remaining rolls from my hand. "It might not be safe."

"I just spent the entire day poisoning my body with a shitload of narcotics and stimulants, and you're worried about a couple dozen antacids?" I laughed. "Fuck off already."

He opened the window and flung the Tums out into the parking lot.

"You suck!" I yelled.

"I'm sorry, baby," he said, caressing my cheek. "Do you want me to go get them?"

I pushed his hand away and flipped him off. I wasn't angry about the Tums, but rather annoyed that I was becoming increasingly more attracted to him, despite my best efforts to resist.

"Do you want to know how old I am?" I asked coolly, glaring at him.

"I couldn't care less," he replied, gazing into my eyes, "I'm already in love with you."

"You are so full of shit it's oozing out of your pores," I scoffed, gazing back.

"I mean it, baby," he argued, caressing my cheek again, "you're the one. Don't you believe in love at first sight?"

"All I believe is that you're a horny motherfucker who's full of shit," I countered, pushing his hand away again, "and by the way, I'm only fifteen."

"Doesn't matter to me," he said, grinning cockily. "I wouldn't care if you were only thirteen."

"You're a dirty old man. You should be ashamed of yourself."

"Hey, is it a crime to prefer veal over beef?"

"When *you're beef* it is."

"Fuck, you turn me on," he growled, pulling me toward him.

"That's your problem, Trog," I countered, fending him off. "If you touch me again, I'll break all ten of your fingers, one at a time."

Suddenly, the door flew open.

"You're still dressed, huh?" Kyle asked, grinning at me. "You must be losin' it, Jake."

"I haven't lost shit, man. This one's a defiant little vixen. I've never seen anything like it. She's Kate the Shrew incarnate."

I flipped him off again and moved to the back seat. He followed.

"You guys ready to roll?" Kyle said, reclaiming the helm.

"Yeah," Jake replied, glancing over at me, "let's get this show on the road."

Upon arriving, we walked through the backyard of one of the houses, where we were greeted by a coke dealer named Gary, who was as slimy as can be. "Well, well, well," he said, opening the screen door, "look who's here. Come on in."

Jake, Kyle, Kiki, and I sat down on the couch, while Gary positioned himself in the love seat opposite. After undressing Kiki and me with his eyes, he reached over the coffee table and handed me a sawed-off McDonald's straw. "Help yourself, sweetheart," he said, pointing toward a batch of freshly chopped lines that were resting on a mirror in front of me.

I snorted a tetrad – two for each nostril – then passed the straw to Kiki.

"Sssssoooo," he hissed through a slick smile, "where did you two come from?"

"We found them at a Carl's Jr.," Kyle said, petting Kiki's hair. "Unbelievable, huh?"

"You don't say!" Gary exclaimed sarcastically. "Which one do I get?"

Kiki and I glared at him. To indicate that I was already spoken for, Jake pulled me onto his lap, which I didn't mind, given the circumstances.

"Aren't you going to let me play with your toy, Jake?" Gary said, waving his forefinger at me.

"She's no toy, man," Jake replied, wrapping his arms around me, "she's the one. I asked for a soul mate and God sent her."

"God, huh?" Gary laughed. "And when did you become religious?"

"About an hour ago," Jake replied, smiling.

"How old are you, little girl," Gary hissed.

Before I had a chance to answer, Jake cut in. "Doesn't matter, man."

"You know Jake's a shameless and incurable womanizer, right?" Gary said, taking the straw from

Kyle. "He's left a trail of broken hearts from here to New York City."

"Don't listen to him, baby," Jake whispered loudly, resting his chin on my shoulder. "He's a mean old son-of-a-bitch who hasn't been fucked or blown in a year. He's only saying that shit 'cause he's sexually frustrated."

Gary grinned archly, then slapped his forehead and said, "Crap, I almost forgot! Candy showed up, and she's *blitzed*. She's been knocking on my door all damn night, looking for you."

"Who's Candy?" Kiki asked.

"My ex," Jake sighed.

Gary and Kyle started to laugh quietly, as though they were privy to an inside joke.

"What's so fucking funny?" I asked.

"Candy's gonna smoke her, man!" Kyle said to Jake. "The second she sees her!"

"What are you talkin' about?" Kiki asked.

"Well, she'd be pissed anyway that Jake's got someone else, but even worse, she fuckin' *hates* blondes," Kyle replied. "She's beaten the shit outta tons since I've known her."

I flipped around and glared at Jake, who was smiling sheepishly. I had a sneaking suspicion I'd been handpicked and brought along for a reason. "What the fuck, asshole?"

"Don't worry, baby," he said, stroking my back. "I won't let her harm one hair on your pretty head."

"How punningly clever," Gary snickered.

"She hates blondes?" Kiki exclaimed, looking over at Jake. "What a fuckin' bigot! That's like hating someone 'cause they're black! Why the fuck would you wanna be with a cunt like that?"

"I know tons of chicks who hate blondes," Kyle said, "and when I ask 'em why, they can't give a justifiable answer."

"That's because they don't have one," Gary said, passing the straw to Jake. "They're pissed off that most men are partial to blondes, including Alfred Hitchcock... and me."

"Amen to that, brother," Kyle said, lighting a cigarette. "The world can never have too many blondes."

"I don't think that's true," Kiki said, taking the cigarette from his mouth and placing it in hers. "Most guys are impartial perverts. They don't give a shit what color a chick's hair is."

"She's right," I agreed.

"And how would you know?" Gary asked. "You're chicks."

"And blonde," Kyle added, lighting another cigarette.

"Because I've had every hair color known to mankind," Kiki laughed, exhaling, "and some that aren't."

"And your point is?" Gary interjected.

"The pigs gawked and wolf-whistled with the same amount of gusto no matter what fuckin' color it was."

"That's 'cause you're a babe," Kyle said, smiling at her adoringly.

"No," she retorted matter-of-factly, "it's because I've had huge tits since I was ten."

The rest of us burst out laughing.

"It's true!" she exclaimed. "Ninety-nine percent of the guys that check me out never make it past my tits! They have no fuckin' clue what color my hair is, and I bet they care even less."

"Blonde, brunette, redhead, bald, makes no difference to me," Jake said, smiling dreamily. "As long as she's fine, I'm into it."

"You're hopeless, man!" Kyle laughed. "No wonder Candy wants to stuff your dick down your throat!"

"And speaking of the Amazon woman from the depths of hell," Gary said, flashing a sinister grin, "you'd better hide your little friend here. If Candy sees her, she'll tear her limb from limb."

"You guys don't know what you're talking about," Jake said, as I took the straw from his hand. "Candy's a mature adult. As soon as I explain the situation, she'll walk away peacefully, and I'll finally be able to get on with my life."

"And what exactly *is* the situation?" Gary asked mockingly.

"That I'm madly in love with someone else," Jake replied, kissing my cheek.

"Yeah!" Kyle laughed. "That'll go over *real* well, man!"

"Come on, baby," Jake whispered, ignoring their remarks, "let's go outside and find her."

"Why," I asked, diving into the mirror again, "so I can die?"

I was no coward, but knew my limitations.

"I promise I'm not gonna let her touch you."

"Bullshit," I replied, standing up and handing the straw to Kiki, "but I'm suddenly feeling masochistic. Let's go, before I change my mind."

Right as we stepped out into the backyard, there was Candy – all six feet, 170 pounds of her – coming through the gate. "WHO THE FUCK IS THAT?!" she yelled, storming over.

"The love of my life," Jake replied, parking his hands on my derriere.

"GET THE FUCK AWAY FROM MY MAN, YOU FUCKIN' SKANK!" she screamed, getting right up into my face, "OR I'LL SMASH YOUR FUCKIN' FACE INTO THE CONCRETE!"

I had a *minor* problem with her attitude, she had malodorous breath that was singeing my eyebrows with every respiration, and I've *never* been fond of being threatened. My temper simply couldn't and shouldn't abide, *ever*. I pushed her as hard as I could. After losing her footing for a moment, she rebounded and pounced with all her might.

When predicting the winner in a catfight, above all, one must consider the tale of the tape. More often than not, the larger girl is going to get the upper hand, unless the smaller girl possesses the fighting skills of Fedor Emelianenko, which most *men* don't, much less women. I was going to be dead within a matter of seconds, but thankfully, Jake was able to contain her rather quickly. As he dragged her into the house, Kyle and Kiki came outside.

"Shit, are you okay?" Kiki asked, helping me up.

I was livid, and determined to get revenge on the bitch. "What the fuck did I get myself into?" I said, straightening my disheveled clothes. "And who the fuck does she think she is?"

"Do you want me to kick her ass?" Kiki asked, cracking her knuckles.

What a loyal friend she was.

"Thanks," I said, scheming, "but I have an even better idea."

Moments later, when the loving couple emerged, Candy appeared to be calm and content, which I found tremendously annoying.

"Watch this," I said to Kiki.

"What are you gonna do?" she asked, laughing.

"Just watch," I replied, walking straight into the hornet's nest.

After giving Candy the evil eye, I wrapped my arms around Jake and began kissing him passionately. Before the bloodthirsty bitch could retaliate, Kyle got hold of her and dragged her to the other side of the yard, where she launched into a murderous verbal assault.

"YOU FUCKIN' SKANK! YOU FUCKIN' SKANK! I'LL FUCKIN' KILL YOU, YOU FUCKIN' SKANK! I'LL RIP YOUR FUCKIN' HAIR OUT BY THE ROOTS! I'LL BREAK YOUR FUCKIN' ARMS IN TWO!"

Her outburst only fueled my retributive objective, and as luck would have it, Jake was an eager accomplice. And so this man, who I'd been fighting tooth and nail, was victorious after all. I jumped up and wrapped my legs around his waist. He cupped my rump in his hands and began thrusting his crotch into mine. I surfaced for a moment and glared at Candy, who was fuming and desperately attempting to break free from Kyle's hold. I smiled, flipped her off, and went back under. It was poetic. Even if she'd gotten loose, ripped out every strand of my hair, and broken all four of my limbs, it wouldn't have mattered. I'd already won.

"Let's get the fuck out of here!" Kyle shouted across the yard. "You two go ahead, we'll be there in a few!"

Jake slung my body over his shoulder and strode back to the van. Before my feet had touched the ground, he pinned me against the door and started tearing at my clothes. After stumbling onto the back seat, we steamed up the windows for what felt like an eternity, but turned out to be ten minutes.

"You guys ready to roll?" Kyle said, tearing open the door. "There's another party on the other side of town."

I wriggled out of Jake's clutches, sat up, and tried to fasten my safety belt, but he wouldn't let go. He kept sucking me into his erogenous vortex, and while it was an elysian place to bathe, I had no interest in flying through the windshield if there happened to be an accident.

"Let me put on my seat belt," I said, pushing him away.

He growled and pulled me down again.

"Fuck off, you beast!" I laughed, smacking him across the face.

Without meaning to, I'd unleashed a salacious animal that was impossible to tame. He was a man on a mission, and that mission was clear: he wanted to screw right there on the back seat, and didn't care if there was an audience. I had no intention of having intercourse with him, and now that I'd achieved my retaliatory goal, I really had no use for him. Yes, he was sinfully scrumptious, but I was only two shtups removed from virginity, and as I mentioned, I belonged to another. The fact that I was deluding myself about the latter bit was irrelevant. Besides, Jake was obviously a slut, who knows where he'd dipped his stick. Contracting herpes or, worse yet, HIV was not on my list of goals. I needed to extinguish his flame immediately before he exploded into a five alarm inferno.

"I'm going to hurl," I announced vociferously.

Even if a man is as horny as a three-balled tomcat, he won't want to dine on regurgitated intestinal matter. It stopped Jake dead in his tracks, but he continued to scheme.

By the time we reached our destination, my little white lie had become a nauseating reality. My head was spinning out of control. It was all I could do to keep from tossing my Tums. The last thing I wanted to do was go into a box filled with rowdy drunks and deafening punk rock.

"I need to go home," I moaned. "NOW."

"I'll take her home," Jake said to Kyle. "You guys go ahead. I'll be back later."

Of course he had no intention of taking me home.

"I just wanna make sure you're okay first," he lied. "Here, lay your head in my lap, and close your eyes. I'm gonna take care of you."

Like an idiot, I obeyed.

He began running his fingers through my hair while spewing another dose of honeyed words.

Like a bigger idiot, I made the error of looking up at those entrancing baby blues, which he mistook as an invitation to deliver a kiss.

"I'm warning you," I slurred, dodging his lips, "if I don't get to sleep soon, I'm going to puke all over you."

"So sleep right here, baby," he said, gazing through disingenuous doe eyes. "I promise I won't violate you."

"Do you ever quit?" I snapped in an irritated tone. "I'm not going to fuck you, asshole! You'd better just let it go, and take me home! I want my fucking bed!"

"I want your bed too," he replied, smiling lasciviously, "with you in it."

"You're a horny pervert."

"I know," he said proudly, "does it turn you on?"

"No, it doesn't *turn me on*, it's annoying as shit."

He started to laugh.

"If you weren't so fucking beautiful, you would have been dead a couple of hours ago," I said calmly, closing my eyes. "Now take me home, motherfucker, before I kill you."

His laughter progressed into cachinnation.

I looked up at him with desire and desperation. He was irresistibly alluring, but my nausea had now reached a dangerous level. If I didn't get to sleep immediately, I'd be barfing digestive juice all night.

"Will you *please* take me home?" I begged, grabbing hold of his hand. "I'm not kidding, I really feel like shit!"

"I'm afraid I can't do that, baby," he said, placing his free hand on my face.

"Why the fuck not?"

"'Cause I may never see you again, and that won't do at all. Looks like I'm gonna have to kidnap you and chain you to my furnace."

"You're too fucking much," I chuckled. "Are you always so persistent?"

"When I want something, I am," he replied, caressing my cheek. "And you, I want."

"FUUUUUUUCK!" I whined. "What the hell do I have to do to get you to take me home?"

He slipped his hand up my shirt.

"I guess that was a stupid question," I said, abruptly removing it.

The negotiations continued for several minutes. I finally offered my telephone number in exchange for my release, and promised I'd go out with him the following weekend. After considering the deal for a moment, he agreed.

When we entered my neighborhood, I directed him to a house down the street, so he wouldn't know where I lived. He stopped the car, turned off the engine, and made his final move.

"I'm yours, baby," he cooed, gazing at me with those dreamy eyes, "mind, body, and soul."

I giggled like an eleven year old, despite myself.

"I mean it," he continued, "you've stolen my heart. I wanna spend the rest of my life with you."

Awwww, ain't that sweet? A bit schmaltzy, but sweet nonetheless. Too bad he was full of shit, and if by some rare chance he was speaking from the heart, *no way*! It was fun for one night, but I'd had my fill. Besides, I liked being alive, and as long as I was with him, there would be a price on my head, courtesy of the wrathful Candy.

After giving him a fake number and a goodbye smooch, we parted ways forever.

BLACK LABEL

Despite its relentless attempts to interfere with my destructive disguised as fun lifestyle, I successfully shirked school and nearly all obligations associated with it. I had more important business to attend to, and it made no difference which prefix was attached to the day. Mia and I spent many a school night drugging and partaking in criminal activity with Pluto, Murph, and Chuck, who shared our unquenchable thirst for mischief and action.

Pluto was an amusingly wicked bastard, who never failed to deliver a rip-roaring time. He was also one of the biggest bigots I've ever known. In many ways, he epitomized the fascist breed of skinhead that had surfaced in the 80s, except he was all talk. Apparently, that's changed, but for the purpose of our journey, I'm sticking with what he was when I knew him.

Murph was Pluto's most trusted accomplice. He was equally wild, but far more tolerant and reserved. He rarely spoke, and when he did, never said more than a handful of words at a time.

Then there was Chuck, another neighborhood Catholic child gone astray, who would ultimately meet a tragic demise, via a shotgun, a few years down the road. Although he considered himself a hardcore punker through and through, he had a closet fondness for Sunshine Pop. He said it made him "feel good inside," which is what it was intended to do. I thought the "incongruity" was as "punk" as it gets, but his fellow "punks" begged to differ. Whenever he attempted to sell them on "The 59th Street Bridge Song," fisticuffs ensued.

It was on one of these play dates that I was reminded of how hurtful teasing can be, even when it's meant to be harmless. When our partners in crime arrived, Mia and I were hitting the bong in one of her father's broken-down jalopies.

"Shit!" she exclaimed, after spotting their car in the rearview mirror. "This is the last of it, and it's not enough for three more sets of lungs."

"Quick," I said quietly, sliding down in my seat, "get down before they see us."

"Here, let's finish it off real quick," she whispered, handing me the bong and lighting the bowl. "Smoke, smoke, as fast as you can!"

The guys were approaching the front door, when Chuck spotted us out of the corner of his eye. "Hey, what the fuck?" he yelled, smiling.

"What's up, bro?" Pluto said, turning around.

Chuck pointed toward the car, and laughed, "Oh, you twooooo!"

Mia and I burst out laughing and rolled down the windows, releasing a squall of pungent smoke in the process.

Pluto immediately rushed the car. "You little fuckin' bogarts!" he laughed, leaning into the window. "Kick the fuck down, right now!"

Mia smacked him on the head repeatedly with her free hand, while cachinnating to the point of tears. After a brief but vicious tug of war match, he threw in the towel. The instant he admitted defeat, she handed him the bong with a sweet smile.

A half hour later, Murph's car was idling in the drive-thru of a dairy mart that was infamous for selling booze to patrons under the legal drinking age. While the owner filled the trunk with three cases of beer, Pluto was struck with a brilliant idea.

"Hey, fuck this chink," he said, staring at the South Korean gentleman through the wing mirror. "I'm sick of givin' him my bread. He's not gettin' another cent outta me. As soon as he's done loadin' the shit, let's bail."

"The license plate?" Murph asked, glancing over at Pluto.

"Don't let him close the trunk, bro. The second the shit's in there, hit the fuckin' gas."

"Nice," Murph said, grinning.

It sounded like a fail-safe plan, and I had to agree with my racist friend, it certainly wasn't going to break the guy.

"Hey," Pluto called out to the unsuspecting proprietor, "how 'bout throwin' in a coupla bags of Doritos while you're at it?"

The instant the chips were in the trunk, Murph hit the gas and peeled out. I looked out the back window and saw the poor owner screaming and shaking his fists in the air. Pluto leaned out of the car and flipped him off with one hand, while making the cunnilingus sign with the other.

Ten minutes later, we arrived at our destination: Forest Lawn Cypress, the final resting place of Eddie

Cochran, and at the time, Karen Carpenter. After scaling the cement wall, we, the living dead, spent the evening whooping it up with the departed.

Around midnight, we were en route to Bob's Big Boy for a late dinner, when Pluto sniffed the air and uttered the following three words: "I smell bacon."

The police department was well familiar with our gang. Since the area's modest population consisted primarily of "normal" law-abiding citizens, it was quite easy to single out the troublemakers. As expected, the cop made an immediate U-turn and pulled us over.

"Ah, fuck," Chuck said, peering out the rear window. "It's that fuckin' dickwad, Smith."

"Shit," Pluto said, turning around as inconspicuously as he could. "That fuckin' chink must have called the pigs."

"He's a jap," Chuck said, lighting a cigarette.

"You're both wrong," Mia interjected. "He's Korean."

"Jap, chink, gook, what's the fuckin' difference," Pluto said, keeping an eye on the cop, "they all look the same to me."

"That's because you're an imbecile," she retorted.

Murph let out a muted chuckle. He appeared to be completely unfazed by the fact that we were about to be arrested for theft, not to mention the DUI charge he'd be facing.

Smith, the cop, was now standing at Murph's window. "Where you headed?" he asked, scoping out the inside of the car with his flashlight.

"Bob's," Murph replied, calmly.

"Case of the midnight munchies, huh?"

"Yeah, something like that."

Smith's radio suddenly went off. "Don't move," he said, walking back to his car.

Here we go again, I thought. The store owner's description of Murph's rare and unique car must have been spot-on. I figured we were screwed and going to straight to jail. I wondered what my mother's reaction would be this time, if any. By now, her slackness had morphed into indifference, probably out of frustration. I looked over at Mia, who rolled her eyes and flashed a pouty frown.

Moments later, Smith returned to the window, wearing a solemn expression on his face. "Isn't Jimmy Foster one of yours?" he asked, after clearing his throat.

"Sorta," Pluto replied, yawning nervously. "Why?"

"He was found dead approximately one hour ago. It appears to be a suicide."

I'd first met Jimmy Foster through Jamie, who'd known him since elementary school. The three of us were in the same P.E. class at high school. I didn't know him well, and could never form a strong opinion about him in any way. I did notice that he was invariably out of place, and desperately searching for acceptance, which had aroused both my sympathy and empathy. His most recent goal was to be a member of our gang. I didn't know what his home life was like or what other demons he was battling, but over the past several months he'd endured ceaseless teasing and roughhousing, all in an effort to belong. Granted, it was done in a prankish manner, but perhaps he'd taken it harder than he'd let on. Nobody likes to be ridiculed or bullied, and for some, it can be unbearable.

"You're shittin' me!" Pluto exclaimed.

"What the fuck happened?" Chuck asked in disbelief. "I swear I just saw him earlier, skatin' down the boulevard!"

"Hanging," Smith replied matter-of-factly.

"Aww, no!" Mia cried, placing her hands on her cheeks. "That's a baaad trip, man! When?"

"Don't know."

After a moment of silence, Murph blurted out a rather stupid question that was bound to irritate the power-tripping hardass: "Umm, can we go now?"

Amid all the somberness I'd momentarily forgotten that Smith had pulled us over for a reason.

"'Cause I'm really fuckin' hungry," Murph added, as if the first utterance weren't damaging enough.

The rest of us cringed in our seats, as the words spilled out of his typically *closed* yap.

"You are, huh?" Smith said patronizingly, glaring at Murph, as though he were about to pistol whip him.

"Uh, yeah," Murph replied, turning around and looking at us for support. "Aren't you guys too?"

We ignored him and stared at Smith, waiting for his reaction.

After a brief pause, he replied gruffly, "Get lost. And when you're done at Bob's, go straight home."

"Yes, sir," Chuck said, saluting him.

"I'll be watching you," Smith added, looking at his watch. "I'm giving you till one, and if I catch you out here even *one minute* past, you're mine. Do you understand? *Mine*."

"Gotcha, bro," Pluto said through a fake smile. "Thanks for lettin' us go."

Smith's lenience couldn't have been more out of character. Jimmy's death must have momentarily thawed his frigid heart. Once the patrol car was out of sight, the mandatory anti-police rant ensued, followed by deafening silence.

I wasn't sure what the others were thinking or feeling, but I was confused and shocked. I couldn't believe Jimmy had actually hanged himself. There was never the slightest indication that he was depressed, let alone suicidal. He seemed to take life in stride. Even during the merciless hazing, he was always smiling. I wondered if his family knew yet. Did he leave a note? What kind of apparatus did he use? How long did it take for him to choke to death? How many hours had his body been hanging wherever it had been found? Who found him? Had he been planning it for a while, or did he wake up that morning and decide to end his short life? Or was it spur-of-the-moment? What was he on when he did it? Or was he sober? My morbid trance was abruptly interrupted when Pluto broke into song.

"*Needles stabbed into the walls... the executioner's curtain call... fighting back he found his life drowning... and there was no way out... 'cause Jimmy hung himself, Jimmy hung himself... it happened just the other day...*"

If you aren't familiar, it's a D.I. tune called "Richard Hung Himself," with a callously distasteful modification to the chorus. Without giving it a single thought, all five of us burst into hysterical laughter and picked up where Pluto left off.

Our dismissal of the tragedy in such an insensitive manner was reprehensible. Jimmy was obviously tormented inside for god knows how long. I'll never know his reasons for checking out early, but have to wonder if the cruelty he'd suffered didn't contribute to his despair. I'd been there myself only a few years prior, and could easily see why some may opt for the ultimate defensive measure. When one's trapped in a seemingly endless onslaught of abuse, it can feel as though there's no alternative.

Ironically, Jimmy finally gained that long sought-after acceptance in death. After years of struggling, he became the most popular kid in the city. For a couple of weeks, at least. Strange how people who were rarely thought of before, if at all, suddenly "matter" once they're dead. Everyone claims to have known and loved them. Whenever a comrade or former classmate died, he immediately gained an army of best friends, many of whom had never acknowledged his existence prior. Another way humans can assert their importance, albeit one of the sickest of all.

Leaving the party early. Having spent the better part of my childhood with an ambitiously suicidal mother, as well as wrestling with my own death instinct throughout my teenage years, my thoughts on the issue are conflicting. While there are certainly instances where checking out is the most merciful course of action, I believe that if the choice is being driven by drugs, other people, or an entirely surmountable situation (including adolescence) there's absolutely no justification. I read somewhere that suicide is the third leading cause of death among teenagers. How tragic, pointless, and above all, preventable. If only they could ride out that impressionable and often tortuous stage of life. What seems earth-shattering to a kid can appear in a completely different light once he's arrived at the other side. Perhaps if Jimmy had reached adulthood, he would have chosen to live.

PHLEGETHON

LIDÉRC

In order to tell the story as thoroughly and accurately as possible, I'm going to rewind to the summer evening when it all began. Lisa and I were walking through the local shopping center, en route to her house, when someone let out a loud wolf whistle. We turned around, and saw two young men standing next to a suped-up car.

"Should we go over there?" Lisa asked, checking them out.

From where I was standing, neither looked particularly attractive, but perhaps they had drugs.

"Yeah, why not," I replied, taking her hand and leading the way.

"Hello, beautiful girls," the scrawny one said, grinning like a used car salesman.

"Hey," Lisa and I replied nonchalantly.

They were a curious pair. The beefy one was grouchy and aloof, while the scrawny one was the polar opposite. They introduced themselves as Rance and Ed, respectively.

"You kinda look like a new waver," Rance said, after giving Lisa the once-over. "I hope you ain't into the fuckin' Cure."

"I fuckin' hate the Cure with a passion!" she exclaimed, smiling.

She was lying. *I* was the one who fucking hated the Cure with a passion. She was clearly trying to impress the guy, so I held my tongue.

"Good answer," he grumbled, forcing a smile. "They deserve your hatred."

"I know this rich poseur chick who thinks the Cure's a killer *punk* band," she laughed, snapping her gum. "Isn't that hilarious? The Cure, *punk*?"

"The Cure's all that punk ain't," he scoffed, "and any dude that likes 'em is a fuckin' faggot."

"No shit." Ed agreed, lighting a cigarette. "It's a queer band all the way."

"Are you gonna give me one of those fuckin' smokes or what?" Rance growled.

"Hey, you girls got me thinkin' now," Ed said, handing Rance a cigarette. "Maybe you can explain somethin' that's been buggin' the shit outta me."

"What's that?" I asked with piqued curiosity.

"How come chicks always buy into fads?"

"What do you mean?" Lisa asked.

"It seems like they lap up whatever's popular, and ditch whatever ain't, even shit they were gaga over the week before. Why the fuck is that? If I like somethin', I ain't gonna stop likin' it 'cause some self-proclaimed authority tells me it's out."

"'Cause they're mindless fuckin' sheep," Rance interjected, "that's why."

Lisa and I glared at him.

"Present company excluded," he added, forcing another smile.

"I've been trying to figure that out since kindergarten," I said, "and I still have no clue."

"So, you agree?" Ed asked.

"Hell yeah," I replied. "I mean, guys get caught up in fads too, but girls do seem more apt."

"And the powers that be know it!" he exclaimed. "That's why women's shit costs way more than men's. Their hair, their clothes… all that shit."

"Maybe girls feel like they need to be accepted more than guys do," Lisa said musingly.

"I don't give a fuck what they like," Rance scoffed, "as long as they don't try to force their stupid shit on me."

"Or eighty-six my LPs 'cause they ain't cool anymore," Ed added.

"Some chick did that?" Lisa asked in disbelief.

"To a buddy of mine."

"What did he do?"

"Dug 'em outta the trash, then booted her trendy ass out the back door! See ya!"

Lisa and I laughed.

"Ah, you girls got a sense of humor," Ed said, smiling. "That's a good thing."

"Hey," Rance said, changing the subject, "we're on our way to a party, you should come along."

"And who's throwin' this party?" Lisa asked.

"Some confederatos of mine," Ed replied.

"*Confederatos*?" I said flippantly. "What, are you in the Mafia?"

"Sorta," he laughed. "So, what do ya say? It's gonna be a blast… kegs, bands, pits, chips, dips, chains, whips…"

"You game?" she asked, glancing over at me.

Had they mentioned cocaine, I would have been.

"I'm shot," I yawned, "maybe some other time."

With that, they said goodbye, then hopped into their car and pealed out.

As usual, summer ended before it began, and the dreaded fall semester came rolling around, marking the beginning of my high school prison stint. On the first day, Lisa and I ran into Rance on our way to History class. I never expected to see him again, and certainly not there. Apparently, he had a crew of students peddling drugs for him on campus. I can't recall exactly how it happened, but within a week, he and Lisa were inseparable.

On the surface, their relationship appeared to be fine, but in reality, it was a multicar train wreck waiting to happen. Rance was a possessive, jealous tyrant, and Lisa was his chattel. He controlled her every move, critically scrutinized her physical appearance, and insisted that she not use any drugs other than alcohol. What a hypocrite. He was a dealer, for crying out loud.

Shortly after they became an item, Rance was arrested on a probation violation and sent back to jail. It turned out that he had a long rap sheet, and had been in and out of the slammer since childhood. Since he was pathologically paranoid and distrustful, he forbade Lisa to go out while he was away, not even with her girlfriends. It was a ridiculously unreasonable and impracticable demand that was begging to be violated, which was precisely what happened. Before the cell door had slammed shut, Lisa was invited to an intimate gathering by a cokehead acquaintance named Tim, who was absolutely smitten with her. I was asked to come along, as was Kiki. Remembering Rance's explicit orders, I was a bit apprehensive, but ultimately agreed. My wants were shamefully simple. As soon as I heard the word *cocaine*, I was game.

Needless to say, the outing qualified as a felony in Rance's twisted penal code book, and within days of his release, I found myself carrying the can. It was a school day. I'd cut my first four classes and spent the morning at the beach with Tai. Around one, I was back on campus, sparring with my defective locker, when Lisa appeared out of nowhere, crying hysterically and sporting a monstrously swollen black eye. I was in a drug-induced haze, but conscious enough to realize that something terrible had gone down.

"Rance knows! Rance knows!" she whispered frantically. "He's gonna fuckin' kill me! You gotta tell him that Tim's *your* friend, and that I just came along, and that I didn't do *any* blow! Pleeeeeaaaaase! He's gonna kill me!"

Before I had a chance to digest or respond, Rance came tearing around the corner, threw me up against the lockers and got right up into my face, like a rabid pitbull.

"I'm only gonna ask you this once," he snarled. "Who the fuck's Tim? And what the fuck happened that night? Answer me right now, and tell the fuckin' truth! I swear to fuckin' god, if you lie, I'll break your fuckin' neck!"

I loved Lisa, and when I love someone, I'm fiercely loyal and protective. Besides, I never thought in a billion years that Rance would lay one finger on me, so I was willing to take the fall. I told him, in so many words, that Tim was indeed a friend of mine, that I'd pressured Lisa into coming along that night, and that she didn't snort one granule of cocaine.

"Is that the truth?" he growled.

"Yeah!" I replied emphatically. "You know I wouldn't lie to you!"

"You better not be lyin'! I swear to fuckin' god if I find out you are, I'll hunt you down and kill you!" Then he gave me a swift backhand across the face.

I was caught completely off guard. My gut instinct was to strike back, but he had an alarmingly ferocious look in his eyes I'd never seen before. I was afraid he'd waste me if I so much as *breathed*. He held the menacing glare for a moment longer, then grabbed Lisa by the arm and stormed off.

I didn't return to school until the following week. When my mother inquired about the faint contusion on my cheekbone, I told her I'd had a fight with Lisa. I also told her I'd been stricken with the stomach flu, and needed to remain in bed, near a toilet. In reality, there was no bug. I was starving myself, and on those rare occasions that I did eat, I puked. Before long, I was down to an emaciated ninety-eight pounds, which threw my mother into a state of panic. And with good reason, since she'd been battling an eating disorder for most of her life. Without my consent, she made an appointment with an uptight shrink whose practice was run out of a mansion. After discussing the matter with Tai, I decided it was in my best interest to come clean with Dr. Mahler II, at least to some degree. I didn't tell her about my drug addiction, but did recount every lurid detail of the Rance incident, which turned out to be a complete waste of time. While I truly believe that psychotherapy can be beneficial, and even save lives, the woman was absurdly incompetent. She stared at me in silence for one hour straight, while I squirmed in my seat, struggling to avoid eye contact. She was as creepy as can be. She didn't say more than five words the entire time, and when all was said and done, her diagnosis was as stock as they came: "You are suffering from an eating disorder, and this young man, Rance, is the catalyst."

I thought she was full of shit. It wasn't Rance's responsibility to ensure that I was eating properly, nor did he stick his fingers down my throat. Moreover, I refused to give him credit for my engagement in yet another form of self-annihilation. I can only conjecture about why I took up the potentially lethal hobby. Perhaps it was a learned behavior from watching my mother subsist on pills, laxatives, and candy? I only know that I continued engaging in it because I liked being thin. Thankfully, it was an ephemeral phase that I climbed out of unscathed. Now let's rewind a bit…

A week after the blow-up, Lisa called to assure me that Rance would never touch either of us again. Sensing my reluctance, she put him on the horn.

"Sorry I had to hit you," he grumbled, "but it was the only way you'd learn your lesson."

I was speechless.

"Don't worry," he continued, "I ain't gonna hit you or Lisa ever again. I swear on my mom's grave."

He was lying through his venomous fangs, but the dead mother reference aroused my sympathy.

Christ, I could be naïve.

Throughout the duration of their relationship, I witnessed the most unspeakable cruelty. Rance battered Lisa and viciously so. Merciless psychological abuse and beatings that often culminated in Lisa and I locking ourselves in the bathroom, while Rance raged on outside. He'd inevitably coax her out with an insincere apology, and then remain on his best behavior until the next assault, which was chronically imminent. There was always an excuse and a false promise, but I knew he wouldn't stop pulverizing her until she completely disintegrated. I cared deeply for Lisa, and wanted desperately to help, but I was petrified and powerless. Besides the fact that I was drowning in my own morass, and in no condition to save *anyone*, she was deaf, unresponsive, and seemingly brainwashed. It was a textbook case of battered woman syndrome if there ever was one, except she wasn't a woman, but a neglected kid, which made her even more susceptible.

Ironically, Rance and I formed a platonic friendship. It was not intentional on my part. He initiated it, and I was too frightened to protest. It happened on a school day, merely weeks after he'd assaulted and threatened to kill me. I'd just returned from another play date with Tai, and there was Rance leaning against my locker, lying in wait. I tried pulling a U-turn before I was spotted, but vigilance was one of his strong suits.

"Hey!" he yelled, forcing a smile. "Where are you goin'?"

"Nowhere," I lied, walking toward him. "What's up?"

"What are you doin' right now?"

"I'm supposed to be in P.E. but I blew it off. Now I'm trying to decide if I want to skip History too. I'm already flunking anyway."

"Shit, you keep ditchin'," he chuckled, "and you'll end up on the five-year plan."

"I can't help it," I said, shrugging my shoulders. "School fucking sucks… always has, always will."

"Are you hungry?"

"Famished. How did you know?"

"'Cause you're a fuckin' pothead."

"No argument here."

"Come on," he said, motioning with his head, "I'll buy you lunch."

We went to the local grease pit, ordered a feast fit for stoners and dug in.

"Man, you can eat!" he exclaimed with a slight frown. "Doesn't your mom feed you?"

"Sorry," I said, shoving a handful of fries into my mouth. "I'm a pig. Is it grossing you out?"

"Nah, if you were a fat fuckin' cow it would, but you ain't, you're skinny."

"Too skinny?"

"What do you weigh?"

"About a buck… give or take a penny."

"You could stand to lose a few," he said, staring at my protruding, coat-hanger clavicles. "You'd be perfect at an even ninety."

Perfect at an even ninety? Maybe if I were a foot shorter. "Perfect" doesn't exist, and I already looked as though I'd served time in Dachau. Had I dropped another ten pounds, my organs would have failed. If you're a well-proportioned or underweight person, and someone tells you "you could stand to lose a few," plant your foot up that person's ass immediately. Or better yet, season them to taste with salt and pepper, and *eat* them.

"But you got a great ass," he continued, smiling.

I tore open a few packets of mayonnaise and squirted them onto my bun, blatantly ignoring the unwelcome remark.

"Don't worry," he said gruffly, "I ain't tryin' to hit on you, it's just an observation. You're always paradin' around our place in that fuckin' shoestring bikini. It's kinda hard to miss."

I was extremely uncomfortable with where the conversation was going. I wanted to tell him, but resorted to self-deprecation instead. It came naturally, and I knew it would lighten the mood.

"That's because it's so enormous," I said, taking a bite of my cheeseburger and chomping on it, "you'd have to be blind to miss it."

He burst out laughing. I'd never seen him laugh so hard. "You're fuckin' crazy, you know that? But it's good. Most females piss me off, but you make me laugh. You're alright, I like you."

"I like you too," I lied, shoving more fries into my mouth.

I didn't like him, but was afraid to tell him how I really felt. Perhaps if I had, the awkward tete-a-tete would have ended right there, instead of taking an intimate turn.

"You know, females never get me," he said diffidently, looking down at his food. "The only one that ever did was my mom."

I glanced up, and was unexpectedly moved by what I saw. He looked so sad and vulnerable I couldn't help feeling compassion for him. I thought he was utterly devoid of emotion, but his mother's death had obviously wounded him deeply.

"But you're different," he continued, now gazing into my eyes. "You seem to *get* me. I don't know how or why, but you do."

I smiled commiseratively before diving headfirst into my root beer float with extra ice cream, courtesy of the pervert who owned the place.

"I take it back!" he laughed, snatching the float from my hands. "You *are* a fuckin' pig! You keep puttin' away all this shit you're gonna turn into a lard-assed cow!"

Not if I could help it. As soon as I returned to campus, I planned to regurgitate the entirety of my stomach contents into the first toilet I could find. In order to do so successfully, I needed the float, which acted as a lubricant and blending agent.

"Give it back," I demanded. "I need it."

"Okay," he said tauntingly, holding it just out of reach, "but only if you promise to hit the gym hard tonight. I don't want you turnin' into a whale."

"Okay, I promise," I said impatiently. "Now give me the fucking float, please."

He smiled and slid it across the table.

Much to my dismay, that nosh-up represented a turning point in our relationship. Without meaning to, I'd gained his trust. He also became exceptionally protective, as though I were his second wife in a bigamous marriage. Even more to my dismay, *I* began to trust *him*, even though he still scared the shit out of me. Looking back, I knew deep down that he was inherently wicked, no matter how "nice" he pretended to be, but I was blinded by fear.

It was on a Friday night that I learned his motives were not only ulterior, but sinister as well. A number of the gang had gone to a gig at a local club. Afterward, the party continued at Ed's. By sunrise, everyone except Rance and I had zonked out. We were sitting on the couch, watching television, when he whispered the following into my ear: "I'm gonna fuck you." The remark itself was upsetting enough, but the tone of his voice was beyond unnerving. I pretended I didn't hear him, hoping he wouldn't repeat it. After a brief, but loaded pause, I stood up, said goodnight, and left the room.

Over the course of the next month, there were numerous sexual overtures, which I simply ignored. I figured he'd eventually grow bored, but nothing could be further from the truth. I was now his prey, and once he set his sights on a target, he'd pursue it ruthlessly until it succumbed. He told me time and time again, in vulgarly graphic detail, how he was going to have his way with me, whether I was a willing participant or not. It can probably be attributed to youth, denial, and my drug-soaked brain, but for some reason, I didn't take his threats seriously. I was a kid who thought she was smarter than any adult on the face of the earth. I may have been more streetwise than the average kid, but I was about to find myself in a situation where all the street smarts in the world wouldn't have helped.

It was a temperate, relatively uneventful night. Rance, Lisa, and I had spent the evening indoors, drinking and watching videos. I'd also snorted a quarter ounce of cocaine that Rance had slipped me when Lisa wasn't looking. Around one, I popped a pair of Valium and retired to the guestroom, as I'd done on numerous occasions. After tossing and turning for an hour, I fell deep into the arms of Morpheus. Not long after, I was jarred awake by a muted choking sound. I opened my eyes to find a half-naked Rance lying on top of me, with one hand over my mouth and the other around my throat.

"I'm gonna fuck you," he whispered forcefully, "and if you scream or fight me, I'll fuckin' kill you."

Realizing it was not a nightmare, my visceral reaction was to defend myself, but I sincerely believed he'd choke the life out of me.

He ripped off my clothes, forced my legs apart, and gored me. It was inconceivably excruciating. I felt as though I were being fucked with an enormous wood rasp, with each thrust more agonizing than the previous. It seemed impossible that he could be deriving any degree of pleasure, but he was hissing amorous words into my ear throughout. Worse yet, he'd somehow deluded himself into believing that I shared his feelings and was relishing the moment. It was so unthinkably horrific I was rendered aphonic and paralytic. Unfortunately, my mind was operating at full capacity. I'd always been adept at

163

shifting into denial mode amid stress and trauma, but the current situation was simply *too real*. I closed my eyes, gritted my teeth, and waited for the unbearable torture to end.

He began panting heavily, stabbing me harder and deeper, until I could feel every centimeter of him, as though he'd torn straight through to my intestines. Then he came.

I instantly went limp, as though I'd been injected with a potent muscle relaxant.

He started stroking my hair gently, while placing soft kisses on my lips.

I lay there silent and motionless, with my eyes affixed to the ceiling. My unresponsiveness enraged him, undoubtedly because it counteracted the sick and twisted fantasy he'd created in his horrifyingly fucked-up mind.

"Look at me!" he whispered angrily, grabbing my face. "Look at me, right now! Look me in the eyes, damn it!"

I couldn't, even if I'd wanted to.

"If you tell *anyone* about this," he threatened, tightening his hand around my throat again, "I'll fuckin' kill you! You know me! Don't think I won't do it!"

I started to choke. He glared at me until my eyelids collapsed, then removed his hand, and left the room, quietly closing the door behind him.

I was in severe pain, but immobilized by shock. Within minutes, I began to panic. Fearing he may return for a second helping, I quickly got dressed and slipped out the side door.

I'd never been more relieved to be back in that dump of a house. I dragged my enervated carcass up the stairs and into bathroom, then stripped and looked myself over. There was a large red mark in the shape of Rance's hand running across my throat. As I averted my gaze downward, I saw the dried remnants of his venom peeling away from my inner thighs. I didn't take the stereotypical shower you see in most films involving rape, where the victim scrubs herself raw, then slides down onto the floor in tears. It was not a celluloid drama, it was reality, and I couldn't fall apart, because I was numb. After throwing on some clean night clothes, I went into my mother's room, climbed into her bed, and stared at the ceiling until I dozed off. For the first time in ages I felt like the child that I was.

Later that day, I received a disconcerting call from Lisa.

"Hey, where did you guys go?" she asked, skipping the usual chitchat.

I wondered what she meant by *you guys*.

"Who?" I asked confusedly.

"You and Rance! I woke up an hour ago, and couldn't find you guys. Where did you go?"

It was terribly unsettling. Where did *he* go, and why? Had he returned to the crime scene, discovered an empty bed and gone out looking for me?

"I don't know about him," I said, feigning composure, "but I went home."

"Why?"

"Because I felt like puking, and couldn't sleep in that fucking bed."

"Oh!" she laughed. "I was totally freaking out! I thought some fuckin' psycho climbed through the window and kidnapped you!"

There was indeed a psycho, only he didn't climb through any windows.

"So, you don't know where Rance is?"

"No clue."

"What time did you leave?"

"Around three."

"And you didn't see him?"

"No."

"I wonder where the fuck he is! I'm gonna make a few calls. Catch you later."

"Okay, bye."

After analyzing the perplexing conversation for the rest of the day, I came to the conclusion that I'd never be able to breathe a word about the assault. Although Rance's death threat certainly played a part, I knew *no one* would believe me, least of all Lisa, and I'd be branded a lying, traitorous slut by my male comrades whose loyalty lay with the rapist. Fully believing I had no other choice, I stuffed the skeleton into my already overcrowded closet and drugged myself into oblivion.

A week later I met Lisa at Thrifty Drug Store to discuss an undisclosed "important" matter she'd phoned about that morning. I had no idea what to expect, but hoped she'd given Rance the boot. After grabbing some ice cream, we sat on the bench outside, where a flock of old ladies were chattering on about how wonderful Ronald Reagan was.

What happened next was utterly surreal.

"Rance told me you fucked him," my rapist's battered, brainwashed girlfriend said out of the blue. "I got no problem with it, but how come *you* didn't tell me? You know you could have."

I couldn't breathe. Her words were like a sucker punch to the solar plexus. That bastard had the audacity to tell her that *I fucked him*? I couldn't begin to guess why, and if he told *her*, who else did he tell?

She was staring, waiting for a response, but I was speechless.

"I have to go," I mumbled, standing up and walking away.

She called out after me.

I dumped my ice cream cone in a garbage can and kept walking.

In the days that followed, Lisa telephoned repeatedly, but I didn't take or return any of her calls. I wasn't angry with her, but my indignation toward Rance had reached new levels. I now **HATED** him with every fiber of my being, and until he was out of her life, I couldn't be a part of hers. Shunning them proved to have an analgesic effect, and before long, I fell into a semi-fugue state, which helped erase the grotesque nightmare from my mind. Until the day came when I was forced to face it head-on.

Mia, Pluto, Chuck, Murph, and I were loitering in her front yard, hitting the bong, when Rance drove up. I was already feeling queasy from the Vicodin/Kamikaze cocktail I'd ingested earlier. When I saw him, I nearly vomited.

I quickly got up and said to Mia, "I feel like shit. I need to lie down."

"Okay," she said, holding in an enormous toke, "but my bed's a mess, use the other room."

Before Rance got out of the car, I made a dash for the house and retreated to the bedroom at the end of the hallway. No more than ten minutes had passed, when I awoke to find that monster lying on top of me, like an incubus, holding a pocketknife to my throat. Perhaps it was Dutch courage, but I honestly didn't give a shit if he sliced my throat from ear to ear. There was *no way in hell* he was going to violate me again.

I lifted my knee into his gut, causing the blade to nick my throat, which startled him more than me.

He recoiled for a split second, then threw the knife aside and slapped me. "Didn't you like it last time?" he snarled, pinning down my arms with his knees, and tearing at my clothes. "Come on, you fuckin' cunt, don't make me hurt you!"

I spat on him and yelled for help, but he put his hand over my mouth.

Miraculously, Whitman – who was on the other side of the house – heard the ruckus, and came rushing in. Then he darted across the hall to his bedroom, and returned carrying a loaded shotgun, which he pointed directly at Rance's head. "Get out of here!" he yelled. "Or I'll shoot!"

"Okay! Okay!" Rance exclaimed, putting his hands in the air. "Just put down the fuckin' gun!"

"Get out of my house!" Whitman yelled, shoving the barrel into Rance's back.

"I'm goin', I'm goin'! Chill out, old man!"

Seconds later, I heard Rance's car peal out.

"What the hell happened in here?" Mia asked, rushing into the room with an understandably bewildered look on her face.

Fear, confusion, and mortification prevented me from telling her about the rape itself. Some months later I confessed to a handful of people, and needless to say, Lisa was not among them.

Lisa eventually mustered up the strength and courage to leave Rance, but it was by no means a clean or amicable break. He dragged it out for ages, and made her suffer the entire time. He even tried blowing up her house with a self-made bomb, which, luckily, failed to detonate. He finally relented, but remained a forceful presence in her life. As is common with abusive relationships, he just couldn't let her go. His friends claimed that he was crushed, but his behavior indicated otherwise, for shortly after the "devastating" split he raped two other girls, one of whom was an acquaintance of mine. He was clearly a sociopathic, homicidal time bomb who belonged in a cage. I went out of my way to avoid him, but it was nearly impossible. We still moved in the same circles, and he refused to leave me alone. Every time I saw him, I was overcome by suffocative fear and vindictive rage. I wanted to turn tail and attack at the same time.

You may be wondering why I didn't call the police. I wanted to, but was convinced it was not an option. To say that rape is a "problematic" crime would be an understatement. Unless there's material evidence, it's typically her word against his, and the fact that my rapist and I ran with the same gang didn't help. I also had a longstanding and justifiable distrust of the law, which only solidified my decision to remain mute. I knew they would *never* believe my story. Why the hell would they believe a strung-out juvenile delinquent? And isn't every female junkie a worthless whore? They would assume that I fucked Rance for a fix and enjoyed every second of it. Again, I was convinced that calling the police was *not* an option. I thought I had no options at all, and had never felt more helpless. If given the chance to do it over, I don't know if I would have acted any differently. Perhaps if I'd had some guarantee that it would have led to justice. All I can say with absolute certainty is that I wished for Rance's death on a daily basis, and in a perfect world, I would have disemboweled him with a razor-sharp, multi-tined pitchfork and gotten away with it.

Eight years after that permanently life-altering night, I was in a new place, geographically and emotionally, when I received a telephone call from Mia's sister, delivering the most cathartic tidings I'd ever received. Rance was dead. Apparently, he woke up one morning, realized what an abject piece of shit he was, and ate a bullet. The news was like an antidote. Although I would have preferred pulling the trigger myself, or bashing in his head with a baseball bat, I felt as though a massive psychological carcinoma had been excised from my soul.

Rance was the only human being I've known personally that I feared and **HATED**. He was a contemptible, incorrigible beast who tormented others seemingly for kicks. It was only going to be a matter of time before he murdered someone. As far as I'm concerned, fellating that gun was the most considerate act he ever committed. My experiences shape my opinions, and the scarring nightmare you've just read about is responsible for my ambivalent views on capital punishment. I no longer hate Rance, and the only reason I feel that way is because he's dead. His death delivered my freedom from the bile that had been eating away at my soul for ages. I was never going to be able to release it as long as he was still breathing, despite exhaustive attempts. Although the pain and indignation will never go away, the hatred was buried along with the bogeyman.

HAROLD P. BROWN

I rarely saw the Locals anymore. Most of them were knee-deep in tempestuous, drug-fueled relationships, and some had started to procreate. Tai and Jamie were still a couple, but their once loving union was now riddled with ugliness. There were daily knock-down-drag-out altercations, which typically ended with them breaking up. Then each would go out and paint the town red with the goal of making the other green. I was often called upon to abet both parties, but usually ended up with Jamie.

On one such occasion, she and I found ourselves at a party. The first few hours were spent in the company of two loathsome yet generous wannabe womanizers, snorting away to our heart's content. When the well ran dry, they invited us back to their place. Naturally, we inquired about whether there would be more cocaine, and when they said "No," we said "No."

Minutes later, we were approached by a pair of tall, sturdy, heavily inked skinheads, who I'll call Alex and Pete. I immediately picked up an unsettling vibe. Perhaps I'd seen every episode of *Star Trek* ten too many times, but these guys were mechanically inexpressive, like aliens from a gelid, tenebrous planet located in an unidentified galaxy.

"This place is fuckin' dead," Alex uttered in a phlegmatic tone. "There's supposed to be a party nearby with bands. You girls wanna check it out?"

Maybe it was the aftereffects of the rape, but I was inexplicably apprehensive about getting into a car with these two, which speaks volumes, considering I'd get into a car with just about anyone. "Would you excuse us for a second?" I said, pulling Jamie aside to confer.

"Yeah," Pete mumbled, "no problem."

Sure enough, Jamie was apprehensive as well. "I don't think we should go with them," she whispered, before I could say one word. "They look like fuckin' thugs."

"You read my mind. Did you notice the ink?"

"Yeah," she said, glancing over at them discreetly, "they must be in some kinda Nazi gang. What should we tell them?"

"That we have a midnight curfew," I whispered, also glancing over at them discreetly.

"Do you think they'll buy it?"

"Only one way to find out," I replied, locking her arm in mine and walking back over.

"So, what's the word?" Alex asked, cracking his knuckles.

"Thanks for the invite," Jamie replied, smiling, "but we have to be home by midnight or we'll be grounded for fuckin' ever."

They didn't respond.

"It fuckin' sucks being fifteen," she added with a nervous laugh.

"You're only fifteen?" Pete asked, staring straight into her eyes, as though he were testing her.

"Yeah," she replied, staring back at him unflinchingly.

A moment of nerve-racking silence ensued.

"So, you're not comin' then?" Alex asked, cracking his knuckles again.

"We'd love to," I replied, returning the knuckle cracking, "but can't."

"Thanks anyway," Jamie added.

"No problem," they mumbled in unison, walking away without saying goodbye.

"That was easy," I said, watching them head for the door.

"Thank fuckin' god," Jamie sighed in relief. "Do you think they were pissed off?"

"I couldn't even tell if they were *breathing*, never mind pissed off."

"No shit," she laughed. "Fuckin' scary!"

Before they were out of sight, three clean-cut, conservatively dressed frat boys came walking up. I'd noticed them earlier, because they stood out like a bulbous pustule on a baby smooth ass. From here on out, they shall be known as Manny, Moe, and Jack.

"Hey, how's it going? Manny said through a pleasant smile. "We're on our way to another party. Do you wanna come along?"

"What do you think?" Jamie asked, looking over at me.

"Sure, why the hell not," I said, looking around the room. "This place is a fucking morgue."

After some dreadfully boring chit chat, the five of us piled into their black, four-door BMW – me in front with Manny, and Jamie in back with Moe and Jack – then headed toward our destination via surface streets.

About two-thirds of the way there, a vicious argument broke out between Jamie and Jack. At first I thought they were yelling because the stereo was too loud, but quickly realized that the situation was far more serious.

"Hey!" I said, turning down the music and flipping around in my seat. "What the hell's going on back there?"

"Fuckin' asshole won't stop grabbing my tits!" Jamie yelled, pushing Jack away.

He grabbed her again and began screaming unintelligibly at the top of his lungs. It sounded as though he were saying: "*Shit bitch motherfuckin' cunt dyke!*" over and over and over again. Before I could digest and react, he opened the door and attempted to shove Jamie out onto the street. It was appalling, and the fact that Moe wasn't intervening was even more appalling.

I stretched my body over the console and onto the back seat, then dug my fingernails into Jack's arm. "*Do something, you idiot!*" I yelled, looking over at Moe, who appeared to be paralyzed. "*He's going to fucking kill her!*"

Moe just stared at the horrific spectacle with his mouth agape. And Manny was completely oblivious to the situation, as the car continued to accelerate.

I quickly reached over and attempted to yank the key out of the ignition.

"Wait, wait… what are you doing?" Manny asked confusedly.

"*Stop the fucking car right now!*" I screamed, grabbing hold of his throat. "*Before he kills her!*"

"*Okay! Okay!*" he shrieked, pulling over to the side of the road. "*Let go!*"

Before the vehicle had come to a stop, Jamie rolled out onto pavement and ran for her life. Jack immediately gave chase and tackled her from behind. She didn't stand a chance.

"*You motherfuckin' dyke!*" he screamed over and over again, while mauling her like a cougar.

I rushed to her aid, while Manny and Moe just stood by and watched, as though it were a staged wrestling match.

"*Do something, you fucking cowards!*" I screamed, pulling on Jack with all my might, while Jamie squirmed beneath his powerful frame.

They refused to intervene, making it perfectly clear that I'd have to take matters into my own hands. Without giving it a single thought, I removed my right shoe, jumped onto Jack's back, and drove the chrome heel into his skull repeatedly, with no concern whatsoever about killing him. In fact, at that moment, I *wanted* him dead.

"*No bitch is ever gonna hit me!*" he yelled, bucking me off like a crazed bull, and pinning me on the concrete near the gutter. "*I'll fuck you right up!*"

I attempted to defend myself, but he outweighed me by at least a hundred pounds. He smacked my face so hard I thought my jaw had dislocated, and began shaking me violently, while ejaculating another garbled stream of profanity. I could taste blood and feel loose tissue flapping around inside my mouth. The slap had split open my lower lip, causing a sharp stinging sensation, but I didn't have time to hurt, I had to save myself. I tried wriggling out of his hold, but it was no use. I might as well have had a grizzly bear on top of me.

It may sound superficial or even vain, but I was worried about my face, it was all I could think about. Earlier in the year, one of the Locals had sustained several facial and mandibular fractures in a fight. The poor bastard was in excruciating pain, subsisting on Vicodin and chilled Southern Comfort through a straw for weeks on end. He had a deep, gravelly voice, and since he couldn't move his mandible, he sounded exactly like Boris Karloff in *The Bride of Frankenstein*, which made him the butt of everyone's mockery, including mine. When the jaw wires were finally removed, he was gaunt, gorked, pissed off, and uglier than ever. The prolonged and agonizing ordeal had permanently changed him, and for the worse. I prayed that Jack wouldn't hit my face again. I didn't care what he did to my body, as long as I wasn't left crippled or paralyzed.

Right at that moment, I caught sight of a pair of headlights belonging to a pickup truck that had pulled over to the side of the road, merely feet from where I was lying. A handful of cars had driven by and honked, but no one had stopped. Seconds later, two tall, shadowy figures jumped out and rushed to my aid. It was none other than Alex and Pete.

Alex grabbed Jack and body slammed him to the ground, then pummeled him mercilessly. It was barbaric and criminally one-sided, but well deserved.

Realizing that Jack was nearly unconscious, Alex stopped and looked over at me with a menacing expression on his face. "Do you wanna get a few shots in before I finish this motherfucker off?"

I wanted Jack dead, but since that wasn't an option, I performed a clog dance on his rib cage and spat in his face. It felt orgasmic.

At some point during the fray, Manny and Moe had taken refuge in the yuppie-mobile, which Pete was encircling like a ravenous lion at feeding time. Despite his best efforts to lure them out, they remained locked inside, shitting their cotton panties.

Jack was now a humbled, gory mess, a far cry from the ferocious beast who'd materialized out of nowhere. As I stood over him, with one foot on either side, I contemplated whether I should kick him in the face for good measure.

"Okay," Alex said, putting his hand on my shoulder, "he's had enough."

I looked at him, then back at Jack. Then I gathered up my shoes and joined Jamie, who was sitting on the curb, nursing a cigarette with a trembling hand and mouth.

"Are you okay?" she asked, placing her free arm around my neck.

"Yeah," I replied, taking her hand in mine, "how about you?"

"I'm cool."

Alex helped Jack to his feet, then grabbed him by the seat of his pants and shoved him toward the BMW. "Take this piece of shit and get the fuck outta here!" he yelled.

Manny reluctantly emerged. "Dude!" he yelled, motioning at Moe. "I need some help here!"

After peering out the window for a moment, with a look of utter terror in his eyes, Moe emerged, with even more reluctance. Once Jack was loaded into the car, they drove off into the night.

It'd all happened so fast I couldn't gauge what I was feeling, other than the obvious rage and physical pain. Hopping into vehicles with strangers was routine for my girlfriends and me, but we'd never come close to being assaulted. The nightmarish thought was always in the back of my mind, but I'd envisioned the monster resembling Henry Lee Lucas, not Theo Huxtable.

As Jamie and I sat there on the curb, trying desperately to arrest our soaring epinephrine levels, the two men we'd pegged as cold-blooded thugs came over and offered much needed consolation. Alex sat down next to me and gently rubbed my back, while Pete did the same for Jamie. I wrapped my arms around Alex, kissed his blood-smeared cheek, and thanked him profusely.

"Don't mention it," he said matter-of-factly, and after an impeccable comedic pause, "so, *now* will you come to that party with us?"

Jamie and I burst out laughing.

"I'm just fuckin' with you," he said, punching my arm playfully. "Come on, let's get you home."

I learned another harsh lesson that night, and the truth is I've had more run-ins with "normal" men over the years. Especially when they get wasted and convince themselves that they're badass studs. I'm guessing it's due to their lack of hard experience and the fact that they've never had the shit beaten out them. It's no coincidence that they're also the first to threaten to call the police when faced with the possibility of having their clocks cleaned, which would, in fact, be the quickest and most effective cure for their (mis)behavior.

FELIS SILVESTRIS
SUMMA CUM OPPROBRIUM

School was an ever-increasing nuisance that refused to fuck off. Throughout my freshman year, I ditched more often than not, causing my already poor grades to slip dramatically. By the end of the second semester, I'd flunked History and English, and earned an unprecedented F- in Physical Education. Yes, it does exist, and I have the report card to prove it.

I'd come to realize that the people in charge had limited power. Sure, they could assign detentions and Saturday work details, but couldn't force me to attend. And I viewed suspensions as bonus vacation days, the more the better. In other words, the faculty's iron hands were tied by my arrant lack of regard for the rules and potential consequences.

One month into my sophomore year, I'd had enough. I hated school more than ever, and having convinced myself that it was not conducive to my wellbeing, I dropped out. Risky move, since I was technically violating the law. But I was adept at forging my mother's signature, and even more adept at diverting the school's automated phone calls. Moreover, the powers that be were absurdly oblivious. It was a one-sided game if there ever was one. Or so I thought.

It was on a cool autumn morning that an actual human being called to report my multiple truancies.

An unforeseen snag indeed. Worse yet, my mother's boyfriend beat me to the phone.

When my mother came home that evening, the first words out of her mouth were: "The Dean of Attendance called today. He said that you've been truant for over a month! Is that true?"

There was no sense in lying, the jig was up.

"Yeah," I mumbled, "it's true."

"You're in serious trouble, did you know that? They're going to send you to juvenile hall! Is that what you want?"

"Hell no!" I exclaimed.

"I didn't think so. We have an appointment with the Dean and a probation officer tomorrow morning. He thinks we may be able to reach a compromise."

I knew exactly what that compromise would be. I'd be transferred out of the "normal" high school and into another institution tailor-made for delinquents, which was relatively agreeable, since those places typically had shorter days. But what if I was mistaken? What if I *did* end up in juvenile hall?

Five minutes into the meeting I turned on the waterworks, hoping it would hit a soft spot, which it did, thankfully. After an hour-long lecture, they handed down a comparatively lenient sentence: one year of probation and a ten month stretch at Meanwell, a year-round probation school located ten miles away. That's right, no summer vacation for me.

The Dean wrapped up the festivities by shaking a contract in front of my face and stating sternly, "If you do not abide by the conditions stated in this agreement, you will be sent to juvenile hall!"

Knowing damn well that I'd dodged a major bullet, I snatched the paperwork from his hands, and signed it immediately, before he and the probation officer changed their minds. Then I emptied out my locker, and bid the "normal" high school adieu forever. I was scheduled to start at the new place on Monday, and was dreading the three bus commute, which meant I'd have to wake up an hour earlier, but it beat the alternative. At least I wouldn't be waking up behind bars.

Before setting foot on the campus itself, I knew Meanwell was the school for me. Every morning before class, the students would congregate at the grocery store parking lot across the street to exchange drugs and get high. It was tragic, but what do you expect? When you dump a bunch of incorrigible delinquents into the same habitat, they're certainly not going to influence each other in a positive way. I can see why prisoners are rarely rehabilitated.

Meanwell was stocked with characters straight out of a black comedy. One of my favorites was a long-haired, flannel-clad Hessian named Jay, who'd recently served a stretch for bludgeoning his mother with a Wiffle Ball Bat. I repeat, a Wiffle Ball Bat. His security blanket was a dog-eared paperback copy of Golding's *Lord of the Flies*. He was never seen without it. He was never seen reading it either. He also held full-length conversations with himself, and performed medleys of barnyard animal sounds from his desk at the back of the classroom. For reasons unknown, he thought I was Rebecca of Sunnybrook

Farm, a misconception that was immediately shattered when we collided in the pit at a party one night. He was so delightedly astonished, come that Monday, he began lavishing drugs on me. I have myriad fond memories of Jay, including the time he climbed onto my desk, assumed the fetal position, gazed at me with his lopsided eyes, and asked, "Why do you have a heart-shaped ass?" repeatedly for ten minutes straight. Perhaps my most cherished memory was the time he rescued a group of female students from a flasher who was whacking off in front of the campus one morning. Well, "rescued" isn't quite accurate. After an unsuccessful attempt at tackling the creep, he chased him down the boulevard for several blocks while singing, *"No apparent motive, just kill and kill again! Survive my brutal thrashing, I'll hunt you till the end! My life's a constant battle, the rage of many men! Homicidal maniac!"* at the top of his lungs. The kid was a riot. Clearly psychotic, but highly entertaining.

On a more serious note, continuation schools do not get the recognition and praise they deserve. Meanwell was so much more than an academy for rejects, and I felt privileged to be a member of the student body. Not only was I allowed to work at my own pace, but "normal" pedagogics were virtually nonexistent. Because of my deep-seated issues with strict authoritarians and rules, it turned out to be the ideal educational environment. For the first time in my life, I excelled scholastically, proving to myself and others that I was not learning-disabled after all. I found that when I didn't have a drill sergeant breathing down my neck, barking orders at me, I *wanted* to learn, and earned high marks to boot.

Blind though they were to their pupils' morning ritual, the teachers were all exceptional human beings. Every student at Meanwell was unstable to some degree, and some were downright volatile individuals who could have snapped without any warning. Instead of censuring or imposing punishment, the teachers did their level best to understand our shortcomings and cultivate our talents. They also enriched our young minds with learning materials that "normal" high school students were not exposed to. Rather than putting us to sleep with a tedious educational film on American history, they stimulated us with compelling cinema, such as *The Deer Hunter*, *Easy Rider*, and *Medium Cool*. And while "normal" high school students were plodding through *The Scarlet Letter*, *Ethan Frome*, and some watered-down biography that never should have been penned in the first place, I was devouring *Last Exit to Brooklyn*, *Ham on Rye*, and *Hellfire*.

God knows I'm no genius. I'm perpetually scatterbrained, to say that my comprehension skills are deficient would be an understatement, and at best, only twenty-five percent of what I do assimilate remains in my long-term memory. That said, I honestly believe that the education I received at Meanwell was on a par with or better than that offered at any "normal" secondary school in the state. Of course, some have begged to differ, but that's another story, which I'll refrain from telling at the moment. Ah, what the hell, you've talked me into it. Let's just say that I was denied a much needed scholarship to a prominent Southern California business school by a clique of uptight, pompous, condescending sorority alumnae, simply because I didn't wave pompoms, sing in the glee club, run for student council, or take the SATs. Furthermore, I'd committed an unforgivable sin by failing to blow hundreds of dollars on a hideous satin dress I'd never wear again, only to waste an entire night among a horde of "normals" in a five-star hotel ballroom. Apparently, the fact that I'd been admitted to the highly competitive program, along with the exceptional grade point average I'd maintained during my junior college years was not enough to deem me worthy of the elitist plutocrats' dough. My parents could not afford to help me with the astronomical tuition, and while I was offered financial assistance in the form of work-study, loans, and a grant, the scholarship incident had left such a rotten taste in my mouth I was altogether repulsed by the establishment. It may sound childishly bullheaded, but even if those bitches had changed their minds and begged me to take the money, I would have told them to shove it up their shriveled twats. It was a matter of principle. Who the hell did they think they were sizing me up in such a discriminatory manner? I'd done nothing wrong, yet they were interrogating me as though I were the prime suspect in an unconscionable crime. Christ, I was pissed off. I was angrier at myself, though. I should have known better than to put myself in the hot seat. What kind of questions did I expect them to ask? These women epitomized "normal," and therefore, were only interested in "normal," symbolic achievements. When in high school, a proper young lady was expected to associate with clean-cut and well-behaved teenyboppers, take part in a variety of extracurricular activities, and attend the prom. Most of my playmates were twentyish, disorderly criminals, my extracurricular activities were limited to drugging, stealing, vandalizing, and raising hell, and on prom night, I was at a nightclub wasted out of my mind. It didn't matter that I'd ultimately gotten my act together and was striving to better myself in every possible way, including working my ass off to earn a college degree. Oh no, all that mattered was that I did not receive a "normal" high school education. Needless to say, it was not the only time my "abnormal" background returned to haunt me, and it's no wonder I tried to erase my past. The "normal" world is teeming with insentient, judgmental, self-righteous hypocrites who haven't a shred of tolerance for anything or anyone that is "abnormal." Well, guess what? The "normal" world can kiss my heart-shaped ass!

Going to a new school was always difficult, but at least I wouldn't be entirely friendless. Some of my comrades had already been transferred to Meanwell, and another arrived a week after me.

Maxine was a dangerously precocious, Nat Sherman smoking girl who had the perfect setup. Neither of her grossly negligent parents wanted to assume the responsibility of raising her, so they rented her an apartment and cut her loose.

Then there was Earl, fresh out of juvenile hall. I'd heard rumors that he'd joined up with a neo-Nazi gang while inside, but never bothered asking him about it. I suppose I didn't want to know. And if he had temporarily, I'm sure he'd only done so to protect himself from the other, equally violent factions. Anyone who's been an inmate in a correctional facility will tell you that in order to survive you're often forced to take actions that may conflict with your beliefs, including aligning yourself with a group of extremists. The way I see it, unless you've been in that situation yourself, you have no right to opine, judge, or criticize.

You're probably wondering what Earl had done to get himself locked up. Well, in his freshman year, he'd gone on a lunchtime shooting spree in the riverbed directly behind the "normal" high school. Contrary to what you may be thinking, his victims weren't students, but seagulls. It was a front-page story in our typically dead enclave. The area was swarming with cops and news vans, everyone believing that there was a homicidal sniper on the loose, when in reality it was just a baby-faced kid with a latent aversion to our salty-feathered friends. Like everyone else, I was curious to know why Earl had embarked on that avian massacre, so I asked, and here's what he had to say: "I dunno. I just don't like 'em. Never have." Hmmmm, had they shat on him one too many times? I wondered.

Shortly after his release, Earl found his calling as a cat burglar. The kid was a crackerjack of a thief, almost as if the racket had *chosen him* instead of the other way around. He'd slip in stealthily, like a chilly draft through a sagging door, and clean out the places in a matter of minutes. Then he'd fence the loot for cocaine, which he'd generously share with yours truly. It may be difficult to believe, but he was a really nice guy. I recently looked at an old snapshot of him, and apart from the sack of weed covering his muzzle like a feedbag, he looks fairly innocent. I always wondered where he made that wrong turn in life. He was so young, yet so troubled, which was probably why we got along so fabulously. I never felt as though I had to check myself in his presence. He accepted me as I was, and I him. A girl couldn't have asked for a better drug buddy, but unsurprisingly, it was to be short-lived. Earl was ultimately nailed for breaking and entering, and promptly returned to the slammer. I didn't hear much about him until summer of 2006, when I was deeply saddened to hear that he'd accidentally overdosed a few years prior. I'm still trying to confirm his death, but if he did indeed buy the farm, he's only one in a staggeringly long line of former comrades who died tragically and prematurely.

Just prior to Earl's re-incarceration, Maxine and I began to hang out more frequently. She was mourning the loss of her ex-boyfriend, Ray, who'd recently been gunned down by the law. I was shocked when I heard the news, since he appeared to be such a calm and gentle soul. By his own admission, he was a drug-gorging party animal, but as far as I could tell, he was easy-going to a fault and far from violent. You're probably wondering what

Ray had done to get himself riddled with bullets. Well, I never got specific details, but allegedly, he'd refused to pull over for a minor traffic violation, then led the cops on a high speed chase, and tried to run them down after he'd been cornered. His kith and kin suspected there was more to the story, and there probably was, but it wasn't as if they could prove it. The only people who knew the truth were the officers at the scene, and of course Ray, but he wouldn't be talking any time soon.

One temperate Saturday night, Maxine and I went out to dinner at a restaurant near her father's place. I was perusing the tome of a menu, struggling to make a decision, as usual, when she kicked my leg under the table.

"What the fuck?" I exclaimed, looking up at her.

"Shhhh," she whispered, ducking behind her menu, "whatever you do, don't turn around."

"Why?"

"You're not gonna believe who just sat down behind you."

"Who?"

"Rood."

Rood was an impish manchild who was invariably up to shenanigans. I never knew his age. He claimed to be twenty-five, but looked forty-five. I never knew how he earned his living either, for it seemed as though he spent half his time on a skateboard and the other half on a surfboard, but was never strapped for cash. He was a hoot and a half to party with, but impossibly obnoxious, which made it extremely difficult to take him in large doses.

He also suffered from a severe case of "Instant Horny Octopus, Just Add Booze Syndrome."

"You're shitting me," I whispered, also hiding behind my menu, even though he could only see the back of my head. "Who's he with?"

"That dude… you know… the one with the short brown hair?"

"That narrows it down."

She started to laugh.

So did I.

"Shhhh," she whispered, "they're gonna hear."

"Maybe that's not such a bad thing," I said quietly. "They can foot the bill for our meal, and knowing Rood, he's probably holding."

I was referring to cocaine, by the way.

"You think so?" she asked, peering over her menu discreetly.

"There's a seventy-thirty chance," I said, peering back at her.

"Yeah, but if he isn't, we're never gonna be able to ditch him. We'll be stuck with him and his fuckin' tentacles till dawn."

"Ugh," I sneered, "I hadn't thought of that."

"And *you're* the one he's gonna lavish his affection on, 'cause I fucked him already."

"You *did*?" I exclaimed.

"Shhhh. Unfortunately."

"When?"

"A coupla weeks ago. I thought it'd help me forget about Ray."

"Did it work?"

"Fuck no! It only made me miss him more."

"Really? Why?"

"'Cause it was the worse fuckin' sex I've ever had," she whispered, rolling her eyes, "easily."

"Are you serious?"

"*No contest*," she replied emphatically. "He's hung like Secretariat, I'll give him that much, but he shot his fuckin' load before I could blink."

I burst out laughing.

"Shhhh," she giggled, "they're gonna hear us."

"What should we do?" I asked, struggling to stifle my laughter. "We can't hide behind these fucking menus until they leave, and I'm famished, I need food."

"Just lemme think for a sec," she said, chewing on her thumbnail. "I'll come up with somethin'."

Much to her frustration, she wouldn't have an opportunity to think for a sec, or come up with anything, for right at that moment, Rood spotted her.

"Max!" he yelled. "I thought that was yoooo!"

She simpered and waved.

"Shit, I didn't recognize ya with yer hair down! And who's that with ya?"

I turned around, revealing my identity.

"Hey, sweetheart!" he yelled even louder, with a disturbingly wide grin. "How fuckin' cool is this! It's like serendipity or somethin'!"

"Yeah, or somethin'," Maxine mumbled.

"You remember Keith, right?" he said, pointing at his companion whose face was now one centimeter from mine.

"Yeah, sure" I replied, leaning away. "How's it going, Keith?"

"Pretty good," he said, leaning forward and peeking down my shirt. "How's it goin' with you?"

"I've been better," I replied, shielding my chest with my menu.

"Well shit!" Rood yelled. "There's no reason for two fine-lookin' girls to dine alone now, is there?"

"Mind if we join you?" Keith asked, still attempting to cop a gander at my chest.

Maxine and I didn't respond.

"We'll buy you dinner," he added with a pitiable smile.

"Okay," Maxine sighed, motioning with her hand. "Get the fuck over here."

They gathered up their utensils and menus, and walked the three steps it took to reach our table.

"Here, Keith," I said, tugging on his shirt, "you can sit next to me."

I had to choose one or the other, and he was the lesser of two pervs.

Maxine glared at me.

I winked at her.

She flipped me off.

I reciprocated.

"So ladies, what's on the agenda tonight?" Rood asked, reading the menu upside down.

"Not much," Maxine replied, lighting a kelly green cigarette. "We're just gonna chow down, then head back to my pad and watch videos."

"Damn, that sounds fuckin' dull!" he said, reading the menu sideways.

"Do you have something better in mind?" I asked smartly.

"Don't I always?" he replied, raising his eyebrows and grinning.

That "something better" turned out to be a private party at a local drug house. I was a bit reluctant at first, but after learning that the host was one of the most successful cocaine dealers in the area, I changed my tune.

Upon arriving at our destination, Rood rang the doorbell twice.

Seconds later, a frightfully dilated pupil appeared in the peephole. Then the voice behind the pupil in the peephole asked, "Who's there?"

"Geraldo Rivera," Rood giggled.

"Who's with you?" the voice asked.

"The fuckin' DEA, man! Who the fuck do ya think?"

"Just a coupla chicks, Joe," Keith interjected, "they're cool."

"Are you sure?" the voice asked.

"Yeah!" Rood laughed. "Now open the fuckin' door, ya paranoid kook! I'm freezin' my balls off!"

"Maybe if you wore pants for a change," Maxine scoffed, flicking her gold cigarette butt into the air.

Three separate locks unlatched, then the door slowly creaked open, revealing a creature that was the personification of cocaine induced paranoia.

"Hurry up!" he whispered angrily. "Get in here before they see you!"

"Before who sees us?" Rood asked mockingly, looking around.

"The fucking Feds, man! They've been staking me out for a month!"

Rood and Keith started to laugh.

"I'm not fucking around!" he snapped, grabbing Rood by the arm and yanking him over the threshold. "Get the hell in here before they see you!"

Once inside, Maxine and I were introduced to the other guests. There was a ball team, all men in their mid to late twenties, except Joe, who appeared to be in his early thirties.

"Here," he muttered, handing Maxine a loaded crack pipe, "help yourselves."

"Thanks," she said, accepting the gift with a smile, "don't mind if we do."

"And make yourselves comfortable," he added, pointing toward the loveseat. "It's gonna be a long night."

The next few hours were spent freebasing relentlessly, then Joe and some of the others started to mainline. Maxine had dabbled with needles before and found it exhilarating, but was squeamish about injecting herself, so Joe played doctor. I was encouraged to join in on the fun, but politely declined and stuck with the pipe. Again, I had no intention of crossing over into that doomed dimension. The purgatory I was trapped in was hellish enough.

As I explained several chapters back, cocaine often provokes the overwhelming desire to **DO SOMETHING!!!!!** no matter how pointless and nonsensical that activity may be. What Joe and crew proceeded to **DO!!!!!** over the course of the next hour was a case in point. Even though the house was already immaculate, they cleaned it frantically and meticulously, like a team of raving, mysophobic maids. One of them was vacuuming, another dusting, another cleaning the windows, another washing the dishes, another scrubbing the bathroom from floor to ceiling... all of them working at hypersonic speed. It was like watching an infomercial in fast forward mode, or better yet, an undercranked Benny Hill skit. When the madness finally ended, Maxine and I gave them a standing ovation. Then Rood came over to the loveseat and planted himself in between us.

"See those chicks over there?" he asked, pointing toward a pair of haggard looking women who were standing by the door with Keith.

"Yeah," Maxine said, taking a drag on her thin red cigarette, "what about 'em?"

"They want me and Keith to go back to their place with 'em. Is that cool?"

"Whatever floats your boat," she said, exhaling. "Just make sure you double wrap your cocks before divin' in. The brunette looks like a walkin' herpes sore."

"Ya think so?" he asked, glancing over at the brunette. "I think she looks more like a genital wart."

"You should know," Maxine scoffed.

"Look who's talkin'!" he retorted.

"Skank!" she shot back.

"Takes one to know one!"

They fell silent for a second, then burst out laughing.

"You guys are fucking nuts," I laughed, shaking my head.

He kissed Maxine on the cheek and asked, "Sure yer not gonna be pissed off?"

"Fuck no!" she replied, looking around at the roomful of men. "You dudes gotta go where the action is, and it sure as hell ain't here."

"Ya can say that again," he grumbled, leering at me.

"Quit looking at me like that, you fucking pig," I said, pushing him.

"Ooooh, baby!" he said, grinning lasciviously. "I love it when ya talk dirty to me!"

I smacked the side of his head.

"Resist me all ya want, sweetheart, but I'm not givin' up. I'm gonna get ya in the sack yet, then I'll show ya what a *real* man can do."

"Don't hold your breath," I snickered, remembering the juicy tidbit Maxine had revealed earlier.

"Here," he said, slipping me a Grant. "Joe's gonna set ya up all night, and when yer ready to split, call a cab."

"Thanks," I said, stuffing the bill into my bra and smiling. "Now get the fuck out of my sight."

He sprang to his feet and signaled to Keith that he was coming.

Keith gestured for him to hurry up.

He flipped Keith off.

"Maybe I'll drop by yer place next week, Max?" he said nonchalantly.

"I won't be there," she replied, exhaling.

"Why, where ya goin'?"

"Anywhere you're not."

"Ouch!" he laughed, holding his hand on his heart. "Yer fuckin' cruel!"

She hissed at him.

"Awright, girlies," he said, still laughing, "I'm outta here."

"Later," Maxine and I replied in unison.

Keith waved at us from the door.

We waved back.

And they were gone.

As I mentioned, Joe was a highly successful dealer who specialized in crack. Although he ran a closed shop, he was open for business twenty-four hours a day, seven days a week, and was definitely not hurting for customers. Throughout the night, that doorbell must have rung a hundred times, and I couldn't help noticing the diversity of his clientele. When crack had become a nationwide epidemic, the media had led the public to believe that it was a solely a ghetto problem. As usual, the media was completely off base. I was in a chic little bungalow in the whitest of neighborhoods, and only one black person came knocking the entire time I was there.

Never one to pass up an opportunity to make new connections, I spent a good portion of the night schmoozing, and as luck would have it, my efforts paid off. Around midnight I made the acquaintance of a tall, sinewy, sable-haired bull who I hoped to exploit in the near future. His sonorous voice and imposing presence oozed masculinity and commanded attention. He had a strong, euphonic name, like that of a mythical Celtic warrior. It rolled off the tongue beautifully, which is why I've never forgotten it. My mother probably hasn't forgotten it either. His business card was one of many she found while conducting an unconstitutional search and seizure on *the one day* I forgot to lock my bedroom door. For legal reasons I can't use his real name, and since I can't come up with a worthy substitute, I'm simply going to call him the Scotch-Irishman.

"So, how long have you known Joe?" he asked, leading me back over to the loveseat.

"I just met him tonight," I replied, sitting down Indian style.

He sat down beside me, and strategically wrapped his arm around the seatback, placing his chiseled face merely centimeters from mine. Thankfully, he wasn't suffering from halitosis. In fact, his overall scent was quite pleasant, a sublime blend of fresh spearmint, Chanel Por Monsieur, and manly musk.

"And what do you think of him so far?" he asked, eyeing me discreetly.

"He seems pretty cool," I replied, sensing that he was eyeing me, "and he's definitely not stingy."

"With *you*, he isn't," he said, pointing to his face with his thumb. "With this mug, I'm lucky he even *sells* it to me."

I chuckled. Not at his dumb joke. He was far from homely and knew it. He was being affectedly modest or perhaps clever.

"You must be Swedish, Danish, or Norwegian," he said, after studying my face for a moment.

"I'm none of the above."

"Really?"

"Yeah, really. I'm Irish and German with a trace of Alsatian on my dad's side and a trace of Bohemian on my mom's."

"Is that so? You look Scandinavian."

"Yeah, I guess so. Except for my humungous fucking noggin, it's Irish all the way."

"It's not big at all."

"Easy for you to say, you don't have to schlep it around."

"Looks just right to me," he said, smiling.

"You should have your eyes checked."

He burst out laughing.

"Whoa!" he exclaimed. "You're a strange one! I have to tell you, it's a little disturbing!"

"How kind of you to notice," I smirked.

"I am so sorry," he said sheepishly, placing his hand on my thigh, one inch from my crotch. "I meant *intriguing*, not disturbing."

"Yeah, sure you did," I said, moving his hand away from my privates in a gingerly manner. "You don't have to apologize. I know I'm a fucking weirdo. Do I scare you?"

"Absolutely not," he replied emphatically, staring into my vastly dilated pupils. "You fascinate me."

I had eye contact with him for all of five seconds before averting my gaze to the center of the room, where Joe was giving Maxine another injection. An awkward lull ensued, which the Scotch-Irishman promptly broke.

"I'm a lot older than you, and should know this, but where in the world is Bohemia?"

"Czech Land."

"Oh, okay. I thought it was a counter-culture district in the Bay Area."

I chuckled again.

"I'm not joking," he laughed. "Ignorant, isn't it? I guess it goes to show that college degrees are overrated."

I chuckled once more and asked, "What are you?"

"Three-quarters Scotch-Irish and one-quarter Cherokee on my mother's side."

"Hmmmm, interesting," I said, cracking my knuckles.

It wasn't that interesting. In fact, the whole conversation was about as exciting as shaving your armpits, but when you're totally wired-uh, the dullest, most trivial conversations seem riveting.

"My mom's boyfriend is part Cherokee," I continued, cracking my neck, "one-third, I think."

"Is that so?"

"Uh-huh. She's been obsessed with Native American culture since before I was born."

"It's interesting that you used the term Native American," he said, after a brief pause.

"Why? That's what they are, technically speaking, except they didn't call this shithole America."

"Yes, I know, but most people refer to them as Indians."

"And it makes no fucking sense. They're not from India or the Indies."

He tried to respond, but I cut him off.

"When I was a little kid, my dad took me to meet Iron Eyes Cody."

"How does your father know Iron Eyes Cody?"

"He doesn't. He teaches at Cal State Long Beach, and Iron Eyes Cody came to the campus powwow a few years back."

Yes, it was before Espera Oscar De Corti's true and unmistakably Italian ancestry was revealed.

"Oh, I see," the Scotch-Irishman said, nodding.

"Anyway, when it was my turn to meet him, he pulled me onto his lap and asked if I was doing my part to keep America beautiful. I told him I'd never littered once in my whole life. Then I asked him if he preferred being called Indian, American Indian, or Native American."

"And what did he say?"

"That all three were cool with him, but he knew people who hated being called Indian."

"I would imagine he's grown accustomed to it. He's been known as the Crying Indian for years."

"Yeah, that's what all the palefaces were calling him, and he didn't coldcock anyone over it."

"Was that it then?" he asked, grinning.

"Of course not, he was a captive listener."

"That poor man," he laughed. "What did you do to him?"

"Nothing," I replied innocently. "I just asked him if he preferred playing good guys or bad guys."

"And what did he say?"

"That he liked playing both, but wished there were more good-guy roles available for Native American actors."

"I have to agree with him there. Hollywood has always pigeonholed them, and in a negative way."

"Yeah, I think that's what he was implying."

"So, what happened next?"

"I told him he should find himself a nice squaw, and maybe then he wouldn't be so sad."

"You didn't," he laughed, placing his hand over his face.

"Yeah, I did," I said, smiling.

"What did he say... that he *had* one, and she was the *cause* of his grief?"

"No," I laughed, "but that would have been hilarious if he had. He didn't say anything. He just laughed and patted my head, then gave me a cherry lollipop and sent me on my way. To make a long story longer, a week later I found out that his wife was dead, and I felt like shit about what I'd said."

"That is so sweet," he said, grinning warmly.

"No it isn't!" I exclaimed. "It totally fucked me up! I still feel guilty about it!"

He burst out laughing again.

"I'm fucking serious!" I said, glaring wildly. "Why do you think I remember it so clearly? It's been haunting me for years!"

"It's all right," he said in a tranquilizing tone, while gently rubbing my upper thigh. "Just take a deep breath and relax, before you have a stroke."

"I don't know how to relax," I said, redirecting his hand toward my knee. "That word's not in my vocabulary."

"I'm sure it doesn't help that you're as high as a damn kite."

"I am coked-up, but it makes no difference. I came into the world a restless spaz, even when I'm sound asleep, I'm not relaxed."

"And why is that?"

"Because I'm a neurotic freak who belongs in a loony bin," I replied bluntly, "and I'm sure all the acid I've been dropping is only making me worse."

"Then why do you do it?"

"Because I'm a self-destructive masochist," I replied, even more bluntly.

He didn't react, so I kept rambling.

"If I ever run into the genius who said that acid isn't addictive, my knee and his gonads are going to have a little talk. That drug scares the shit out of me, but I can't stop taking it. If that's not an addiction, then I don't know what the fuck is."

He was noticeably uncomfortable. I often had that effect on humans, and still do at times. I haven't the faintest idea why, but most people are put off by spontaneity and sincerity, even those who consider themselves receptive and unshockable. They seem to prefer the safety and comfort of façades. I didn't want to repel the potential drug ticket, and it was too late to backpedal, so I spit out the first thing that popped into my jumbled head.

"So, how about them Dodgers?"

He stared at me with a puzzled look on his face, as though he weren't sure if he should laugh at my stupid quip or answer the question literally. He did neither. He simply smiled, then returned to the original topic seamlessly, as though we'd never digressed.

"You know, some Native Americans actually prefer the Indian label, but I think it's inappropriate."

"You do?" I asked, cracking my knuckles.

"Absolutely, but try telling that to the general public. They're very attached to Columbus's misnomer."

"I think the general public's been watching too many John Wayne flicks."

He laughed and asked, "You mean you're not a John Wayne fan?"

"Not really. I don't hate him, but I don't like him either."

"That's funny."

"Why?"

"Well, John Wayne was one of Orange County's most famous residents. They even named the airport after him."

"Yeah, I know," I said smartly. "It's not my fucking fault. If it were up to me, I would have named it after Leo Fender."

"Leo Fender? How about Dick Dale?"

"That would have been cool too."

"So, I guess you don't like westerns, huh?"

"Are you fucking kidding?" I exclaimed. "Some of my all-time favorite films are westerns!"

"But you don't like John Wayne? That's a little contradictory, don't you think?"

I smirked and replied, "Whatever you say, Pilgrim."

"You're a real wiseass," he said, leering at me, "and you have a dirty mouth."

"I can't help it," I said, returning his leer. "Is it offensive?"

"A little."

"Good."

"Good?" he laughed.

"Yeah, good."

Another awkward lull ensued, which he broke more quickly than the first.

"I hope you don't mind my asking, but how old are you?"

"How old do you think I am?"

"It's difficult to tell, but if I had to venture a guess, I'd say twenty-one."

"I wish! It would make my life a hell of a lot easier."

"Does that mean you're younger?"

I nodded.

"How much younger?"

"The truth?"

"Please."

"I'm fifteen."

Like every other ephebophile I'd encountered, it didn't faze him at all.

"Would you like to go out sometime?" he asked.

"Yeah, why the hell not," I replied, masking my relief that he'd finally asked the awaited question.

"Are you sure you don't want to know how old I am before deciding?"

I studied his face for a moment. He couldn't have been a day over twenty-five. I had no intention of touching him anyway, so his age was irrelevant.

"Not really," I replied indifferently.

"I'm thirty-seven," he blurted out guiltily, as though he were revealing some unthinkably horrific secret. "I'm old enough to be your father."

I didn't respond verbally or otherwise. I simply gazed at him blankly, as though I were in a catatonic state.

"Say something," he said, laughing nervously. "You look a little thunderstruck."

"Don't flatter yourself," I scoffed. "I don't shock that easily."

I was lying. I was thunderstruck, dumbfounded, and flabbergasted, but he was far too valuable to let go, thirty-seven or not. I quickly pulled myself together and tried to act impassive.

"There must be something running through that mind of yours," he said, staring at me inquisitively.

"There is," I replied, smacking my lips. "I was thinking about how yummy an ice-cold beer would taste right now."

"Is that all?" he laughed. "I thought you were going to tell me to take a hike! Don't move. I'll be right back."

Less than a minute later, he returned with a frosty bottle of Beck's, one of the only beers I could stand.

"So," he said, sitting down, "are we still on?"

I chugalugged the entire bottle, then let out a long, resonant belch and replied, "Sure, Pops."

What a graceless slob. For the record, I no longer burp in public, but at the time it was second nature.

He laughed while shaking his head in what appeared to be disgust, then handed me his business card and a pair of unmarked capsules that resembled miniature jelly beans. "Those will help you come down," he said with a shifty smile.

Without looking at it, I shoved the card into my pocket, then examined the capsules for a moment and asked, "What the fuck's in them?"

"Just a mild soporific."

I looked at him dubiously.

"They're perfectly safe," he said, brushing my tousled hair away from my face with his long fingers. "Nothing I wouldn't give my own mother."

Maybe he despised his mother. Maybe she was a mean, vicious, wretched, spiteful, straight-razor toting woman who beat him mercilessly with a rolling pin as a boy.

I stared at the pills for a moment longer then carefully tucked them into the coin pocket of my jeans.

"Look," he said, checking his watch, "I have to run, but will you call me in a couple of days?"

"Yeah," I replied coolly.

"Is that a promise?"

"Yeah, I promise I'll call you by Tuesday."

"I look forward to it."

"Yeah, me too," I mumbled.

"And please don't overdo it tonight," he added. "It'd be a shame if you died before our first date."

With that, I expected him to go on his merry way, but much to my surprise, he placed his hand behind my neck, pulled me toward him, and planted a firm smooch on my mouth. Although his move was somewhat aggressive, he kept his lips closed and his tongue to himself, which indicated that: 1) he wasn't overly pushy, and 2) it was going to be a cinch to string him along.

After removing his mouth from mine, he began caressing my face with his forefinger while gazing into my eyes amorously. For a split second I thought about snapping his finger in two, but I was mesmerized by his hypnotic brown eyes. Suddenly, I felt explosively hot, and when I went to switch on the AC, it malfunctioned. What can I say? He was not hard to look at, and I was always a sucker for a smooth, deep voice. Too bad I was in the midst of adolescence while he was on the brink of middle age.

He kissed me once more, on the cheek, then stood up and headed for the door. Before exiting, he turned around and said sternly, "Remember, do *not* overdo it tonight!"

I found his tone annoying. He sounded like a strict, overbearing father. We'd just met, and he was already fitting me with a collar and leash.

I flashed him a saucy smile and the bird.

He grinned, waved, and blew me a kiss, then walked out.

I wish to god I'd heeded his admonition, but I was an incurable, reckless glutton. I smoked more crack on that particular night than any other, before or after. That sooty glass tube became an extension of my dry, viscid lips. I was so wired I could actually see my toiling ticker pulsating through my bony chest. Breathing became a laborious task, and my thorax felt as though a two-ton hippopotamus were perched upon it.

By five a.m. I was convinced I was a goner, and it drove me into a state of unmitigated panic. Before anyone noticed, I slunk into Joe's bedroom, climbed into the sack, pulled the covers over my head, and swallowed the pills the Scotch-Irishman had given me, hoping they'd alleviate the maddening discomfort. Whatever was in those magic beans did the trick. Within twenty minutes I was out cold.

A short while later I awoke to a familiar, yet troubling sound. Familiar in the sense that I'd heard it before, and troubling because of its close proximity. I couldn't place it at first, but after listening carefully for a minute or so, I was able to make an accurate identification. Joe and Maxine were fucking violently right there next to me! I opened my eyes a bit to see if I was hallucinating. After all, I'd just spent several hours inhaling toxic fumes, but unfortunately, it was no chemical induced illusion. The two maniacs were virtually on top of me, in the anvil position, while the bed shook, rolled, and creaked, as though it were in the midst of a catastrophic earthquake.

Her legs were wrapped around his neck, and he was pounding her like a madman as she moaned in ecstasy, "Oooooooooh, Joe! Oooooooooh, yeah! Fuck me, baby! Fuck me harder!"

She repeated the lustful chant over and over again while he chimed in periodically with, "Oooooooh yeah, baby! Fuck yeah!"

I was pissed off, mortified, and slightly nauseated. I hadn't asked to be a spectator, and it was far more graphic and sickening than any skin flick I'd seen. I wasn't sure if I should ignore them or get the hell out of that bed. Before I had a chance to decide, they climaxed simultaneously, and what a repugnant harmony that was. Not wanting them to know that I'd witnessed one second of the nasty duet, I played possum until I dozed off.

Around two that afternoon, Maxine and I hopped into a cab, and although I was definitely tempted, I refrained from mentioning one word about her romp with Joe. I figured if she wanted to talk about it, she would. I couldn't help wondering how they'd wound up in bed, though. Was she crassly propositioned or did she willingly offer herself? Either way, I thought she was crazy. Putting out was not mandatory. The trick was to resist until the benefactor became frustrated, and consequently tightfisted, then move on to the next mark. Besides, Joe wasn't exactly Steve Reeves, and his personality stunk. What could be the attraction? Rumor had it that Maxine was pathologically promiscuous, but I always took such rumors with a grain of salt, particularly when they were coming from the mouths of men. In this case, however, the rumors turned out to be true. I soon learned that Maxine was a self-proclaimed nymphomaniac, who'd have sex with any man who was *up* for it, free of charge. I dug this girl immensely, and if she was hooked on penis, more power to her. But I was automatically found guilty by association, which only rubbed salt into the wounds caused by the rape, since sleeping around was the most reprehensible offense a girl could commit. Yes, I'm being sarcastic, although there is some truth to that statement, albeit twisted. For some inexplicable reason, promiscuous women have always been viewed with far less tolerance than promiscuous men, and often stigmatized by *both* genders. It's a flagrantly sexist double standard that makes no sense whatsoever. As far as I know, most STDs are unisex and one size fits all, so why the hell is a loose man hailed as a virile stud, while an equally loose woman is branded a filthy slut? It doesn't add up, but such is the way of the world.

When I last saw Maxine, she was drug-free, pregnant, and planning her wedding. More important, the girl who'd been treated as an inconvenience by the people who'd brought her into the world, had finally found security and unconditional love.

I have the innate ability to conjure up the exact emotions from nearly every significant moment of my life. Even when I can't recall the other details, the feelings are always vivid and crisp, as though I've just experienced them. I've found it to be both an asset and a curse, depending on whether the emotions are pleasant or afflictive in nature. Shame falls into the latter category, and if given the choice, I'd rather shove a scalpel into my abdomen than suffer its degrading impalement. That said, the feeling is not entirely without purpose. I firmly believe that a spoonful of shame can be healthy, but by the same token, an overdose can be fatal. I've never forgotten that night at Joe's, because it was the most shameful situation I've ever found myself in. Even though I was merely an innocent bysleeper, who happened to be in the wrong bed at the wrong time, I still felt like a miserable, unwilling crack whore, who *allowed* herself to be violated, when her gut feeling was to eviscerate the son of a bitch. In my wounded mind, it was tantamount to sexual assault, and the rawest nerve in my being was not only touched, but brutally manhandled. I was so deeply hurt and utterly ashamed it prompted me to question my ruinously self-indulgent lifestyle for the first time. Up until that point I'd been driven solely by two motives: the overpowering urge to use drugs, and the desperate urge to use whoever I could to get those drugs.

As my fifteen-year-old carcass lay on that cum stained mattress of a thirtysomething, whacked out drug trafficker, who'd just shot semen into my fifteen-year-old friend after shooting cocaine into her veins all night, I found myself reminiscing about Washington D.C. and the final family trip before dumping the homemaker for the homewrecker. Although the clan had visited our nation's capital on numerous occasions, the purpose of the last trip was to trade in our beat-up Ford station wagon for the used Dodge van that would bring us to California. I don't know why the memory popped into my mind other than that it carried me away to a simpler, happier time, a time when I desired ice cream, bubble gum, and a Lincoln Memorial snow globe, rather than acid, coke, and speed. I couldn't believe where life had taken me. I was a naïve child whose days had merely begun, yet I felt like a cunning adult with one foot in the grave. My relationship with drugs was like a viciously abusive marriage, but no matter how many times I was battered and raped, I couldn't bring myself to leave. I drew the line at sodomy, though, and vowed right then and there to never return to Joe's place again, no matter how desperate I got. I also passed on the Scotch-Irishman.

When you're a chemically dependent and manipulative leech, you must switch off two things to achieve greatness in the sport: your conscience and your pride. The former posed no problem, it had conked out ages ago, but the latter was stuck in the **ON** position. I was a devious, opportunistic hustler, who probably deserved to be shot execution style, but miraculously my dignity was still intact. I hadn't the slightest intention of divorcing drugs, but if I expected to maintain my self-respect, it was time to rethink my game. I simply couldn't conduct myself in such a disgraceful manner any longer. At least that's what I temporarily fooled myself into believing. Who the fuck was I kidding?

Less than two weeks later, I found myself sitting across from the Scotch-Irishman at an upscale eatery. I'd chosen the restaurant specifically for its privacy and low-key ambiance. Brightly lit, overcrowded dining rooms made me edgy, self-conscious, and paranoid. More important, I'd chosen the restaurant because the object of my obsession worked there. I hoped that when he got a load of my handsome, virile escort, he'd become overwrought with jealousy and challenge him to a duel. What an immature fool I could be. His heart belonged to another. And besides, it was his night off.

The Scotch-Irishman and I feasted on grilled halibut and a variety of side dishes, which I washed down with a slice of decadent cheesecake drowning in fresh whipped cream. The conversation during dinner had been relatively tame, but over dessert it took a rather wild turn.

He leaned forward, placed his forearms on the table, and fastened his arresting brown eyes onto my face. I was blissfully immersed in my rich, creamy cheesecake, but his commanding presence was too hard to ignore, especially when I could sense that he was staring at me seductively. I glanced up to discover much more than your average come-hither look. He was gazing at me rapaciously, as though he were about to devour me headfirst, like a white chocolate Easter bunny. I smiled modestly, and gave him a look which indicated that I was listening.

"Look," he said, "let's stop beating around the bush. We both know why we're here. I have an insatiable drug habit, and a lot of money. As far as I can tell, you have an equally insatiable drug habit, and judging from your age, no source of income. Correct me if I'm wrong, but I would imagine this puts you at a disadvantage. I don't know how you've supported your habit in the past, nor do I care to know, but from now on, I'll be more than happy to take care of your needs provided that you take care of mine."

"What do you mean?" I asked innocently, looking up at him with doe eyes.

I knew *exactly* what he meant, but was curious to hear his response.

"I'll spell it out for you. It was no accident that I approached you at Joe's. I have a thing for blondes, especially underage, sassy, wayward blondes. I find you very attractive, and forgive my forwardness, but I'd like to fuck your brains out, repeatedly."

I started choking on the bite of cheesecake I was masticating. I admired candor, but needless to say, this was a bit excessive.

"Are you all right?" he said, pushing my glass toward me. "Here, have some water."

I took a couple of sips.

"Are you all right?" he reiterated.

I nodded, then ducked back into the sanctuary of my cheesecake.

"As I was saying, you arouse me something fierce. You're provocatively insolent, uncouth, and naughty. You need to be tamed and disciplined, and I want to be the man who carries out the task."

I couldn't believe my ears! It was too absurd to be true! I felt as though I'd been dropped into the middle of a raunchy, twisted version of *Pygmalion*! I'd dealt with my share of perverts, but this bloke took the Dundee cake! His frankness and effrontery were unprecedented! Christ, I'd pegged him wrong! Perhaps if I were legal and we were madly in love, I would have found it alluring, in a kinky way, but he was a complete stranger who was only a few years younger than my favorite uncle from Ann Arbor. No doubt about it, the suave Scotch-Irishman was a slimy, degenerate pig. I was insulted, not only by his words, but by their implication. But you know what? I had it coming and then some, although admitting that I was getting my just deserts didn't make it any easier to swallow. I hoped that he was finished, but unfortunately, I hadn't heard nothin' yet.

"Here's my proposal," he continued, "I'll supply you with all the drugs you want, as long as you grant me the pleasure of fucking you whenever I want, starting tonight. I'm a very busy man, I probably won't require your services more than twice a week, but when I do call I expect you to be available, open-minded, and prepared to do whatever I ask. My time is limited, I can't afford to be chasing you around, so I'm going to give you a pager, and I want you to leave it on. Have I made myself clear?"

"Crystal," I replied.

"Well, do we have a deal?"

I scooped up the last chunk of cheesecake with my spoon, stuffed it into my mouth, and let it melt slowly on my tongue.

"Speak up," he said, smiling lasciviously. "I don't think I can restrain myself much longer. I've had a painful hard-on since I saw you strut in here in that dress."

"Oh yeah?" I said teasingly, glaring at him.

"Oh yeah," he sighed. "I've never had a fifteen year old before. I'm dying to get inside your tight little cunt, only I can't decide what I want to do first... make sweet love to you in the missionary position or bend you over and fuck you like a bitch."

My blood had already passed the boiling point, but the moment those words crossed his lips I was consumed with murderous indignation. It took every ounce of self-control I had to keep from leaping over that table and severing his carotid artery with the hilt of my spoon.

I wiped my mouth with my napkin, scooted out of the booth, picked up my unused dessert fork, and proceeded to drive it into his hand, the same hand that had been caressing my face just two weeks prior.

"*FUCK!*" he yelped, retracting the wounded paw, and holding it with the other.

I leaned over the table and growled, "*Eat shit and die, you motherfucking pig.*"

Then I walked out of the restaurant and up the street to 7-11, where I called a cab. I had exactly zero dollars and twenty-five cents, so I directed the driver to Mia's house. Thankfully, she was home, and covered the fare.

As we walked into her house, she asked the expected question. "What the fuck happened? I thought you went out with Daddy Bigbucks tonight?"

When I tried to explain, I broke down and cried like a helpless infant sitting in an acidic shit-filled diaper. I thought I was so tough and thick-skinned. What a joke. I was nothing more than a damaged little girl who grew up way too fast, hid behind a shuck of moxie, and infused her still-developing body with anesthetics so she wouldn't have to feel.

MAH NÁ MAH NÁ

I thought jocks were thoroughly uninteresting, save the fact that they weren't as virtuous as they let on. They had their parents, teachers, and coaches fooled into believing that they were boy scouts, when, in fact, most of them were inveterate drug users. I also found it amusing that they were beguiled by the "bad girls." Sure, they had their apple-pie prom-queen cheerleader sweethearts, but it was the fast-living rebel chicks they lusted after. They must have assumed that drugging, raising hell, breaking the law, self-mutilation, and slutty garb was synonymous with promiscuity and kinkiness. A creepy, freakishly enormous lineman comes to mind, who I believed was retarded, in the literal sense. Rather than hitting on my girlfriends and me, he'd blatantly stare in the same manner Lennie admired Curly's wife before pawing and shaking her to death. I was not at all surprised to learn that he'd once attempted to rape a girl after forcing her into the bathroom at a party.

Jock parties were mind-numbingly boring snobfests, but also teeming with drugs. On a Friday night in late autumn, Kiki, Mia, and I found ourselves at one of these snooty socials. An hour into it, I was approached by a succulent hunk of beef who I'll call Biff. He was five years older and came from wealthy stock. I knew all about him and his Deca Durabolin pumped cronies. They had a reputation

219

for being sought-after ladies' men. I thought they were arrogant meatheads.

"Are you taking applications for a boyfriend?" he said, after introducing himself.

I've always found pickup lines repulsively artificial, but I was wired and he was a captive listener. After chatting for a spell, I realized that he wasn't such a jerk after all. Granted, he was about as boring as they came, but he made me feel safe. He also smelled *incredible*, like fresh laundry that had been washed in soft water with Tide then dried on medium with three sheets of Bounce. His face was average, but his well-developed and chiseled upper body was busting out of his aromatic, vanilla shirt, and it was a delectably seductive vision. After what felt like an hour of painfully insipid dialogue, he asked for my telephone number, which I gave without hesitation. My hasty decision was based solely upon his physical attributes. Yes, it was sickeningly superficial, but sometimes you have to follow your libidinous instinct.

Biff wasted no time in calling, which earned him additional points. When I gave someone my number and said to call, I meant it, but for reasons unknown, most people took forever, which didn't jibe with my awareness of elapsing time. Biff reached out and touched me the following afternoon with a dinner invitation. I accepted, but made it perfectly clear that I had no intention of becoming seriously involved with him or anyone else. He made it equally clear that he had a longtime girlfriend named Bambi, who was attending college out of state. I had qualms about dating someone who was spoken for, but I'd met Bambi once, through a male friend at the gym, and she was a first-class supercilious bitch. She refused to shake my hand, spoke to me in a patronizing tone, and glared at me in disgust, as though I were a puddle of gamy, chunky Shih Tzu vomit that wasn't even worthy of being mopped up. While she was torturing my poor friend with vapid, self-admiring chin music, I contemplated grabbing her by the hair and ramming her overinflated head into the dumbbell rack. She represented all that I despised about the upper crust, and therefore, was undeserving of my guilt. After hanging up with Biff, I gave my conscience five minutes to say its piece before coming to the following conclusion: fuck Bambi and the high horse she rode in on. I decided to use her boyfriend for sex, but not in the conventional sense. In the months following the rape, I'd flinch whenever a man touched me, even my own father. It was extremely distressing and potentially crippling. I was only a kid. I didn't want to be disabled by intimacy issues for the rest of my life. The only solution was to face and eradicate the incubus before it became a permanent resident.

As expected, the first roll in the hay didn't go too well. I was apprehensive and tense, and simply lay there like a corpse, while Biff worked his magic. Miraculously, my unresponsiveness didn't scare him away, and I was pleasantly surprised when he called the very next day. I grew to trust the meathead, and after a week of trysts, had an awe-inspiring, prolonged multi-orgasm that nearly knocked me unconscious. Although I'd hobnobbed with the garden variety, I'd never made the acquaintance of that hallowed Spot in the female body whose existence is doubted by some. It was an excellent sign. I was certain I'd been permanently ruined by the rape, but was obviously mistaken.

Shortly after that glorious, life-changing night, Biff and I started to see each other on a daily basis. Again, my reasons were as superficial as they came: he was financially generous and magnificent in bed. In addition to his fat wallet and sexual prowess, he was always in possession of a sackful of potent weed. Our time together was spent smoking pot, drinking, dining at expensive restaurants, and humping maniacally. That was the extent of it.

A month into it, he presented me with a plump gold necklace and announced, "I broke up with Bambi. I don't care about her anymore. I wanna be with you exclusively."

Although truly flattered, I was not remotely interested. Being fuck buddies was one thing, but embarking on a monogamous relationship? The sex was mind-blowing and surprisingly curative, but on an intellectual level, Biff was subpar at best. Not to mention our dissimilar interests. And I couldn't stand the music he listened to. It was driving me up a towering, electric razor wire fence. I was never a Springsteen fan, and if I had to suffer through one more nanosecond, I was going to hurt someone.

Rather than rejecting Biff's heartfelt proposal, I told him I'd think about it. After doing just that, I concluded that a relationship with him wasn't such a bad idea after all. While contemplating the matter I'd made a conscious effort to focus on his positive attributes, which were as follows:

1) He was endearingly protective
2) He was always in a chipper mood
3) He treated me like a queen
4) He taught me some nifty new tricks
5) He'd decontaminated me

For that final reason alone, it seemed only fair that I give it a shot.

Our sexually intoxicating yet otherwise tedious romance thrived for weeks, until the night came when Biff crossed the line. We were sitting in his car, reeling from the divine, shamelessly public intercourse we'd just had, when he began to study my face in an analytical manner. Since he typically eyeballed me for a spell after injecting his juice, I thought nothing of it, although his gaze did seem more intent than usual. I smiled at him, then lay my head back on the seat and closed my eyes.

Moments later, he uttered the following words: "You should let all of those piercings grow in, 'cause my mom doesn't really like the whole Nazi punk rock thing."

"What did you just say?" I exclaimed, sitting up.

"I said, my mom doesn't really like the whole Nazi punk rock thing," he repeated calmly, "I think you should let your..."

"I heard you loud and clear!" I yelled, interrupting him.

"Did I say something to upset you?" he asked innocently.

"I'm not upset, I'm fucking pissed!"

"Really? Why?"

Truth be told, I took greater umbrage at his nitpicking suggestion than at the Nazi implication.

"I'll tell you why I'm pissed!" I yelled. "*No one* tells me what to do, least of all some pampered mama's boy! You don't hold title on me, what makes you think you have the right to control me?"

He placed his hand on my face in an effort to placate me.

I pushed it away and resumed my tirade. "*You* hit on *me*, remember? You knew *exactly* what you were getting! If you want a fucking Barbie doll, god knows there's no fucking shortage! All you have to do is take a spin through your neighborhood! Aren't I good enough for you the way I am? You sure as hell haven't complained while you've been fucking me into a stupor every night!"

"Look," he interjected, "let's just..."

"As for *the whole Nazi punk rock thing*," I yelled, cutting him off, "since when the fuck are punk rock and fascism bedfellows? Educate yourself!"

"Hey, all I know is that some of those skinhead dudes are really messed up."

"No shit, Sherlock, but they're a whole nother breed of cat."

"I don't see how," he scoffed. "If it looks like a punk, walks like a punk, and quacks like a punk..."

"How fucking original," I retorted snidely. "You're a regular fucking quipster, aren't you?"

"What?" he asked, turning his body toward mine. "Isn't that what it's all about? Dressing up like a weirdo, beating the crap out of each other, and hating society?"

"No," I replied, turning my body toward his, "and it may be difficult for you to grasp, but not everything has to be *about* something. Some things just *are*."

"That doesn't make sense," he said, shaking his head. "It has to be about something."

It was like Abbott and Costello doing Beckett. I was beyond frustrated, and it was all I could do to keep from smacking him.

"It isn't about anything specifically," I said, in a futile attempt to explain. "It's whatever the fuck you want it to be, and that's what makes it so cool."

"I don't get it."

"There *is* no prescribed set of rules, and anyone who does follow one is missing the whole point."

"I still don't get it," he said with a dopey look on his face.

It was like discussing international relations with a half-witted, three-year-old jingoist. He was deaf, at sea, and halfway to Catalina. At first I thought it was because he was stoned, but quickly realized that he was disturbingly insular and slow on the uptake. I knew he was a bit dense, but had no idea he was so narrow.

"It's really fucking simple," I said in an irritated tone, "but somewhere along the way it got distorted, and now everyone thinks it's about tattoos, piercings, mohawks, misanthropy, and violence."

"That *is* what it's about," he argued. "I've seen that movie *Suburbia*."

"Then you know," I said sarcastically, "because movies are *always* a hundred percent factual. You'd better not go to sleep tonight... some psycho with bad skin and a red and green striped sweater might slash your throat and gut you."

"Hey, I'm only going by what I've seen," he said, grinning, "and some of the people you hang out with look exactly like those fuckups from that movie."

"Yeah," I agreed, "and some of them don't, but they're all on the same wavelength... and so am I."

"What wavelength is that," he laughed, "the freak show wavelength?"

He meant it in jest, but it rubbed me the wrong way, prompting me to say the following: "I don't know why I waste my breath. You're too fucking stupid for your own good."

"Come on now!" he exclaimed. "There's no reason to get bitchy about it!"

It was the most emotion I'd ever seen him show. Next to an orgasm, that is.

"You want bitchy, motherfucker?" I snapped, holding my fist up to his face. "I'll give you bitchy!" I wanted to bop him right in the nose.

"Okay," he said, placing his hand on my fist, "just calm down!"

"Fuck you!" I yelled, pulling away. "Don't tell me to calm down, you fucking cocksucker!"

"Hey, don't talk to me like that!"

"I'll talk to you however the fuck I want!" I yelled, shoving my face up into his. "What the fuck are you going to do about it?"

We glared at each other for a moment before turning away. A brief pause ensued. Then he placed his hand on my thigh and tried to make amends.

"Let's just chill out and start over," he said in a calm voice.

"No," I said, removing his hand, "I don't want to start over. In fact, I'm not even sure if I want to see you anymore."

"Why," he exclaimed, "because I want you to make a few improvements?"

"*Improvements*?" I yelled. "You're a petty fucking asshole, and I don't give a shit what you want! If you don't like me, just come right out and say so!"

"I *do* like you!" he argued. "All I'm trying to say is that I want you to meet my mom, and she's not gonna like all that junk! Can't you just take it out?"

"No, *I can't just take it out!*" I said mockingly. "I don't give a flying fuck what your mommy likes! I don't want to meet her skanky ass anyway! And you know what, fuckface? You've pissed me off so much I'm going to ram *more* metal into my body! While I'm at it, maybe I'll tattoo a giant swastika on my forehead! Do you think your mommy will like that?"

I was obviously kidding about the swastika.

We fell silent and stared at the house in front of us for what seemed like an eternity. Then Biff offered a lame apology.

"Look," he sighed, "I don't wanna fight, but will you at least think about taking the junk out?"

I glowered at him.

"Okay, forget it," he said, raising his hands in defeat. "I'm sorry I brought it up in the first place."

I accepted his rotten, blighted olive branch, but suggested that we cool it for a spell. He argued at first, but ultimately agreed. Then I demanded that he take me home.

Without saying goodbye, I got out of the car, went up to my bedroom, washed down a pair of Valium with a lukewarm Kamikaze, climbed into bed, and bawled for an hour straight. Although he hadn't meant to, he'd hurt my feelings deeply, and not because he'd asked me to grow in my piercings. To his credit, not once did he bring attention to our differing socioeconomic backgrounds, but merely *being with him* rekindled those dormant feelings of insecurity and shame. I was embarrassed by my Career Academy haircut, my basse couture clothing, my dilapidated shack that looked as though it were about to collapse, my mother's enormous '76 Buick Regal that stood out like a steaming mound of elephant shit on a pristinely manicured lawn... Biff wasn't to blame in any way, but for the first time in three years, I felt grossly inadequate. My confidence had been annihilated, and once again, I was that "ugly, grody, weird, white trash loser." Only now, the jeers were coming from inside my head.

A couple of days after the pointless quarrel, I received a telephone call from Biff.

"Um... how's it goin'?" he said, sounding uncharacteristically anxious.

"Fine," I yawned. "How's it going with you?"

"Um... fine. Um... I need to talk to you."

"So talk," I said curtly. "I'm all ears."

"Um... no... um... I mean, in person."

"Okay, come on over."

"Um… okay. I'll be there in… um… ten minutes."

I could sense from his nervous tone and the plethora of "ums" that he had something weighty on his small mind. I couldn't begin to guess what it was, and couldn't wait to find out. Ten minutes later, he pulled into the driveway and honked the horn.

As I was getting into the car he asked, "Um… so, how's it goin'?"

"I thought we already established that *it* was going fine?" I replied gruffly, slamming the door. "Get to the point already."

"Okay," he said, after letting out a deep sigh. "Um… I really don't know how to tell you this, so I'm just gonna say it. Um… Bambi and I are getting back together, so um… I can't see you anymore."

Admittedly, I was shocked, but also relieved.

"Okay," I said, gently tugging on the necklace. "Does that mean you want the chain back?"

He looked at me as though I'd told him to go fuck himself. I think he was expecting a more histrionic reaction. Perhaps he thought I'd get down on my knees and implore him to reconsider, but on the contrary, I was grateful. I had no illusions about my relationship with Biff, and knew from the outset that our days together were numbered. I know I'm repeating the obvious, but we came from different sides of the tracks, metaphorically and literally. He resided in a palace on the west side of the boulevard, while I dwelled in a rattrap on the east side. He was rich, Christian, conservative, and "normal," while I

229

was broke, atheist, anarchistic, and mental. It was only going to be a matter of time before our sultry, forbidden romance reached its inevitable end, and I didn't want to be the one who broke it off. I always had a terrible time being assertive with men. Complaisance and pugnacity came more naturally. When it came to ditching a guy, I was slightly bipolar: if he was a good egg I'd handle him with kid gloves, if he was an asshole I'd handle him with boxing gloves. Biff fell into the former category. Even though he was painfully shallow and dull, he'd never been anything less than a saint. I couldn't help having feelings for him.

"No," he replied, forcing a smile, "I want you to keep the necklace."

"Are you sure? Because you can have it back."

"No, it was a gift. I want you to keep it."

I wondered how much I could get for it at Paco's pawn shop. It had to be worth some serious change.

"If you insist," I said, smiling angelically. Then I placed my hand on his thigh and asked, "Hey, do you have any more of that skunk bud left?"

"Um, yeah," he answered confusedly. "Why, do you wanna get high?"

Here's what I thought: "No dingbat, I'm so fucking heartbroken I want to place a plastic bag over my head and suffocate myself." And here's what I said: "Yeah, why the hell not?"

After engaging in one final smoke-out session, Biff and I parted ways forever.

NATURE WAS ON CALL

On one of my last romps with Biff, I crossed paths with a creature called Baron, who was a charter member of a legendary gang that my girlfriends and I aspired to associate with. I was once asked to describe them in ten words or less, and here's what I came up with: the Wild Bunch meets the Marx Brothers.

Biff and I had just pulled into a local gas station, en route to dinner, when Baron appeared out of nowhere, tapping on my window.

"Fuck!" I yelled, jumping in my seat and placing my hand over my heart.

"Shit, sorry!" he said, smiling and waving. Then he walked around to Biff's window.

"What's up, bro?" Biff said, unlocking the back door. "Hop in."

"How the hell do you two know each other?" I asked, flipping around in my seat.

I couldn't help wondering, since punks and jocks were sworn enemies.

He looked at me, then at Biff, then back at me, as though he weren't sure if I could be trusted.

"She's cool, bro," Biff said, introducing us. Then he explained that Baron supplied him and his fellow meatheads with drugs.

After shooting the breeze for a spell, Biff went inside to get a soda. The instant he was out of sight, Baron moved up to the driver's seat.

"Hey, sweetheart, what the fuck are you doin' with this tool?" he said, smiling flirtatiously. "He doesn't seem like your type."

I rolled my eyes and replied, "How would you know what my type is?"

"I'm pickin' up a strong vibe, and even though you kinda look the part, somethin' tells me you ain't no princess."

I didn't respond.

"If you ask me, *I'm* more your type," he said cockily.

"Well, I *didn't* ask you."

"How old are you?"

"None of your business."

"Are you legal yet? 'Cause that's all I need to know."

"Hey!" Biff laughed, opening the door. "Are you trying to steal my girl?"

"How old is this one?" Baron asked, keeping his eyes set firmly on my face.

"Fifteen," Biff replied proudly, as though he were talking about his daughter, rather than the underage kid he was fucking. "Nice, huh?"

Baron climbed over the console, and planted himself in the back seat. "So, where are we headed?" he asked, grinning slyly.

"Well, *we're* headed to a restaurant for dinner," Biff laughed.

"Mmmmm, sounds good to me," Baron said, rubbing his stomach, "I'm starving."

What ensued was sheer madness. Biff tried repeatedly to get Baron out of the car, but he refused to budge. Even crazier, he was brazenly hitting on me, right in front of Biff. He was spewing out quotations by Sir Walter Scott and Lord Byron, among others, and at one point, I turned around to talk to him, and his two front teeth were suddenly missing. I was broken up for several minutes.

"Did you lose something?" I asked, after regaining my composure.

He explained that he was wearing a removable bridge, because his choppers had been kicked down his throat by one of his oldest and dearest friends.

"You think this is bad?" he laughed. "You should see what I did to him! I thought I fuckin' killed him! There was blood everywhere, and it took a shitload of stitches to seal his head shut. There's still a huge lump, you can see it through his hair."

"What the fuck were you fighting about?" I asked, still laughing.

"Fuck if I know," he said, shrugging his shoulders. "I can't remember that far back."

As the minutes passed, I quickly realized that Baron was right. He and I were indeed far more compatible than Biff and I would ever be. Sure, he was a certifiable lunatic, but I was one step away from Danvers myself. He was also hilarious and alluringly dangerous. By the end of the night, I was more determined than ever to know him and the rest of his gang.

As luck would have it, a week after Biff and I called it quits, Mia and I ran into Baron while leaving a warehouse party. He was with a heavily-inked, wild-eyed freak who had an obscenely dense head of thatch. It was plain to see that if he dunked his head into a sink, the water would simply glaze the surface of his brush cut, like morning dewdrops on a spring meadow. My father started losing his hair at nineteen. I couldn't help wondering: with all the young men out there suffering from premature alopecia, was it really necessary for one guy to have that much grass?

"Hey jailbait," Baron said, scooping me up in his arms. "Are you still runnin' around with that rich, two-timin' prick?"

"Do you see him here?" I scoffed.

"That's what I wanna hear!" he laughed. "Didn't I tell you it wasn't gonna work out? What a tangled web we weave...?"

"Only about a billion times," I replied, rolling my eyes.

"And I was right, wasn't I?"

"Yeah," I replied reluctantly, "you were right."

"I'm always right," he said with a boyish smile, "and don't you forget it either."

"I'm sure you'll remind me if I do."

"You're cool with it anyway, aren't you?" he said, putting me down. "I mean, it's not like you were in love with him, were you?"

"Fuck no!" I snapped back.

"Whoa, take it easy!" he laughed. "I was just askin'. I don't know what the fuck you were doin' with a clown like that in the first place. You're way too good for him."

I *really* needed to hear that. I'd spent the past week thinking I was a horribly inferior creature who would never be good enough for anyone. I should have thanked him, but didn't.

"This is LT," he said, pointing toward his deranged-looking friend, who was now gazing up at the starlit sky with his head cocked back and mouth agape. "I know he looks like a fuckin' psycho, but he's harmless. He just dropped an eighth of a sheet a coupla hours ago."

"Are you fucking kidding?" I asked in disbelief. "Is he okay?"

"Yikes!" Mia exclaimed. "That's insane, man!"

"He's cool," Baron laughed. "His brain's a little fried. It takes at least that much for him to trip." Then he wiggled his fingers in front of LT's face, while whistling the theme from *The Twilight Zone*.

LT remained still, his bulging, manic eyes affixed to the sky.

"So, who's your cute friend?" Baron asked, eyeing Mia. "She looks sweet enough to eat!"

I introduced them.

"Me and Manson here are heading over to our buddies' pad for a private get-together," he said, still eyeing Mia. "Do you wanna come with? I promise we won't chop you up and dump your remains in a remote location."

Mia and I looked at each other, exchanging thoughts telepathically.

"Sounds like a plan," she said enthusiastically.

A half hour later, we were sitting in an apartment, where Mia and I met, and were embraced, by the rest of the inner circle. It marked the beginning of yet another leg of the journey.

EYEGORE

ffiliating with the gang proved to be beneficial in terms of having a reliable source of chemical sustenance, as well as mischievous fun. It wasn't all shits and giggles, though, far from it. Besides the obvious, there was no shortage of violence. While there were occasional scraps with outsiders, the majority seemed to occur within. I witnessed the worst incident while spending what should have been an uneventful evening with Mia, Vince, LT, Igor, and Lucas at one of the marked territories.

Vince was not a member of the gang, but rather a loveable long-haired rocker who lived at the opposite end of my street. I'd known him since moving to the area. To my knowledge, he and I were the only kids in our neighborhood who came from broken homes, except in his case, it was his mother who'd split. Our relationship was truly unique. For reasons unknown at the time, there was not a modicum of sexual tension, which enabled us to connect mentally and emotionally without any interference. In addition to having mentally unstable, 12-Stepping mothers, we shared an intense love for music, roller coasters, vomit-inducing carnival rides, mystical and macabre art, necromantic games, ice cream, chocolate, cereal, cats, cartoons, horror flicks, G.L.O.W. and classic television shows... and drugs, of course. He didn't care for most of the guys that the girls and I ran with, and it wasn't merely the usual "long hairs hating punks and vice versa" scenario. True, they did tease him relentlessly, but I'd later learn that some of the homophobic jerks were hitting him up for sex behind closed doors. He also hated the heap of trouble that accompanied the gang, and his concerns were not groundless. The majority of my arrests took place when I was in their company. Although I was equally guilty, they were usually responsible for attracting the police in the first place, whether through uncontrollable public intoxication, violence, warrants, or some other red flag.

LT was one of the few that Vince liked and got along with. He was the most spirited creature I've ever known, and the ultimate daredevil, welcoming every foolhardy challenge that came his way. Whether it was eating a plateful of peanut butter and crackers sans liquid while suffering from a severe case of cottonmouth, or executing the perfect Adolph that would've been the envy of any professional trampolinist. The former feat was performed on a fourteen-foot trampoline, and was a spectacular sight indeed. Except he didn't land on his feet... or on the trampoline. Given the cartoonish nature of the tumble, I instinctively doubled over in laughter, but soon realized that he wasn't moving. I was certain he was dead, or at the very least paralyzed, but within seconds, he jumped up, brushed himself off, and performed an encore. LT's fearlessness and vivacity were matched with equal parts of compassion and humility. He was bright, deep, sensitive, and wanted to save the world. Not in an artificial, kudos-hunting manner. He genuinely wanted to help others. He'd been given up for adoption at birth, which had left him with the standard "abandonment" issues, but never wallowed in self-pity. While his folks were financially well-off, he held down a regular job, drove a jalopy, and favored nature over the trappings of wealth. He always stopped for hitchhikers, and whenever he spotted a climbable tree, he'd pull over and scale it like a macaque, even if it was in the middle of a congested street. I loved him dearly. He was one of a kind, and so much more than the chemically-dependent ex-con society had reduced him to.

Igor, the most recent import, was a spleenful, hardcore, militant nihilist, who was always angry about some injustice, (mis)perceived or otherwise. It could have been "more bullshit from politicians" or the fact that the "stupid fucking skank at the Jack in the Box drive-thru" didn't give him enough ketchup and napkins.

Lucas was the polar opposite, a quiet soul with an angelic veneer who was perhaps more troubled than any of the others. I didn't see him often, since he seemed to spend most of his time behind bars. I wasn't sure if it was a form of self-sabotage, if he had difficulty functioning on the outside, or if he actually enjoyed living in a cage.

What was supposed to be a fun night of drugging and high jinks transmogrified into a gruesome nightmare when Igor and Lucas began bickering like an old married couple. These altercations were routine, occasionally escalating into brutal slugfests, which was the case here. After shoving and punching each other for several minutes, they rolled down into the concrete riverbed, grappling all the way. Mia, Vince and I followed, cheering them on. Arguably not the wisest course of action, but much like a rough-and-tumble hockey fight, these scraps could be a source of thrilling entertainment.

Then came the near fatal turn. Igor got to his feet, stood over Lucas and began kicking him in the face repeatedly with his steel-toed boot. Vince yelled for LT, who flew down and shoved Igor aside, but it was too late. Lucas was still alive, but his eye was not so fortunate. When he stepped into the light, a horrifying sight was revealed.

"Oh my fucking god!" Vince yelled, placing his hand over his mouth.

Mia, LT, and I let out a collective gasp. None of us were strangers to gore, but it was the worst battle wound I'd *ever* seen. Lucas' upper eyelid looked as though it had been chopped with a hatchet, and the orb appeared to be hanging out of its socket.

"What? What? What? What? What?" Lucas repeated confusedly.

"Are you okay, man?" LT asked, placing his hand on Lucas' shoulder. "I mean, can you stand and breathe okay?"

"Yeah, I'm cool," Lucas replied, reeling slightly to the left. "What the fuck happened?"

"Maybe he should sit down," Mia said to LT, pointing at an empty crate a few feet away. "Here, Lucas, sit down for a minute."

With LT's help, he staggered over to the crate and plopped down. "Dude, my fuckin' eye hurts like hell," he slurred, instinctively placing his hand over the gaping hematoma.

"Don't touch it!" LT snapped. "We gotta get you to a hospital, man!"

"Yeah, but I got a warrant… maybe more than one," Lucas said in a frustrated tone. "The hospital will call the fuckin' pigs for sure, and I ain't ready to go back in yet."

Throughout it all, Igor remained silent, pacing back and forth on the other side of the riverbed.

"I know, man, but your eye looks really fuckin' bad," LT said calmly. "You gotta let someone take care of it."

"Yeah," Mia agreed, "you have to go to the hospital, and *now*. You don't want to be blind for the rest of your life."

That was all Lucas needed to hear. "Is it really that bad? Aww fuck it, man," he grumbled, standing up. "It hurts like a motherfucker. Alright, let's go."

The five of us crammed into the four-person car and raced to the emergency room. I was the smallest and therefore, had the privilege of sitting on Lucas' lap. His eye was now the size of a tangerine, with an irrepressible efflux of blood streaming down his face, saturating my clothes in the process. I was tempted to place LT's hoodie over it to suppress the bleeding, but was afraid the eyeball would pop out if I so much as touched it. The eye was clearly a goner, a thought that made me physically ill. Lucas would spend the rest of his days wearing a prosthesis, simply because he and Igor had knocked back ten too many and gotten carried away. What a senseless and completely preventable tragedy. Yet another incident in which goodtime John Barleycorn had proven to be a catalyst for ugliness.

"I'm so fuckin' sorry about the blood," Lucas mumbled over and over again.

I wasn't sure if the graveness of his condition had fully registered. He did take a brief look in the mirror, but it was almost as if he didn't see the same monstrosity the rest of us saw. Perhaps it was the drugs. Or maybe he was scared and in denial.

"Don't worry about it," I replied softly, "it's just a little blood." Then I did my best to assure him that the injury wasn't as horrific as it looked, and that he was going to be fine. "It's just the swelling and blood that's making it look so bad," I said, gently patting his back. "Some antiseptic and a few stitches are all it needs." Of course I was lying, but what the hell was I supposed to do? Tell him they were going to gouge out his eyeball and insert a marble in its place?

By the time we reached the hospital, Lucas was queasy, presumably from the rapid blood loss. LT put the car in park and left the engine running. I quickly jumped out, and once Lucas was on his feet, jumped back in. LT escorted him through the double glass doors, sat him down in one of the chairs, and split before he was seen.

"That was fuckin' gnaaaaarrrrrly," Vince said, as LT got back into the car.

"I know, man!" LT agreed, putting it into gear and flooring it. "Way gnarly!"

"I hope he's going to be okay," Mia said.

"Me too," I said, glancing down at my blood soaked clothes. I looked as though I'd committed a homicide. I hoped that a cop wouldn't cross our path, since I'd have a hell of a time explaining why I was covered with blood. "Whatever you do," I said to LT, "don't get pulled over."

Igor had yet to mutter a single word.

Lucas' eye was ultimately saved, although the scars remained until he took his last breath. He spent the better part of his life incarcerated in a prison of addiction, from which he was released, by his own hand, in early 2011. Yet another former comrade pointlessly crushed by the jaws of self-annihilation.

THERE ONCE WAS A SCHIZO NAMED STROTHER

The Morgans were brothers, and the tenants of that apartment I mentioned a couple of chapters back. Adam was the eldest, and most amiable. He could outdrug anyone, but still managed to be somewhat responsible. Then there was Eric, the largest, loudest, and toughest of the three. His greatest gift was his supernatural ability to belch and fart simultaneously… on cue. Joe was the youngest and most pleasing to the eye. He had an agreeable disposition with a strong fiery streak. They were a peculiar brethren who lived by an absurd code. Whenever one of them was arrested, he'd give one his brothers' names instead of his own. Since all three had mile-long criminal records, and were constantly in court or jail, it couldn't have been more pointless, but they did it regardless.

The girls and I quickly became fixtures at the Morgans'. They were a blast to hang out with, had drugs galore, and the company they kept opened more doors on the connection front. One night Kiki and I were there, engaging in the usual, when a pair of those connections came knocking.

"Hey," Eric said, opening the door, "about time. Come on in."

It was a drug trafficker named Keleko and his out-of-state colleague, who was in town for the week. I glanced over at them from the couch, where

Kiki and I were nursing the crack pipe. Keleko was certainly an impressive looking creature, in a Hellenistic way. Standing over six feet and carrying at least two hundred pounds of solid, chiseled muscle, he looked as though he'd been sculpted from clay. He also had the thickest, most venous neck I'd ever seen on a human being. After saying their hellos and taking a fat wad of cash from Adam, they made a bee line for the couch.

"Hello, ladies," Keleko said, extending his hand. "I'm Keleko, and this is my colleague John."

Kiki and I offered our hands and names.

"Why don't you guys have a seat," Kiki suggested, smiling flirtatiously.

"I have a better idea," Keleko said, returning her smile. "Are you hungry, by any chance?"

"We're on our way to the most amazing sushi place," John added.

"I could probably eat," she said, glancing at me. "How about you?"

The decision had been made before we'd even been invited, but it was important that we not appear too eager.

"I can try," I replied coolly.

"Alright then," Keleko said, extending his hand and helping us up from the couch. "Shall we?"

While heading down the stairs to their car, I turned around and saw Joe standing in the doorway, scowling. I figured he'd either smoked too much crack or was PMSing. I smiled pertly and gave him the finger. He glared at me for a moment before slamming the door closed.

Our destination was an upscale Japanese restaurant located a couple of cities over. The owner was a friend of Keleko's, and went out of his way to ensure that our dining experience was superb. As the hours passed, and our blood alcohol levels spiked, Keleko became a bit affectionate, but never came close to violating any boundaries. In fact, he was the consummate gentleman, which I found incredibly refreshing.

Around midnight, the four of us retreated to a nearby hotel and began freebasing relentlessly. Keleko claimed that his house was under surveillance, hence the need to rent a room. He told a sensational tale about police helicopters encircling his property while he hid under the dining room table with a loaded shotgun, waiting for the fuzz to bust down the door. It sounded too farfetched to *not* be true.

A couple of hours into the revelry, I was struck with the worst case of food poisoning I've ever had. I barely reached the bathroom before my entrails came gushing out like water from a broken fire hydrant. After disgorging every last drop of bile, I began to retch violently, resulting in a merciless migraine, for which decapitation was the only cure. Since that wasn't an option, I reached for the pipe. I had nothing to lose. Even if it killed me, at least the headache would be gone. Deliriously feverish and vomiting convulsively, I could barely hold down *oxygen*, yet continued inhaling the toxic fumes anyway, while running to the bathroom in between rounds. I was going to croak right there in that hotel room. It was an unconscious decision at first, but quickly (d)evolved into a deliberate, almost masturbatory act of self-obliteration. At the peak of it, I can remember lying in a fetal ball on the bathroom floor, gasping for air, while heaving violently, and thinking, *"I'm done, it's time to go, please just let me fucking go..."* before crawling back to the main room and guzzling another goblet of hemlock.

I somehow managed to survive until dawn, and despite my tenacious resistance, Keleko insisted that we check out before *I* checked out. He claimed to be concerned about my safety, which likely meant that he didn't want to end up with a(nother) corpse on his hands.

Upon arriving at my mother's house, Keleko carried me to the front door.

"So," he said, placing me down gently, "are you going to give me your phone number? Or do I have to beat it out of the Morgans?"

"Not necessary," I slurred, struggling to hold down the bile that was creeping up my esophagus. "Do you have something to write with?"

He reached into his pocket and pulled out a pen, which I used to scribble the digits onto his palm. I didn't view him as a potential romantic interest, but rather as an invaluable connection, which I had a bookful of.

"Other than you getting sick," he said, looking at his hand and smiling, "tonight was a blast. Let's do it again soon, please."

I nodded and mumbled what was supposed to be an expression of thanks.

"It was my pleasure," he said, hugging me tightly. "Please take care of yourself. I'll call you later to see how you're doing."

I waved at Kiki and John, who were sitting in the car, then stumbled inside and barfed my guts up once more before passing out until later that evening.

The following weekend, Mia, Kiki, and I went over to the Morgan's with LT and Baron. Before I'd even crossed the threshold, Joe was in my face.

"I can't fuckin' believe it," he said, shaking his head. "You really let me down."

"What are you talking about?" I asked, completely confused.

"Oh, come on," he said snidely. "You know exactly what I'm talkin' about!"

"No, I don't."

"Oh, yes you do!"

"You're an idiot. Just tell me what the fuck you're talking about, in plain English."

"I can't believe you fucked Keleko for a fix!" he exclaimed. "I thought you were better than that! Man, was I wrong!"

I was not only shocked, but *outraged*, and dangerously so. "Where the hell did you get that idea?" I asked angrily. "Did Keleko tell you that?"

"No, he didn't necessarily *tell* me, I just know that you did."

I wanted to break Joe's jaw. It was a tossup on which offense was more infuriating: some lout claiming I'd slept with him when I hadn't, or some deaf, presumptuous fucktard calling me a liar when I was telling the truth.

"I don't know what the fuck Keleko told you," I yelled angrily, "but I did *not* fuck him!"

"Well, you can deny it all you want, but I know what I know!"

And I knew what I knew: I wanted to *kill* Joe with my bare hands. "You fucking cocksucker!" I yelled, getting right up into his face. "If you don't take it back, I'm going to kick your fucking ass!"

"Oh yeah?" he screamed back, taking a step forward. "What's stoppin' you, sweetheart? Come on, let's go! Take your best fuckin' shot!"

What ensued was one of the nastiest altercations I've ever engaged in. I was clearly spinning my wheels. Joe was never going to yield, but my pride wouldn't let me cry uncle. *No one* had dominion over me, no matter what he shelled out, and I wouldn't even *kiss* a man unless I felt an emotional connection with him. That raw nerve had been manhandled yet again, and I was beside myself with pain and fury.

"Apologize, fuckface," I threatened, "or I will never speak to you again!"

He glared at me for a moment then stormed off to his bedroom, slamming the door behind him.

After three weeks of mutual snubbing, Joe finally broke the silence, but not with an apology, which I thought I deserved. I let bygones be bygones anyway. Until Halloween night.

Mia and I were at a bash with Pluto, Chuck, Eric, and Joe. Around midnight, we were standing in the backyard near the keg, when it started to rain. Joe had been in a disagreeable mood all night, severely exacerbated by his state of shitfaced drunkenness.

What little sense he did have had been washed away by a river of Moosehead, causing him to make the colossal mistake of rehashing his baseless Keleko theory. Another vicious argument erupted. Then, without any warning, he doused me with thirty-two ounces of lager.

I didn't say one word, because even *a thousand words* wouldn't have been enough to express the monumental rage I was feeling. I simply wound up and clipped him smack-dab on the nose.

"What the fuck did you do that for?" he yelled, recoiling and pulling his shirt over his nose to stop the bleeding.

I glared at him, fully intending to launch into a verbal assault, but it was an absurdly comical sight, the tough, hard-bitten punk reeling from a bloody nose that I'd caused with my girly fist. I completely lost it, as did the others. They were howling, crying, and falling all over each other.

"Bro, you had that comin' for so long!" Eric screamed through the laughter, high-fiving me.

"I can't believe a chick made my nose bleed!" Joe mumbled, looking at me with his long-lashed doe eyes. "No one's ever made my nose bleed! I think you broke it, you bitch!"

I flipped him off.

"Get your ass over here!" he demanded, motioning with his free hand.

Not knowing if he was planning to retaliate, I took refuge behind Eric, which was the safest place to hide. He was one of the only people I knew who could take Joe in a fight.

Joe burst out laughing, which I took as a sign that he couldn't have been too wrathful. I decided to take my chances and emerged.

"You're fuckin' crazy!" he laughed, lifting me off the ground with a bear hug.

"Are you finally going to drop it, fucker?" I said, holding up my fist. "Because there's a shitload more where that came from."

"Yeah, whatever," he grumbled, pushing me away. "I oughta kick your punk ass. Why the fuck did you hit me?"

"Because you deserved it, fuckface," I replied matter-of-factly.

Joe never mentioned Keleko's name in my presence again, and Eric added the Halloween anecdote to his repertoire, sharing it with anyone who would listen.

Intergender battery. Some people seem to think it's acceptable for a woman to strike a man, but not vice versa. I don't think it's any different than a smaller, weaker man sucker punching a larger, stronger man, and if the former *initiates* the assault, the latter has every right to defend himself. I shouldn't have hit Joe, and wouldn't have blamed him if he'd fired back. Thankfully he didn't, because I probably would have been hibernating for the remainder of the year.

Fast forward to 1999. It was a Sunday morning. I was standing in line at Von's supermarket, when I felt a gentle tap on my shoulder. I turned around, and lo and behold, there was Joe. By now I was in full denial mode about my past and expending every ounce of energy struggling to fit in with "normal" society. When he said my name, I replied: "Sorry, you must have me confused with someone else."

It was pathetically lame. Unless he was suffering from amnesia, there was no way he would believe that I was someone else, but I was desperate, and my deaf-mute act wasn't going to fly with him.

"No, it's you," he insisted, shaking his head. "I could never forget you."

He was bound and determined to make me admit it, while I was equally resolved to do the opposite. Even if I'd been locked in a room, and forced to listen to "Macarena" at ear-splitting decibel levels for twenty-three hours straight, I wouldn't have caved.

The infantile exchange escalated, and was frighteningly familiar. It felt as though he and I were right back in that apartment, arguing vehemently and pointlessly, only now, I was fighting to preserve my fabricated Doris Day persona. Joe was no pushover, he could wrangle with the best of them, but he was no match for my Taurean obstinacy. He ultimately became frustrated and moved to another checkout line.

DORALICE

The rape had engendered a murderous rage toward any behavior that could be perceived as sexually offensive, and I didn't fuck around. Physical and verbal transgressions were met with the same zero tolerance policy. *No one* had the right to violate me, and I'd only be a victim if I allowed it, which I had no intention of doing, *ever again*. I'd spill blood first. Thankfully, the incidents were scarce, presumably due to the way I carried myself, as well as the plank I had on my shoulder.

One of the most memorable episodes occurred on a crisp winter afternoon. Mia and I were wandering around the neighborhood, pilfering change from unlocked cars, when a black super stretch limousine pulled up. Down rolled the driver's side window, revealing a marginally creepy yet seemingly friendly face.

"Hello, girls," the face's mouth said, through a thick, unidentifiable accent.

"Hey," Mia and I replied in unison.

"Do you need a ride somewhere?"

"Is it free?" Mia asked, smiling.

"Yes, of course!" he replied enthusiastically, while unlocking the doors. "Get in, get in!" Once inside, he asked "Where to?"

"PCH?" Mia said, looking over at me.

"Sounds good to me," I replied, eyeing the portable gin mill.

"Sure," he said, glancing at us through the rearview mirror, "and help yourselves."

"Thanks, don't mind if we do," Mia said, closing the privacy divider.

I turned on the stereo and cranked it up, then proceeded to mix a pair of screwdrivers, while Mia rolled a joint.

"Man, I could get used to this," she said, breaking up a bud on the bar top.

"Tell me about it," I agreed, stirring the drinks.

We were cruising along blissfully – savoring the joint, sipping our libations, Getz/Gilberto wafting out of the speakers – when the driver took an unexpected turn.

"I wonder where he's going," Mia said, rolling down the window and peering out.

"Who fucking knows," I said, holding in an enormous toke, "and who fucking cares."

"Yeah, I guess it doesn't matter," she said, rolling up the window. "How about making me another one of those drinks?"

"I'm all over it," I said, exhaling and passing her the joint.

Just as I was twisting off the vodka cap, the driver made a sharp turn into a shopping center, then drove around to the back lot and parked.

"Okay, where the fuck are we?" Mia asked. "And why the fuck did he stop?"

"Good question," I said, handing her the bottle. "Here, I'll ask him." I opened the privacy divider, only to discover that he wasn't there, and by the time I turned back around, he was sitting right next to me.

"Hello, girls! Time to have some *real* fun!" he growled, placing his hands around my waist and pulling me toward him. "Come to papa!"

Yes, that's what he said, verbatim. I almost burst out laughing, but rage quickly stepped in and took over. I didn't want his filthy mitts anywhere near my body.

"What the fuck do you think you're doing?" I yelled, pushing him away.

"I'm just having a little fun," he said, with a disturbing grin that screamed RAPIST. "That's what you want too, isn't it?"

Before I had a chance to reply, he pounced on Mia. I impulsively reached for a bottle of Jack Daniels and cracked him across the skull as hard as I could. The bottle didn't break, but his head did, and there was blood trickling down his temple onto his cheek.

"I'm going to call the police! I'm going to call the police!" he screamed over and over again, placing his hand over the wound. "I'm going to call the police and have you arrested!"

"Oh, no you're not!" Mia yelled, reaching for a bottle of Wild Turkey and striking him again.

That one did it. He was out cold.

"Is he dead?" I asked, shaking him gently.

"I don't think so," she replied uncertainly.

I looked at her, then at him, then back at her. There was a piercingly silent pause, during which she and I engaged in a staring contest, as if trapped in a state of suspended animation. Then, as if on cue, we simultaneously burst into a fit of hysterical cachinnation, even though our predicament wasn't remotely humorous.

"What should we do with him?" I laughed, shaking him again.

"We could strip him naked and roll him out into the parking lot," Mia suggested, giggling.

"That would be hilarious."

"Or, we could take the limo for a little joyride?"

"Not if *you're* driving," I scoffed.

"Why not?" she said in a slightly offended tone. "What's wrong with my driving?"

"You're Mr. fucking Magoo behind the wheel!"

"What the fuck, man! I have my contacts in!"

"Your sight's not the problem!"

"What the fuck are you implying?"

"I'll tell you what the fuck I'm implying! You're the only person I know who just *stops* at a stop sign!"

"That's what you're supposed to do at a fucking stop sign, *stop*!"

"No you're not! You're supposed to stop *and* look both ways to see if any cars are coming! All you do is *stop*! You never look! And then you just floor it like Mario fucking Andretti! One of these days, you're going to kill someone!"

"Excuse me, but who the fuck has the driver's license here? Huh?"

"I still don't know how you pulled that off!" I laughed. "The guy must have had a hard-on for you, because there's no way in hell you passed that test!"

"For your information, I didn't just pass that fucking test, on my own merits, I passed it with flying col…"

The unconscious driver let out a faint groan, causing Mia and me to jump in our seats.

"Let's vamoose," she whispered, opening the door, "before he comes to."

"I'm right behind you."

As we made our way across the parking lot, a navy blue convertible Mustang pulled up alongside us and stopped.

"Is everything okay?" the driver asked, giving us the once over.

I instinctively wondered why he'd assumed that everything *wasn't* okay. Did we have blood spattered all over our faces?

"Why do you ask?" I replied, wiping my cheeks.

"You look very distraught."

"No, everything isn't okay," Mia interjected. "Our limo driver just attacked us."

"Are you serious?" the man exclaimed, visibly shocked. "I have a phone, should I call the police?"

Obviously out of the question for a number of reasons.

"No, that's okay," I said, leaning into the car. "Can you give us a ride home?"

"Yeah," Mia lied through a feigned long face. "We'll call the cops from there."

"Yes, I can give you a ride, but are you sure you don't want me to call the police right now?"

"No, that's cool," Mia and I snapped in unison.

"Alright," he said, moving some items from the front seat onto the floor, "hop in."

I rode shotgun while Mia sat in back. The first thought that popped into my head was: *I hope he's not a psychoperv too.* You never know, they're all over the place. He appeared to be harmless, but so did the limousine driver.

"I'm Diego, by the way," he said, smiling warmly. "And you are?"

Mia and I introduced ourselves as Pola and Schatze, respectively.

"It's a pleasure to meet you," he said, extending his hand.

"Likewise," I replied, shaking his hand.

"Where am I taking you?"

Mia shook his hand and answered.

Once we were en route, Pola and I fed him the story. Not *the* story, of course. He seemed to be genuinely concerned, which confirmed that he was indeed harmless.

When we reached the south entrance of our neighborhood, Pola tapped him on the shoulder and said, "You can let us off here, Diego."

She was a clever girl, always thinking on her feet.

"Be sure to contact the police right away," he said, handing me a business card, "and please call me if you need my assistance at all."

Pola and I thanked the Good Samaritan profusely, and waved reverently as he drove away. Then we walked across the street, plopped down on the curb near the house on the east corner, and fell into a reverie.

"I wonder if he does drugs," I said, after thoroughly examining the business card. "Maybe he'll come in handy at some point."

"Yeah, you're right," she laughed. "Better hang on to that card."

"Are you hungry?" I asked, tucking the card into my pocket.

"I could eat," she yawned. "What are you in the mood for?"

"I don't care," I replied, catching her yawn.

"How about Chang's?"

"Yuck! It was too greasy last time! Besides, we skipped out on the check, remember?"

"Oh yeah, I forgot," she giggled. "Guess we won't be going back there for a while."

"Guess not," I laughed.

"How about the Parasite?" she asked, smiling.

Would you care or *dare* to dine at a restaurant called the Parasite? That wasn't its real name, but should have been. It was a long treasured haunt for the area's seniors, and viewed by many as a hallowed landmark, but aside from the hot chocolate and desserts, the food was almost inedible. Mia, however, absolutely loved the place, which was understandable, since it evoked fond memories of her deceased mother.

"You know how I feel about the Parasite," I said with a sneer.

She started to laugh. "Come on, man! It's not *that* bad!"

"You and your fucking Parasite," I grumbled. "I need a well-balanced meal, not a hot fudge sundae and a piece of pie."

"You're no fun," she pouted.

I gave her the finger.

She reciprocated.

"What day is it, Sunday?" she asked, cracking her knuckles.

"Yeah," I replied, cracking my neck.

"I think Glass is working today," she said, rubbing her hands together. "He's always good for a free meal. Maybe we should pay him a little visit? Those grilled chicken sandwiches with extra Swiss, tomato, and avocado were yummy."

Glass was a manager at one of the local restaurants. He was a detrimentally nice guy who we exploited no end. Drugs, money, meals, rides, you name it. I remembered those sandwiches well. We'd devoured them after a three-day meth-induced fast.

"What are we waiting for," I said, standing up.

Fast forward a few weeks. Mia and I had put the limousine mishap behind us with minimal effort. Although it had definitely traumatized us, chronic self-medicators are typically quite resilient. When the brain is being anesthetized on a daily basis, it's quite easy to displace items in the short-term memory, particularly the unpleasant variety. We'd all but forgotten about it, until one evening, when my sister announced that she was going on a date. When the lucky fellow arrived, Mia and I went outside to check him out, which was standard procedure. Only this time, he looked strikingly familiar, as did his car. Then it struck us. It was Diego, the man in the Mustang. What are the chances? As expected, he recognized Mia and me right away, and told my sister the whole story over dinner. She came home early, and never went out with Diego again.

I think it's safe to assume that the limousine driver survived the assault, and didn't call the police. If he had gone to the authorities, or gone west, for that matter, I'm sure the story would have at least made the local news.

HOW NOT TO TRAP LIONS

I was now off probation and had been transferred to a continuation school that was much closer to home. It was there that I made the acquaintance of a delightful young lady named Sadie, who was a year older, and more important, could drive. Legally, that is. What a gal. She was a tough, foul-mouthed, chain-smoking vamp with the deepest, raspiest voice I've ever heard on a teenage girl. In addition to being disturbingly sharp for her age, I'm convinced she could have taken most *men* in a street fight, never mind women. Every time I hear Nazareth's "Hair of the Dog" I immediately think of her. It was one of her theme songs, and couldn't have been more befitting. She and I hit it off right away and became a lethal duo, frequently ditching class (even though the day ended at noon), committing larceny for both sustenance and sport, and gobbling up whatever drugs came our way. Like me and most of my comrades, Sadie was the product of an absurdly dysfunctional home. Her father was a professional grifter who'd served time for fraud and forgery in a handful of states. As a result, the family was perpetually on the go, never remaining in one place for long. Another exemplary parent.

It was through Sadie that Mia and I met Garth, a manic cocaine dealer who quickly became our latest, and greatest, benefactor. He was not only incredibly generous, but gentlemanly as well. Meaning: he kept his hands to himself. Mia and I assumed that he was impotent or perhaps confused about his sexuality, since he never attempted to hit on the leeches (us included) who were regularly milking cocaine from him. Hugs and the occasional lap sitting were as sexual as it got.

Then there was Stiv, who was dating one of Mia's sisters. He was a sharp, witty, and garrulous character who was always holding an abundance of drugs, which he'd generously share with Mia and me. His munificence was certainly appreciated, but came at a price. While lavishing us with various mind-altering substances, he'd gesticulate wildly and preach like Elmer Gantry with a pharmacologist's attention to detail about those substances' potentially dangerous effects, some of which were complete figments of his imagination.

"Girls, you've gotta listen to me! I know what I'm talking about! I've been alive a lot longer than you! You need to take a good hard look at what you're doing to yourselves! You smoke marijuana *all* day, *every* day! You seem to have this notion that cannabis is totally innocuous, and you couldn't be more mistaken! Tetrahydrocannabinol is a highly carcinogenic compound! It's also been scientifically proven to decimate brain cells and cause cognitive, memory, and learning impairments! If you wanna know the truth, you're better off inhaling tobacco smoke! Fuck, it may give you emphysema and lung cancer, but at least it won't make you retarded! And cocaine? Every time you snort a line or take a drag you're risking your lives! It's like playing Russian

Roulette, for crying out loud! No matter how young and healthy you are, you could drop dead instantly from cardiac arrest or acute respiratory failure! The same goes for methamphetamine, which you girls have been sniffing like Atomic Number Eight! And how about diacetylmorphine? You probably think it's perfectly safe because you don't inject it, right? Heroin is heroin, god damn it! It doesn't give a fuck how it gets into your body! Have you noticed how shallow your breathing becomes after taking a hit? Almost feels like someone's holding a pillow over your face, doesn't it? Did you know there's a very good chance that external respiration will cease altogether? And you know what that means, don't you? That's right! You're dead, gone, kaput, finito! Go directly to purgatory! Do not pass go, do not collect two-hundred dollars! Now, this is what worries me most. I've noticed that you girls have been using a substantial amount of angel dust lately! I don't even know where to begin here! Did you know that phencyclidine causes cerebral hemorrhages? That's right! At fifteen years old, you could suffer a massive CVA that may leave you permanently paralyzed or brain-damaged! And speaking of brain damage, let me remind you for the hundredth time that those tanks of nitrous oxide you've been inhaling are not gonna boost your mental capacity!" Then he'd take a few hearty puffs or snorts of whatever potentially dangerous substance he was sharing at the moment (e.g. marijuana, cocaine, heroin, PCP, nitrous oxide) and continue, "If you knew what was good for you,

you'd quit using drugs right now, before you become addicted!"

Excuse me, *BEFORE* we become addicted? It was unfathomably absurd. I can recall one time in particular, when in the midst of his harangue, he suddenly stopped, reached into his pocket, and pulled out a plastic sandwich bag containing a substance that resembled burnt crumbled cow chips.

"Here, eat these!" he demanded, shoving the bag into Mia's hands.

"What the fuck is it?" she asked, holding it up and examining it.

"Some Lophophora williamsii a buddy of mine grew!" he said nonchalantly, as though he were giving us fresh roasted peanuts.

Mia and I stared at him blankly.

"You know, Injun Dope, Peyote, Bad Seed!" he elucidated, flailing his arm in the air like Mussolini. "You eat half and give the other half to her! Now, where was I?"

It didn't end there either. Stiv also considered himself a soothsayer, and made a habit of prognosticating our futures, which according to him, were far from bright.

"You know, girls, if you keep using all these drugs you're gonna lose your looks! I promise you, before you're old enough to legally drink, you'll be haggard, toothless dogs! I'm not trying to scare you, it's just a fact! I've seen some of the chicks I used to party with back in high school, and let me tell you, these chicks used to be knockouts! We're talking drop dead gorgeous! But now? Man, oh man! It's fucking scary! They look like death warmed over! If you wanna keep your looks, you'd better give up the drugs right now! You two have been blessed, and take it from me, *every* heterosexual male is a sucker for a stacked bod and a pretty face, whether he's an infant or a septuagenarian! Money doesn't grow on trees, and this jungle can be a tough place when you're broke! You girls have to use your beauty to your advantage! But if you keep using all these drugs? Fuck, I don't know what to tell you! You'd better get decent paying jobs!"

Nice that he had such magnificent expectations for us, wasn't it? He'd go *on and on* for what felt like *hours* at a time. I always wondered why he insisted on delivering these homilies while getting us high. Did he somehow get off on it? He was certainly likeable and generous, but obviously a whackjob. Mia and I tried our best to tune him out with hysterical laughter, but the man was a compelling speaker. Unintentionally hilarious, but compelling nonetheless. His raving sermons were not only penetrating, but incisively true.

Enter Grant, Stiv's munificent cocaine trafficking buddy. Needless to say, his chosen profession made him quite popular with the ladies, despite the fact that he'd been disfigured by a thunderbolt as a boy. The near-fatal accident had not only etched a deep lightning-shaped scar into the side of his face, but had also burned off most of his hair. He could easily afford a replacement of superior quality, but instead wore a conspicuously phony ash blonde wig that resembled a ventriloquist dummy's mop. Grant was a mysterious cat, a man of few words, which was fine with the girls and me. He could have been a mute for all we cared, as long as he kept supplying the highest quality blow our money couldn't buy.

Between Garth, Stiv, and Grant, my cocaine habit was stronger than ever, but methamphetamine had become my new stimulant of choice. The fact that it delivered a much longer high meant I didn't have to hustle as hard to feed my addiction. Of course, it was wreaking havoc on my body in a way cocaine never had, as I'd soon learn.

On the music front, the underground warehouse party was in full swing, and plenty of worthwhile bands were playing the clubs and arenas. I was hitting live shows like a morphine drip, and dropping acid nearly every time. It was also the chosen snack for all other diversions: amusement parks, the circus, the cinema, the great outdoors, you name it... even school. I'd come to the erroneous conclusion that life was better on LSD. It wasn't merely another emotional analgesic begging to be abused, but rather a mind-expanding elixir and gateway to an alternate existence. A transcendental, five-dimensional existence that was light years more desirable than the one I'd been floundering in since birth. My childhood dream of metamorphosing into a cartoon or storybook character was the underlying impetus.

Since I was now old enough to be legally employed, I decided to give it a go, and somehow managed to obtain, and *lose*, several jobs. I landed the first with Sadie's help, at a local department store that was also one of my favorite shoplifting haunts. My mother still has the ruby ring I nicked for her birthday one year. Less than a month into the gig, I was caught snorting meth in the bathroom. By the boss, no less. Although I talked her out of calling the police, for self-explanatory reasons, I was canned. As for the others? Well, if you haven't noticed, I was congenitally insubordinate, which can be an "occupational hazard." It didn't matter if I was peddling lingerie or slinging hash, the instant someone wielded authority, I'd tell off the fucker and split. Or, if a more appealing offer came along, which didn't take much, I'd simply walk out.

The most recent job was at a deli, where I didn't even make it through the first day. I tried my level best to stick it out, but damn it, if the owner wasn't the most despotic bastard I'd ever collided with. I'd arrived that morning determined to make it work, but within an hour, it was all I could do to keep from carving the fucker like a Christmas roast.

At noon, I was slicing turkey, struggling to find a reason to stay, when LT and Baron walked in.

"What's up?" LT said, flashing that endearingly maniacal smile. "What time are you done here?"

"Not until five," I growled, glaring at the clock. "What are you guys up to?"

"We're on our way to a party," Baron said, scowling at my boss. "You should blow this shithole and come along."

"Yeah," LT added, rubbing his hands together, "bands, beer, cocaayeena… you should come with, it's gonna be a blast!"

Hmmmm, what a tough decision. Be an abusive, oppressive jerk's peon for minimum wage? Or gorge myself with drugs, and rock out until the early morning hours? I looked at my comrades, who were beaming, and then at my boss, who was squatting over a crate of tomatoes, cracking his own special brand of smile. It was a no-brainer. After filling a bag with chips and premade sandwiches, I tore off my apron and threw it against the wall. "Let's get the hell out of here," I announced, loud enough for my boss to hear.

As expected, the slave driver followed, carrying a Genoa salami in his left hand. "What do you think you're doing?" he yelled, shaking the beef dildo.

"What do I *think* I'm doing?" I said, looking daggers at him.

"Yeah, where do you think you're going? You're not done till at least five!"

I got into the car, popped out of the sunroof, pulled a hoagie from the bag and flung it at his noggin. "*Shove it up your ass, you fat motherfucker!*" I yelled, as LT peeled out.

LT and Baron thought it was priceless, but I couldn't even fake a grin. Instead, I was exasperated and consumed by despair. *Life was not fun anymore*. I was *dying* inside, and the years of incessant drug abuse were beginning to take their physical toll as well. To begin with, my endocrine system was malfunctioning through and through. As a result, I was rapidly gaining weight, even though I was barely eating, and my period – which had only begun three years prior – had ceased altogether.

I was also suffering from chronic insomnia, severe heart palpitations, spontaneous nose bleeds, and ferocious mood swings. My body and mind were in a critical state of turmoil. I was torn about whether I even wanted to do drugs anymore, but it was no longer a choice: *DRUGS WERE DOING ME.*

LETHE

EGG SANDWICH

Whatz up mang? Well, I'm tripping out on this world, and I wanted to write you & tell you that I care and love you much, and tell you that I think you did the right thing and you've got a lot of balls to do what you did. Nobody is going to fuck it up for you, because I know how you crave even that 1 small skunk roach. Be strong and don't do it. It can really fuck up a person's life, and this is only the beginning of ours and you did something about it before it was too late, as we stand by and kiss our squashable asses goodbye from all those stupid, shitty drugs. You are a definite positive influence on us and I have been thinking about a lot of things the past couple of months, especially after getting arrested for shit. I go to court tomorrow for the 1st time & let me tell you, I'm scared shitless and I don't want to go to jail, or be on probation or nothin', but I did something stupid, got caught, and now I'm paying the penalty. – Oh well – ☹ ☺ Fuck it! Anyways, I just wanted to tell you how I felt, and that I'm very happy for you and that all of us are going to be a positive influence on you when you get out. What are friends for? I will give you all the support I can give, because I know it's going to be a bitch at first, but I know you and you can do it. I will pray for you and hope for the best. We all love you and care about you.

See ya whenever

Love, Vince

BOUFFÉE DÉLIRANTE

The calends of march [sic]. I emerged from Slumberland determined to vanquish my demons and reclaim my autonomy. I'd been a slave for one-quarter of my years, and was done in. It was time to break the chains or relinquish life.

I was still half asleep when I walked into my mother's room, broke down, and begged for help. Although she suspected that I drank booze and smoked marijuana on occasion, she had no idea I was a seasoned junkie whose entire existence revolved around drugs. Without prying for details, she immediately began making rehab arrangements. Thanks to her job as a registered nurse I had decent health care coverage, but there was still a lengthy roll of red tape to cut through. As with most insurance companies, I had to be pre-approved before I could seek any treatment that wasn't included in my basic plan, and naturally, the powers that be made it as difficult as possible. It took a tremendous amount of perseverance on my mother's part, and the cheap bastards refused to foot the entire bill, but in the end, I was granted admission to a well-respected facility that was fairly close to home.

The following evening, I passed through the sliding glass doors of Servand Hospital with one goal in mind: to kick the drugs and begin *living*.

Upon entering the ward, I was greeted by a swarm of "normal" yet sweet girls, who went out of their way to make me feel welcome. While it was very kind of them, I felt like Mowgli when he returned to The Man Village. Once my bags were in my room, the girls insisted that I join them in a gabfest. I tried my best to harmonize, and made a conscious effort to use PG-Rated language, which was a major challenge, considering that "fuck" was one of my favorite words.

"Do you know who's totally cute?" one of them squealed. "Charlie Sheen!"

"Oooooooh!" the others agreed. "He *is* cute!"

"Don't you think he's cute?" one of them asked, looking directly at me.

"I don't think any human is *cute*," I replied, "but he was pretty good in Platoon and Wall Street, and his dad's been in some great flicks."

"Who's his dad?" one of them asked with a puzzled expression on her face.

"Who's his dad?" I asked, trying not to sound condescending. "Martin Sheen."

It wasn't registering.

"*The Incident, Badlands, Apocalypse Now*?"

All five of them looked at me as though I were speaking Muong. They fell silent for a moment, as did I. Then one of them squealed, "Oooooooh! My mom's bringing my George Michael album when she visits tomorrow!"

Okay, I'd had enough. Suum cuique, but I was out of my element, and it was exacerbating my already overwhelming anxiety. I excused myself and retired to my room.

The following morning I couldn't get out of bed.

It wasn't that I didn't want to, I was physically incapable. I felt as though I'd been flung out of a fifth-story window, then run over thrice by an eighteen wheeler and lived to tell about it. I'd been feeling out of sorts for quite some time, and had now reached a point where I wanted to sleep forever. Or croak. While it was partially due to withdrawal, I was also suffering from some drug induced health complications, which, if left untreated, could be fatal.

Thankfully, a doctor arrived that evening. After undergoing a physical examination, I was diagnosed with tachycardia, gastric ulcers, and a perforated nasal septum. In layman's terms, my heart was racing out of control, my stomach was full of lesions, and the partition inside my nose was slowly eroding, all courtesy of cocaine and methamphetamine. No wonder I was feeling so damn rotten. After being prescribed a cocktail of medications, I was referred to the common room, where the other patients were in the middle of a group therapy session. I immediately thought: *One Flew Over the Cuckoo's Nest*, and was not into it *at all*. Besides, would they really notice if I wasn't there? I returned to my room instead, where I was knocked flat on my ass by a one-two punch of Truth. First, I spent five minutes scrutinizing my image in the mirror, and was appalled by what I saw. I'd evolved from ugly to downright grotesque. How was it possible that I'd failed to notice the transmogrification? It was inconceivable, but in the span of just months, the meth had laid waste to my physical appearance. My complexion was sallow and wizened, there were unconcealable dark circles and blood vessels under my eyes, my body was bruised and bloated. Stiv's ominous prediction had come true after all: I'd metamorphosed into a gorgon. I quickly averted my gaze before I turned to stone. I then spent five minutes soaking in the environment, and that's when I was struck with the right cross. *Get clean? What the fuck was I thinking?* I had to get out of there, and fast. Since it was an occasionally guarded lockdown unit, it was going to be challenging, but I was determined to escape.

I crept out of my room undetected, then planted myself in the corner behind the double doors until the janitor came along and inserted his keycard. The instant the doors flew open, I crawled past him and made a run for it. As I tore around the corner, heading for the side exit, I crashed into one of the counselors, named Mike.

"Where do you think you're going?" he asked, grabbing hold of my arm.

"None of your fucking business, motherfucker!" I yelled, pulling away from him. "Get the fuck out of my way!"

"Oh yes it is my fucking business!" he said, grabbing my arm again.

I pulled away again and screamed, "Let go, you fucking bastard! I'm not going back there, and you can't make me!"

"Oh yes you are!" he shouted, dragging me toward the ward. "And yes I can!"

I put up one hell of a fight, but was subdued within minutes. He then carried my squirming, flailing body down the hallway and through the double doors. When we reached my room, he tossed me onto the bed and closed the door. Seconds later, I snapped my crackle. It was my first bona fide mental meltdown. I'd experienced unpleasant psychological episodes in the past, but never quite as sudden or severe. Panic-stricken, hysterical, and inconsolable, I felt like a claustrophobic, feral cat trapped in a shoebox without ventilation holes. I was convinced I'd been abandoned by everyone who claimed to care, then locked up in an insane asylum where mad doctors were going to take turns experimenting with barbaric treatments. I flipped out and sobbed for what must have been hours. Mike tried to placate me, but it was no use. I'd slipped over a precipice and was falling at a breakneck speed. At some point, he sent for a doctor who administered a sedative. Then my mother was called.

When she arrived, I explained that I'd made a tremendous mistake, and begged for my release. "I can do it on my own!" I pleaded, hugging her with all my might. "I don't need to be in here!"

"No, you can't," she argued calmly, "and you're my child, I have to protect you."

"I'm done with the fucking drugs, I promise! Just get me the hell out of here!"

She flat out refused my demands. Having waged her own battle with substance abuse, she knew the drill better than anyone. I wasn't going anywhere, but toward recovery.

After three insufferably long days, my condition began to improve, and for the first time in four years, I hadn't the slightest craving for *any* drug. You'd think I would have felt strong and invincible, but instead, I felt precariously vulnerable. Although my body was headed down the healing highway, my spirit couldn't even find the on-ramp. Habitually glutting yourself with chemicals is harmful at *any* age, but I believe it can be far more damaging when you're a child. Those daily doses of poison had interfered with nearly every aspect of my development, including the social. I hadn't the faintest idea how to deal with people when I wasn't hiding behind a mask of intoxication.

On the fifth day I became fully aware of my situation, and it was disconcerting to say the least. I was locked up in a booby hatch with a horde of strangers, and was the only female addict in the place. I didn't consider myself female, but since the staff did, I was expected to mingle with the other members of my gender, who were suffering from eating disorders and depression. Most of them came from relatively stable, well-to-do homes, read *People* and *Seventeen*, listened to pop music, conversed about celebrities, cosmetics, and clothes, and thought Jello Biafra was an exotic dessert at the cafeteria. Again, these girls were sweet, and I genuinely appreciated their hospitality, but aside from our chromosomal makeup and some body parts, we had absolutely nothing in common. Despite their efforts to make me feel equal and at home, I still felt painfully out of place.

In order to attain a sense of belonging, I latched on to a couple of the male inmates who seemed to get where I was coming from. The first was a metalhead named Julio, one of the most sincere and empathetic souls I've ever encountered. He was also there of his own volition, and desperately wanted to get clean. The rest of the junkies had been admitted against their will, and couldn't wait to be sprung so they could recommence their drug abuse. Julio was determined to triumph over his addiction, a common goal that resulted in an immediate bond. The other inmate I took to was an inexplicably charismatic character named Wes, who came from North Long Beach, a crack rock's throw away from Compton. When I say "inexplicably charismatic" it means I'll never be able to explain what I saw in him, beyond the fact that he reminded me of my male comrades. He'd suffered a horrific acid trip the month before, and had been admitted directly from the emergency room. In addition to the feeling of familiarity, he and I shared many common interests. One being drugs, of course, which Wes spoke about in a praiseful manner. It should have been a glaring red flag, but I wanted to give him the benefit of the doubt.

I also became attached to Mike, the counselor. He'd waged his own war with addiction, and had survived the sixties, a decade I'd always found intriguing. He and I would spend a couple of hours a day listening to music, while engaging in intense conversation. I'd been hiding behind impenetrable emotional armor for months. I knew deep down that I was terminally despondent, but couldn't produce so much as one meaningful tear. With Mike's help, I was able to shuck the armor and begin the healing process. Even though he was old enough to be my father, he understood me better than anyone in the place, and I trusted him implicitly.

By the end of the first week, word of my voluntary incarceration had spread to my kith and kin. My father and friends, in particular, were shocked. The former couldn't believe that his youngest child was such a mess, and the latter couldn't believe that one of their comrades had defected. Although many of us had toyed with the idea of seeking treatment, following through was another matter altogether. Most of them were supportive of my decision, and kept in touch via phone calls, letters, and visits, while others were terrified by the very idea of a drug-free me.

As expected, my parents felt the need to incriminate someone. While my father held my mother accountable, my occasionally misandristic mother laid blame on the men in my life. I believe her exact words were: "I want to douse their homes with gasoline and set them on fire." She meant well, but I thought her condemnation was unfair. I'll admit that consorting with pushers and users certainly facilitated my addiction, but I was still solely responsible for my own actions. No one had forced me to abuse drugs, and I've never been one to buy into the victim mentality. I was a weak, broken, and chemically-dependent deadbeat, but *not* a victim. If I ever expected to attain and maintain abstinence, I couldn't afford to become one.

I spent thirty days in Servand, undergoing various forms of psychotherapy and attending two Twelve-Step meetings a day. By the end of the third week, I'd shed twenty-five pounds, my health had improved significantly, and I *thought* I'd fallen in love. In retrospect, I've realized I was *not* in love. I was more vulnerable than I'd ever been in my life, and desperately needing someone who spoke my new language, that of sobriety. And who did I give my heart to, you ask? Wes, the most fucked up person in the joint, as I'd soon find out.

In any event, by embarking on a relationship with him, I'd broken one of the cardinal rules of AA. I was also beginning to have serious issues with the program. Bearing in mind that I was an ultra-defiant kid who viewed booze as an inferior form of poison that I rarely abused, my take was as follows: first off, I couldn't bring myself to say that I was "an alcoholic" because I wasn't. In my mind it was tantamount to confessing to a crime I hadn't committed. I had no problem at all admitting that I was an addict, which made Narcotics Anonymous far more appealing. In line with my "personal responsibility as the path to recovery" stance, I didn't believe that addiction was a disease, which made it difficult to digest what I saw as mumbo jumbo. Having been to meetings with my mother when she'd collected her birthday chips, I was familiar with the program and I admired many aspects, but couldn't ignore the "organized religion" vibe, not to mention what I saw as rules. I had a tremendous problem with being *told* that I could never use drugs again for as long as I lived. Sure, they had ways of sugar coating it, such as "One day at a time," but when it came down to the nitty gritty, orders were still being issued, which didn't jibe with my congenital insubordination. I must have been born with a switch in my head that clicked whenever I was told what to do, because I invariably wanted to do the opposite, even if it was in my worst interest.

At the end of the month I was released from Servand, feeling more hopeful than I had in ages. When I arrived home that evening, there was a brown-leather, gilt-trim Bible and a dozen yellow roses sitting on the doorstep. Gifts from LT. While I was away, he'd run into an old buddy of his named Jesus Christ, who'd ordered him to give drugs the boot. God bless the lunatic. Even though it wasn't my bag, I was elated for him. My decision to get clean had motivated a handful of my other friends as well, including Mia. Life was good. I was feeling uncharacteristically optimistic, which I attributed to my newfound sobriety. Therefore, I felt obligated to attend at least one NA or AA meeting a day, despite my reservations.

One month later, Wes was released from Servand. I was immediately introduced to his circle of friends, one of whom – a Jehovah's Witness turned car thief – spilled the beans. It turned out that Wes had been using throughout his entire stay at the facility. The larcenous Witness had been smuggling in the drugs whenever he visited, which would explain Wes' laudatory slant during those talks I mentioned earlier. I should have broken it off with him and returned to my uncomplicated, single and celibate existence, but somewhere along the way I'd convinced myself that I could save Wes and help him get clean. Christ, I was stupid. Anyone with half a brain knows damn well that you can't change anyone but yourself, and even that's debatable at times. For the sake of my sobriety, I had to distance myself from Wes, which took every shred of strength and willpower I had, because I'd gotten used to having him in my life already. It was difficult, but I loved where I was emotionally and spiritually, and had no intention of letting that slip away. Of course I couldn't abandon him altogether. When I care about someone, I'm loyal to a fault, and Wes was no exception. I continued speaking with him on the phone, but avoided seeing him in the flesh. I suppose I hung on with hopes that he would see the glorious light and convert. Instead, *I* was the one who would undergo change, in the form of reversion.

BEELZEBUB BUILT A QUINZHEE

On Memorial Day weekend LT decided, on a whim, to hit Mammoth for some late season skiing, and insisted that Mia and I come along. Neither she nor I knew how to ski, but when he offered to pick up the entire tab, we couldn't possibly refuse.

Shortly before I'd entered rehab, LT had received a thoughtful gift from a secret admirer: a Molotov cocktail through the windshield of his car. It came with the territory, although still surprising, since he seemed to have a knack for not making enemies. Thankfully, he was in the house when the gift was delivered, but the car was burned to a crisp. He wasted no time in acquiring a new jalopy, which now sat before my eyes. As I mentioned previously, I admired LT's humility, as well as his desire to live a frugal existence. It was commendable, and more important, unfeigned. Having said that, when I saw the heap in which we'd be traveling hundreds of miles, I nearly dropped dead. It was a mid-70s Audi Fox composed of parts from at least a dozen different clunkers. The miscreation had two bald tires, no suicide seat, and appeared to be held together by duct tape and rubber cement. I felt sorry for the car, but was understandably concerned about its ability to deliver us to our destination. Although the drive to Mammoth is picturesque, a portion of it is in the boonies. After pointing that out to LT, I tossed my misgivings into the trunk, along with my bags, and we were off to see the great outdoors.

Frankenaudi was clearly resentful of my cynical attitude, and was hell-bent on running beautifully... until the inevitable happened. While cruising along the abovementioned desolate highway, the front tire on the driver's side blew out. LT pulled over to the side of the dusty road to assess the damage.

"What's the prognosis?" Mia asked, popping her head out of the window.

He didn't answer, prompting us to get out and see for ourselves.

"Why don't you just slap on the spare?" I asked, looking directly at him.

He turned away and began giggling impishly.

"There *is* a spare, isn't there?" Mia asked, stuffing a piece of chewing gum into her mouth.

His giggle progressed into cachinnation.

"You fucking idiot!" I yelled, smacking him upside the head. "Don't tell me there's no spare!"

He laughed even louder, causing Mia and me to laugh as well.

"What the fuck were you thinking?" I asked, after regaining my composure.

"He wasn't thinking," Mia said, laughing out loud. "That's the problem."

"Don't sweat it," he said in his usual optimistic tone, lighting a cigarette and surveying the area. "I'll figure something out."

"Like what?" Mia said, also surveying. "We're in the middle of fucking nowhere."

"We're going to have to thumb it," I sighed. "*If* anyone comes along, that is."

Mia and I planted ourselves at the shoulder of the highway, while LT got back into the car and hid. He'd likely frighten any potential Good Samaritans, and girls tend to fare better at hitchhiking anyway. Less than an hour later, a tow truck came along, with a friendly and helpful driver. It was unbelievably fortuitous. I was certain we were going to die out there, but within a couple of hours the car was patched up and back on the road.

The following morning, we hit the slopes. LT was born on skis and spectacular to watch, like a scene from a Warren Miller film. Mia and I had never skied, and were a spectacle to watch, like a scene from a Laurel and Hardy film. Since it was the end of the season, the only open runs were highly advanced and perilously steep. LT begged us to take lessons. We not only refused, but also flung snowballs and obscenities at him for even daring to suggest it. I didn't blame him for what he did next.

"Okay, have it your way," he laughed, skiing away, "but don't say I didn't warn you!"

Mia and I were now stranded on top of Mont Blanc. The slope was literally perpendicular. When I looked down, I couldn't see the bottom. While sane people would have fled back to the ski lift, my fellow bedlamite and I were salivating. After wiping out for three hours straight, we crashed into a tree. We certainly weren't lacking in determination, but it was impossible to employ the basics, like snow plowing, when traveling at speeds of a hundred miles per hour. Shortly after the final wipeout, two ski patrolmen came along with empty toboggans in tow.

"Hello ladies," the blond said. "We received a report that you were having a little trouble up here."

"That's an understatement," I chuckled.

"Is everything okay?" the brunet asked.

"No," Mia replied, smiling, "we're inept."

"Are you hurt?" the blond asked, smiling.

"She is," Mia replied, pointing toward me.

"What's wrong?" he asked.

"What's right?" I retorted.

They started to laugh.

"I mean, where are you hurt?"

"Wherever there are nerves."

"Do you think you can make it down on your own?" the brunet asked, lifting his sunglasses, revealing a pair of striking green eyes.

"Yeah, we can make it down all right," Mia laughed, "but we may be in several pieces when we get there."

"Are you really that bad?" the blond asked, lifting his sunglasses, revealing a pair of equally striking blue eyes.

"Put it this way," Mia laughed, "Stephen Hawking would fare better on skis."

They laughed again.

"Well, we can carry you down the mountain if you'd like," the blond said.

"Sounds like a blast!" Mia said enthusiastically. "Strap me in, Pirmin!"

The toboggan ride was, without a doubt, the high point of the day. What a rush. When all was said and done, Mia was a bit scratched up, but virtually unscathed. I, on the other hand, had broken my right forefinger, sprained my left wrist, and my ass felt like an enormous, throbbing contusion, making it impossible to sit properly. Other than that, I felt fantastic.

After three sanative, soul-searching days, my comrades and I headed home, feeling refreshed and incredibly hopeful. We'd done the impossible by getting clean, and life was only going to improve with each passing day.

Once back in Los Angeles, we dropped in on a comrade named Woody, who'd recently been diagnosed with HIV. Woody and LT had grown up together and shared an undying fraternal bond. Tragically, Woody was a heroin abuser of the worst kind. After saying our hellos, I parked my bruised derriere on his thighs.

"So, how's Annie doin'?" he asked, staring at me with heavy eyes.

Annie was his estranged wife, who I'd recently seen for the first time in ages. He was concerned about her and with good reason. She'd been busted for trafficking earlier in the year and was due to enter prison any day now.

"She seems to be dealing with it," I replied, shifting my body weight, "and her attorney says she'll probably only serve part of the sentence."

"That's good. She'll do all right in there, she's pretty tough."

"All I know is that I don't envy her," I said, shifting once more.

"Why the fuck are you sittin' like that?" he asked, abruptly changing the subject.

"Like what?"

"Leanin' to one side," he said, attempting to straighten me out. "You're smashin' the fuck outta my nuts and givin' me a Charlie horse!"

"Don't do that!" I yelled, smacking him on the arm. "My ass hurts like a motherfucker!"

"Why? What happened?"

I pointed at LT who was wrestling around with Mia by the stereo.

"Oh no," Woody laughed. "What did he do this time? You can't take him anywhere."

"The fucker stranded us on top of the Matterhorn," I laughed. "Mia figured out how to break her falls, but I kept landing flat on my big fat ass." I held up my wounded paw and continued, "That's why I have this ace bandage on my wrist, I sprained it trying to protect my tailbone, and I broke my finger too."

He took my mangled finger and gently kissed it.

I smiled at him.

"How did you get down the mountain then?"

"A couple of ski patrolmen carried us down on toboggans. It was insane."

"Yeah, those guys can sure ski," he said placing his hand on my rump and grinning. "You know, I'm pretty good with my hands. I bet I can knead those contusions right out. How 'bout rollin' over and lettin' Daddy go to work?"

"How about not," I replied, crushing his hand in mine, "you fucking pervert."

"So, how does it feel to have clean blood and a clear mind?" he asked, slipping his hand out of my vise. "Must be a real trip."

"Incredible," I gushed. "I can't even describe it."

"That good, huh?"

"Better than you can imagine. I haven't felt this good since I was a little kid. Those fucking drugs stole my will to live. I never really thought about suicide, but honestly didn't give a shit if I died."

"Man, I hear you there!" he said. "The only reason I wake up every day is to shoot that dope into my veins. It's my fuckin' lifeblood. It doesn't even get me high anymore, but I can't function without it." Then he let out a deep sigh and continued, "I'd probably be better off dead."

I stared at him blankly.

"So, how many days of sobriety do you have now?" he asked, smiling.

"Ninety-two."

"Wow! Ninety-two fuckin' days without drugs! Man, I wish had that kind of self-control, but I'm a born junkie. I'll never quit, and I guess there's no reason to either."

I found his remark so upsetting I spent the next hour encouraging him to try a Twelve-Step program. I probably sounded like a fanatical Mormon trying to lure a Gentile into the LDS Church, but I couldn't help myself. If Woody was destined to check out early, whatever time he had left should be spent *living*, not merely existing.

By the end of the visit, I was in an achingly pensive mood. It had been a harsh reminder of where I'd come from, and how close I still was. Ninety-two days was merely a blip.

I snapped out of the funk the instant LT started the car. Immediately before the trip, he'd made the *god-awful* decision to listen to Christian rock exclusively. I don't know where the hell he dug up the music, but it was so offensive I would have preferred New Kids on the Block. I loved him dearly, and his enthusiasm toward sobriety was deeply inspiring, but the music crossed a line that should *never* be crossed. I begged him repeatedly to turn it off, but he flat out refused. I finally removed my seatbelt, climbed up to the front of the car, hit the eject button, and after a short yet fierce tug-of-war, chucked the cow chip onto the 405 South. Yes, I was guilt-ridden about littering, but it had to be done.

The following weekend, I collected my ninety day chip at the Servand NA meeting. Shortly thereafter, my dormant junkie was back with a vengeance. Remember Jamie and Tai? Well, one day, out of the blue, I received a frantic, tearful phone call from Jamie.

"You're not gonna believe this!" she sobbed. "My parents are moving to fuckin' Riverside!"

"You're kidding!" I said, taken aback by the news. "Why Riverside?"

"Because my dad finally got a job, and that's where it is!"

Her father had lost his job earlier in the year, and had been searching diligently ever since.

"I don't wanna move to that fuckin' shithole!" she cried.

"I don't blame you," I said, not knowing what else to say.

"And I don't wanna leave Tai, and my school, and all my friends! I fuckin' hate my parents! They can't make me go! I was up all night thinkin' about it, and I know what I'm gonna do. I'm gonna run away! I'd rather live in my car than move to that fuckin' shithole!"

The thought of her sleeping in her car was too much to bear, and I knew damn well she'd do it.

"Why don't you stay at my place for a while?" I suggested, after taking a moment to think. "You know, until you figure something else out."

"Do you think your mom will let me?" she asked, after blowing her nose.

"I don't see why not. When she gets home from work tonight, I'll ask her. Okay?"

"Okay. Thanks. I love you."

"I love you too. And don't worry, we'll take care of it one way or another."

It was a shortsighted decision on my part, but I meant well. Now Jamie, a practicing junkie, was sharing my bed. I lasted four days, and on the evening of the fifth, decided I needed to retrieve certain aspects of my former life. I was missing the camaraderie of the gang, and finding it seriously difficult to readapt to life with my biological family. It felt foreign, as though I'd been placed into foster care. Since alcohol had always been the one drug I'd used "responsibly," I convinced myself that it would be okay to have a drink or three. As anyone who's been there knows, even if booze isn't your drug of choice, its judgment impairing effects can drive you straight into the arms of the old favorites. And that's exactly what happened when I hit a party that night with Mia, Jamie, and Tai. Within days, I was back at Garth's for a cocaine orgy, which genuinely upset the habitués, prompting earnest interventions. I can recall one in particular that was permanently etched into my memory. Right as I was about to snort that first line, the concerned fellow and I locked eyes.

"What are you doin', babe?" he said with an expression of painful disappointment on his face. "I thought you quit? You gave the rest of us hopeless motherfuckers hope! *Please don't snort that line!*"

I was conscience-stricken for all of three seconds before sucking up that powder like a 2000 watt Hoover and demanding another helping, which Garth gleefully served up with a nefarious grin.

The sojourn in the Promised Land was over.

STRAIGHT OUTTA
CO-DEPENDENCY

A vital element was achingly absent. I'd lost my fire and it would take years to recover. After three months of exquisite, treasured, hard-earned freedom, I'd fallen back into servitude. The shackles were tighter than ever, and seemingly unbreakable. I thought it impossible that I could dislike myself more than I already did, but relapsing had propelled my self-loathing into new depths. I'd had a taste of what could be, and it was *pure bliss*. Instead of hanging on to it at all costs, I heedlessly threw it away, and for that, I didn't deserve to *live*, let alone be content with myself. I now believed that my sole purpose for existing was to torture myself while en route to well-deserved obliteration, and I was determined to succeed.

Much to my exasperation, I was now dwelling in a sordid hellhole I'd dubbed "The Snake Pit," and drowning in one of those tempestuous, drug-fueled relationships I'd vowed to avoid. I wanted to love Wes, but he was sucking out what little life I had remaining, making it instinctively easier to hate. He and I were two lost, fragmented souls who couldn't have been more temperamentally incompatible, and common interests can only carry a relationship so far, especially when the primary common interest is drug abuse. While most couples try to avoid conflict, Wes and I pursued and gorged on it, quarreling out of necessity, as though it were a life-sustaining medication, like insulin to a diabetic. We fought and made up, fought and made up, fought and made up, fought and made up, fought and made up, fought and made up, fought and made up. It was *unbearable*, and that godforsaken, crime-infested neighborhood only added to the misery. To say that North Long Beach was (and still is) dangerous and unimaginably bleak would be a gross understatement. I think anyone who's ever lived there would agree that it borders on the apocalyptic, like an alternate universe that exists in a quarantined dome, where even the oxygen is different. I was obviously visually impaired, but not stone-blind. I was fully aware that the relationship was doomed from the get-go, and would threaten to leave at least once a day, but would *allow* Wes to guilt trip me into staying. I tried my level best to remain impassive, but couldn't help feeling sorry for him. His biological father had been killed when Wes was a baby, his mother was clinically insane and had been in and out of institutions for most of his life, his family was destitute and living in squalor, his two youngest brothers had been taken away and placed into foster homes where they were viciously abused… the list of adversities was endless. Then there were the suicide threats that cropped up every other time I expressed my intention to end it. If he really wanted to overdose, hang himself, or slash his wrists, I had no business standing in his way, but couldn't shoulder another load of self-reproach, so I stayed, even though I was terminally miserable.

On a relatively positive note, Jamie was in town with her new boyfriend. She'd only been at my mother's place for a month before her parents came and dragged her to Riverside. Shortly thereafter, she and Tai ended their relationship for good. She didn't remain single for long, though. Within a week, she was committed to a gangster named Juan. Without giving him a fair chance, Wes decided that he didn't like him, but after hearing our plans to get whacked on PCP, he grudgingly agreed to come along on a double date.

Carmelitos was a deplorably rundown housing project that provided one-stop shopping for the area's junkies. Apparently, it's been somewhat renovated in recent years, but is still a far cry from that other walled community where the rich and famous reside. On the night of our double date, there wasn't a trace of PCP to be found in the entire slum, but one of the dealers referred us to an associate in Compton. Finding the place proved to be impossible. After searching in vain for an hour, Juan pulled into a gas station, where a cadaverous looking codger was loitering near the phone booth.

"Hey, check this vato out," Juan laughed, putting the car in park. "He's gotta be holdin' somethin'."

"No shit, dude," Wes said, with a scowl on his face. "Let's go talk to him."

"I think the girls should go," Juan said, glancing over at him. "You and me might freak him out."

"Yeah, I guess you're probably right, man," Wes agreed reluctantly.

He could never admit that someone else was right. It was always restricted by a "probably" or some other qualifier.

"Here, baby," Juan said, handing Jamie a fifty, "go hit him up."

As she and I approached the stranger, I noticed that he was much younger than I'd originally thought. He was shocked to see a couple of white girls walking toward him, and immediately put up his guard.

"Watcha want?" he asked, in a standoffish tone.

"Super Kool," Jamie replied, breaking down his wall with a warm smile.

"Those your men?" he asked, pointing at the car.

"Yeah," I replied, also smiling.

"What tha fuck they gotcha doin' their dirty work for 'em? This ain't no place for two white girls to be walkin' around, tell ya that much."

"Yeah, but if *they'd* approached you," I laughed, "you would have freaked out even more."

"Damn straight!" he laughed, clapping his hands together.

"So, can you set us up or what?" Jamie asked, flashing the bill.

"Hell yeah, I can set y'all up. Got room for me in that lowrider?"

"The front seat has your name on it," I replied.

Upon arriving at his place, he went inside and quickly returned with a triple dose of the poison. Once the sale was complete, Juan insisted that the stranger, who I'll call Half Dead, light one and take the first drag, like a king ordering his courtier to taste the food. When buying PCP from an unknown source, you could never be certain if it was pure, or lethal for that matter. It was not only pure, but inordinately potent as well. Before the first stick had burned out, Juan fired up another.

One time-lapsed hour later, I found myself lying next to Jamie on the living room floor, where she and Juan were staying, with Isao Tomita's *The Planets* wafting from the stereo speakers. Out of the corner of my eye, I saw Wes and Juan standing in the dining room, smoking the remaining Kool. A disastrously ill-considered move. If you've witnessed a PCP overdose, then you know exactly how disturbing it can be. If you haven't? Well, drooling, violent disgorgement, loss of coordination, and demoniac convulsions are but a few of the symptoms. Juan recovered rather quickly, after puking for the fifth time, but Wes looked as though he were about to sprout horns and a tail. At one point I was certain he'd croaked, which scared the shit out of me for purely selfish reasons. All I could think was: *"Shit! Shit! Shit! What the fuck are we going to tell the cops?"* I immediately began performing CPR, but abruptly stopped when he nearly drenched my face with projectile vomit. By dawn, the worst had passed, and after washing down a loaf of pumpkin bread with a quart of milk, he passed out on the kitchen floor.

The nightmarish experience terrified Wes into swearing off PCP forever. I, of course, had no intention of ending my hate-hate relationship with the drug, especially in light of the newfound connection and his perilously potent product. Less than a week later, Jamie and I paid Half Dead a visit. A day that will remain inextricably linked with N.W.A.'s *Straight Outta Compton*, which was pouring into my ears, as I inhaled the poison, feeling as though I were an actor in a formulaic scene dripping with dramatic irony. Unlike the first meeting, Half Dead didn't ask for any money in return, which was how business would be conducted from that point on. Although I can't say for certain, I think he enjoyed the company. Given my predisposition for abusing the hell out of whatever drugs were up for grabs, it was a disaster in the making. PCP and its depersonalizing effects propelled my already unstable mind into a state of nihilistic psychosis that delivered its own form of intoxication. There was a warped and almost shameful feeling of liberation that came from truly not giving a shit. I'm not referring to the "I don't care what anyone thinks! Fuck them all!" bluster that's often ejaculated by people who do indeed care what others think, as evidenced by their need to declare otherwise. I mean, not caring if or when you croak, as long as it's not unduly prolonged or painful. When that fear of death is not only removed, but replaced by its antithesis, a person can become illusively immortal – a delusion that can lead to unthinkably irrational behavior and pseudo-nerve in situations that should be intimidating.

A case in point occurred shortly after that second trip to Half Dead's. I was at a dealer's place, a couple of blocks over from The Snake Pit. When I emerged, there was a patrol car idling across the street. I wasn't holding any drugs, but was on the tail end of a three-day meth binge and had just smoked some PCP laced marijuana. Rather than attempting to circumvent the conspicuous trap, I walked right into it. After a brief interrogation, I was groped, cuffed, and forced into the car, then threatened with bogus charges, ranging from possession to theft, with my release being dependent upon my "cooperation." Meaning: sexual extortion. I can't begin to express the level of rage I was feeling. If I'd been holding a semiautomatic, I would have pumped the entire clip into the bastards without a modicum of hesitation. Any fear I should have been feeling was completely overpowered by my instinctive indignation. Coupled with the cocktail of drugs coursing through my bloodstream, I was a loose cannon. Obviously, I had no intention of indulging them, nor did I want to spend one nanosecond in a cage. They were goons, riding a wave of false power and using duress as a means of "seduction." The only way to extricate myself from the situation was to feign apathy rather than show fear, which would only empower them.

"Sorry to disappoint you," I scoffed, "but I'm not scared. Go ahead and run me in, I really don't give a flying fuck."

"You'll be singing a different tune once you're behind bars," Salt said with a nefarious grin.

"I'll be singing a tune of freedom, because I'll finally be out of this shithole of a neighborhood, and my miserable excuse for a relationship. Let's go."

"Do you know what you're facing?" Pepper said sternly.

"Yes, three square meals and a roof over my head."

The exchange continued in the same vein until they finally realized I wasn't going to break.

"You know we were only kidding about the blowjobs, right?" Salt said, laughing.

"Yeah, we just wanted to teach you a lesson," Pepper added, also laughing.

I didn't find it remotely funny, and guarantee that if I'd yielded, they would have welcomed my "services" with open flies. It was insulting and humiliating, and the fact that I was a minor only seemed to encourage them. I was furious that these motherfuckers who'd taken an oath to "serve and protect" were exploiting their positions of power by demanding sex in return for my freedom.

After sparring with them for a while longer, I told them that my brother knew the Mayor of Long Beach and there would be hell to pay if I wasn't released at once. Of course I was lying, but coincidentally, my brother does know the current Mayor of Long Beach.

"Consider it your lucky day," Salt said, opening the door and removing the cuffs, "but we'll be watching you, and if you fuck up again, you won't be so lucky."

I glared at him and casually walked away. As soon as I turned the corner, reality set in, and I ran like hell.

There are plenty of decent, respectable, and ethical police officers out there, some of whom I've known personally, but my myriad run-ins with the

303

rogue variety ingrained a deep mistrust at an uncommonly young age. I freely admit that when I was violating the law, the cops had every right to do their job. It was what they did "beyond the call of duty" that engendered my justifiable cynicism. My girlfriends and I were often groped and hit on. Then there were those pigs who carried on relationships with friends of mine when they were minors. I mentioned one earlier, if you recall. I had another girlfriend who was only thirteen when she embarked on a torrid affair with a local cop, who'd initiated the illicit dalliance. Granted, she was a shameless slut by her own admission, but it was still statutory rape being committed by an officer of the law. *WRONG*, no matter how you look at it.

WITCH HAZEL

I had accomplished a remarkable feat: I'd earned my diploma a year early via the continuation school's independent study program. Maybe I wasn't such an underachieving fuckup after all. With mandatory education in the dust, my mother strongly suggested that I get and *keep* a job. She was concerned about my future, and with good reason. Although she had no idea I was back on drugs, it was no secret that I was an insubordinate slacker whose employment record read like a rap sheet. I had no interest in resuming my role as drudge, even for one day, but pounded the pavement anyway, knowing it wouldn't lead anywhere. Much to my surprise, I landed a customer service position that offered a sufficient salary, paid vacation time and sick days, health insurance, and weekends off. It couldn't have been more perfect, as far as jobs go. The boss was laid back and easy to get along with to boot, which increased the potential for longevity. Since I was used to keeping vampire hours, the schedule took some getting used to, but thanks to my trusty pal methamphetamine, I adjusted rather quickly. Perhaps the best part about the gig was that I finally acquired a car. Legally, that is. Of course it was a barely running piece of shit with leaking brake lines that nearly ended lives on more than one occasion, but having my own wheels afforded a sense of freedom I'd never known before.

In other news, Mia had a new boyfriend who was twice her age. She'd found him at a fundamentalist Christian church, of all places. He was a cobalt-eyed, square-jawed New Englander with a thick non-rhotic accent. She'd brought him over to my mother's place the night she'd picked him up, but the meeting was brief and uninformative. I was able to determine with absolute certainty, however, that he was a dubious character.

The following weekend, the three of us went to lunch at Marie Callender's, where Jesus Freak – as he shall be known from here on out – wasted no time in starting in on me about Our Lord and Savior.

"Have you been saved?" he asked in a presumptuous tone.

"From what?" I said flippantly.

"Not *from what*," he hissed, holding up his forefinger and smiling disingenuously, "*by whom*."

Was he serious? Listen, I respect everyone's right to worship (or not) as they choose, but take umbrage when someone tries to shove their religion (or lack of) down my throat. I find it annoyingly violative, as though a finger were being poked into my ear repeatedly.

"I'm going to stop you right there," I said calmly. "You're barking up the wrong fig tree, and I don't want to say anything that might offend you, so I suggest you cool it with the Holy Joe shit."

Mia began clapping her hands and giggling gleefully. She'd never once attempted to convert me herself, but derived great pleasure from watching the efforts of others.

"You mean, *you don't believe*?" he gasped, as though I'd just admitted to having sex with Hamadryas Baboons.

"I believe in nihilism," I replied, smirking and giving him the evil eye.

I was not a nihilist in the philosophical sense, but the futile and entirely subjective argument was now underway, thanks to this intrusive prick.

"It's never too late to find Salvation," he said, returning the evil eye.

"From what?" I laughed.

"We are *all* God's children," he continued, ignoring my remark. "He loves every one of us, even if we haven't loved Him."

"That's not what I heard," I retorted with a derisive smile. "Apparently, *he* has a slight problem with homosexuals."

"No, no, no, my dear!" he exclaimed, waving his forefinger in the air. "God loves *all* of His children *equally*, whether they be reprobates, heathens, or believers! He proved this by sending His son to die for our sins!"

"Hmmmm, reprobates and heathens, huh?" I said mockingly. "Well, god damn! That must mean he loves little old *meeee*!"

"Why, of course He does! You're His child!"

"Hey," I said, struggling to maintain a shred of seriousness, "you're obviously very devoted to your religion, and I can respect that, but you're getting on my last nerve."

"Christianity is a beautiful thing!" he blurted out defensively with veins bulging from his forehead.

"Why are you so loath to believe? It's awfully narrow of you!"

Excuse me, *I* was narrow?

MATTHEW 7: 1–5

JUDGE NOT, THAT YE BE NOT JUDGED.

FOR WITH WHAT JUDGMENT YE JUDGE, YE SHALL BE JUDGED: AND WITH WHAT MEASURE YE METE, IT SHALL BE MEASURED TO YOU AGAIN.

AND WHY BEHOLDEST THOU THE MOTE THAT IS IN THY BROTHER'S EYE, BUT CONSIDEREST NOT THE BEAM THAT IS IN THINE OWN EYE?

OR HOW WILT THOU SAY TO THY BROTHER, LET ME PULL OUT THE MOTE OUT OF THINE EYE; AND, BEHOLD, A BEAM IS IN THINE OWN EYE?

THOU HYPOCRITE, FIRST CAST OUT THE BEAM OUT OF THINE OWN EYE; AND THEN SHALT THOU SEE CLEARLY TO CAST OUT THE MOTE OUT OF THY BROTHER'S EYE.

The whited sepulcher had succeeded in getting my dander up, and naturally, I felt obliged to return the favor. If I hadn't been so euphorically stoned, I would have flung the salt shaker at his vexingly sanctimonious skull, but the valium and marijuana cocktail I'd ingested an hour earlier had subdued my hair-trigger temper.

"I believe in a new kind of Jesus," I said in a twangy Southern drawl, "one that can't waste his blood redeeming people with it, because he's all man and ain't got any god in him. My church is the Church Without Christ!"

Mia started to laugh, as did I.

Jesus Freak was miffed. "That's real cute," he said, grinning sinisterly and tapping his fingers on the table. "Someone's been reading Flannery O'Connor."

"Ding ding ding ding ding!" I yelled, clapping my hands.

"You must be one of those flaky, intellectual, bohemian types who smoke grass and read poetry all day long."

"You're right about the flakiness and grass smoking, my bible thumping friend, but I'm a fucking scatterbrain by nature, and I don't like most poetry unless it's accompanied by instruments."

"She means music," Mia interjected.

"And I'm not singling out Christianity," I continued, "I'm an equal opportunity infidel... *all* religions are anathema to me."

Before he had a chance to respond, the waitress returned with a tray holding three glasses of ice water. After ejaculating the daily specials, she went to get iced teas for Mia and Jesus Freak.

"I have to use the washroom, honey," Jesus Freak announced, sliding out of the booth. "If the waitress comes while I'm gone, please order the meatloaf for me."

"Will do, honey," Mia said, smiling girlishly.

As soon as he took the corner, she asked the expected question.

"So, what do you think?"

I cleared my throat and replied, "Would you like the polite answer or the truth?"

She burst out laughing.

"You're not serious, are you?" I said incredulously. "I hope to fucking god you're just amusing yourself for a week or two!"

"Why? What's wrong with him?" she asked, still laughing.

"Where should I start?" I scoffed.

"It's the age difference, isn't it," she said, removing several packets of sugar from the ceramic holder and placing them next to her spoon.

It was a reasonable assumption, but wrong. Now that "maturity" was looming, I'd decided that age was trivial, and if two people were into each other, a number shouldn't serve as a deterrent. Moreover, I'd always known that older men had a lot to offer. And no, I'm not referring to earthly possessions, but rather experience, wisdom, and mental stimulation. They'd always made wonderful friends, so why on earth wouldn't they make wonderful partners? It seemed like a logical inference. I wasn't so sure about Jesus Freak, though. He had about as much sex appeal as Jerry Falwell, and reeked of svengalism. I couldn't figure out what Mia possibly saw in him. I thought he was devious, self-righteous, and utterly revolting. Although I'd just met him, I could clearly see that he didn't possess one *redeeming* quality. I should have lied and told her he was too old, but didn't.

"I wouldn't give a shit if he were fifty, as long as he treats you well."

"Is it the accent?" she asked, chomping on a mouthful of ice.

"Come on, you know me better than that."

"What the fuck then?"

"He's fucking creepy," I said, taking a gulp of water. "I don't know what it is, but something's just not right there."

"What do you mean?" she asked, staring at me searchingly.

"I don't know, he reminds me of someone, but I can't put my finger on it."

"Who?" she asked, smiling and leaning forward, as though she were giving me a hint.

After puzzling over the matter for a moment longer, it struck me like a gamma blast: "He's like a mutant hybrid of RFK and Reverend Harry Powell."

"I know!" she exclaimed, grinning wildly. "Isn't it fucking cool?"

"You're sick," I laughed. "You need help."

She broke into a wicked cackle.

"Have you had a chance to decide?" the waitress asked, placing the iced teas and straws on the table.

I ordered a turkey sandwich and a bowl of cheese soup. Mia ordered a French dip with extra au jus and a salad with Thousand Island dressing for herself, then ordered Jesus Freak's meatloaf.

"Would your father like soup or salad with his meatloaf?" the waitress asked with a phony smile that screamed "*I HATE MY FUCKING JOB!!!!!*"

Mia glanced over and grinned mischievously, then kicked my leg under the table, indicating that she was going to fuck with the poor girl, and that I should play along. "I don't know, here he comes," she said, as Jesus Freak approached the table. "Hey Dad, do you want soup or salad with your meatloaf?"

"Oh, I'll have salad please," he said, sitting down and placing his napkin on his lap, completely oblivious to the fact that she'd called him Dad. "With honey mustard dressing and no croutons."

Before he knew what hit him, Mia threw her arms around him and began lapping at his neck, like a parched kitten. "Mmmmm," she purred between licks, "you taste yummy, Daddy!"

I thought the waitress was going to drop dead from shock. She froze, and gaped in horror.

"Incest is best," I said nonchalantly, shrugging my shoulders.

She dropped her notepad on the floor, and made a frantic dash for the kitchen, stumbling the whole way. Our food was later served by a busboy.

A month later, Mia dumped Jesus Freak and began dating his polar opposite, Sam. As a chum Sam was a hoot and a half, but as a boyfriend he was bad news. His love for Mia was undeniable. Nearly every man who crossed her path fell in love with her to some degree, it couldn't be helped. Sam was lucky enough to have his love requited, but shortly after winning her heart, he metamorphosed into an insensitive, insincere, untrustworthy scoundrel, who took her for granted. I've always wondered why sharing hearts and bodily fluids can change certain people in such a negative manner. I suppose the fact that Mia and Sam's relationship revolved around drugs didn't help either. But enough on that, back to the subject at hand…

Despite being surrounded by scores of lusty, virile men, Mia had kept her maidenhead intact. Early on in our friendship, she and I had taken a virginity oath. Being constantly torn between Hedonism and Catholicism, she wanted to save herself for marriage, while I simply wanted to wait until I'd found "the right one," whatever the hell that meant. As I mentioned earlier, I could be driven into a state of homicidal rage whenever some lying sack of shit claimed I'd slept with him when I hadn't, and unfortunately, there were plenty of lying sacks of shit. The culprits typically fell into two categories: vengeful candymen I'd jerked around, and disgruntled jocks who were probably suffering from steroid-induced erectile dysfunction. The former were simply trying to save face, which I can understand, in a way, although it was still *wrong*. There was absolutely *no excuse* for the latter, though. While it may seem trivial to some, being the victim of a sexual assault can flay even the thickest of skins, and when it comes to healing psychological wounds, one size does *not* fit all. The rumors hurt to the quick, like the incessant teasing had in elementary school, and once again, I couldn't do much about it. People are going to believe what they want to believe, especially when it comes to malicious gossip, which is like a drug for some. In order to cope at the time, I had to tune it out, but I never forgave *or* forgot, and when a handful of the bastards died over the years, I didn't shed one tear. Naturally, and ridiculously, Mia was the subject of similar rumors – an even greater indignity, given her very sincere moral convictions.

It was on a Monday afternoon that she dropped by my mother's place to discuss a matter of biblical importance. I was riding out a mushroom induced hangover, and had called in sick to work that day. Around noon, I was lying in bed, devouring Blaise Cendrars' *Moravagine* for the first time, when I heard a horn honking outside. Being in a horribly unsocial mood, I tuned out the blaring sound and continued reading, hoping the intrusive pest would fuck off, but he/she/it was tenaciously persistent. I finally went to the window to investigate. Peeking through the blinds, I saw a brand new, yet unidentifiable compact car idling in the driveway. I took a closer look, and saw Mia sitting behind the wheel, waving up at me. I finished the page I was reading, then threw on some shorts and shoes, and went outside. She was now sitting in the passenger's seat with the windows down.

"Where the fuck did this come from?" I asked, leaning into the driver's side window and having a look around.

"Hop in," she said, smiling and flashing a fat joint. "I need to talk to you about something."

"Okay," I yawned, "let me get my keys and lock the front door."

"Grab some tunes too," she yelled, as I walked back into the house.

Three minutes later, I was behind the wheel, heading toward the park up the street. "So, where did you get the go-kart?" I asked.

"Mono," she replied, passing the joint.

"Mono?" I asked, taking an enormous drag. "I thought he was in the county hotel?"

"He was. They sprung him this morning and his ride didn't show up."

Mono was her clean-cut, religious, law-abiding brother-in-law's errant identical twin, who'd first come into our lives via the Tecate Flats pandilla.

"Let me guess," I said sarcastically.

She snatched the joint from my hand and began giggling impishly.

What the hell. I suppose he had to get home somehow. I was mildly concerned about the car's ultimate plans, though. Although auto theft had always been a risky business, the stakes had been raised considerably with the arrival of adulthood.

"You're not planning on keeping it, are you?" I asked. "With your shitty driving it'll only be a matter of time before you get pulled over, and then you'll really be fucked."

"No," she replied, exhaling, "the usual drill. I'm just borrowing it for a couple of hours."

"Good," I said, taking the joint from her hand. "If we get popped now, they're not going to call our parents anymore. Those days are over."

"Tell me about it," she agreed, fiddling with the stereo. "It fucking sucks."

Upon arriving at the park, I went to kill the motor, but Mia quickly intervened.

"Don't turn it off," she said, tugging at my arm. "It might not restart."

"What the fuck did he do here?" I asked, admiring Mono's handiwork, which looked like a third-grader's electrical engineering experiment gone awry.

"What do you want?" she laughed. "He was in a hurry."

After taking one more drag each, she extinguished the joint and turned toward me with an anxious look on her face, as though she were waiting for me to start the conversation.

"So," I asked, lowering the volume on the stereo, "what did you want to talk about?"

"I've decided to give myself to Sam."

Not what I was expecting, *at all*. "What brought this on?" I asked.

"I'm hopelessly in love with him," she replied, beaming girlishly. "I've never felt this way about anyone before. He's perfect in every way. He's my soul mate. I want to marry him and bear his children."

"Is that all?" I asked, smiling.

"Yeah, that, and I'm fucking horny," she giggled. "I can't hold out any longer."

"I knew there was more to it."

"So, what do you think?"

"Go for it, if it feels right," I replied, after taking

a moment to think, "but don't forget, you're only a virgin once. Once that cherry's popped, it's popped, you can't re-grow it."

"Yeah, I know," she said, staring at some crows that had gathered around the car.

"And," I continued, "you'll spend the rest of your life knowing that you lost your virginity to Sam, whether you end up marrying him or not."

"Yeah, I know," she repeated, still staring at the crows.

"That's some pretty heavy shit, Miss Catholic Guilt. Can you live with it?"

"Live with what?"

"Knowing that you lost your virginity to Sam, you fucking space cadet! Have you heard one word I've said?"

"Yeah, I heard you," she grumbled, frowning. "Leave me the fuck alone, I'm thinking."

"Don't hurt yourself," I said, smiling. "I can see smoke coming out of your ears."

"Clean my dick!" she snapped back.

"You finally brought that one out of retirement, huh?" I laughed.

Her irritable scowl turned into a wide grin. "You know it was always my favorite," she said in a Liberace voice.

"So, what's the verdict?"

She didn't respond.

"I don't have all day, you know."

She turned up the volume on the stereo and began singing along with Al Green, who was blaring out of the speakers.

"Listen," I said, raising my voice over the music, "it's not like you have to make up your mind right this second. Mull it over for a while, that's what I'd do. Believe me, Sam's not going anywhere."

She stopped singing, turned down the volume, and looked directly at me with a blank expression on her face.

"Okay?" I said. "Are you finished with me now? I want to get back to that book I was reading. It's fucking insane."

She stared at me for a moment longer, then abruptly flipped around and retrieved a canvas tote sack from the back seat. "Should we see if we can break our record?" she asked, grinning and shaking the bag.

"Is that thing filled with quarters?"

"Damn straight."

As lousy as I felt, I couldn't refuse. "Why the fuck not," I sighed.

"Woooo hoooo!" she exclaimed, beaming and clapping.

After returning the hot car to Mono, we walked up to the bowling alley and spent the rest of the day playing a record-breaking game of Double Dragon.

BURIDAN'S ASS
TAP DANCING AT
MORTON'S FORK

I was plodding through one of the most miserable and squandered years of my short life. Engulfed by unbearable agitation, agonizing despondency, and crippling irresolution, the only "noteworthy" events were dreadful at best.

Wes had been working on my last nerve for ages. It was only going to be a matter of time before I murdered him. It was on a scorching Saturday afternoon that our perpetual bickering took the inevitable violent turn. We were en route to pick up Vince for a day at the beach, and already running late, when Wes insisted on making a pit stop at the local grease joint.

"What the fuck are you doing?" I asked, turning down the stereo. "He's waiting for us."

He ignored me and parked the car.

"Fucking asshole," I sighed, staring out the window as he opened the door.

When he went inside, I climbed over the console and reclaimed the helm. Ten minutes later he emerged with a boxful of food, a king-size cola, and a strawberry milkshake. As he approached the car, I thought about how much I *hated* him. I was never in love with him, but did feel love for him. The same kind of love one would feel for a malodorous, mangy, three-legged mongrel with cataracts. It was probably out of pity at that point, but I did have feelings for him, even though I wanted him to drop dead right there. I couldn't find a single reason for him to continue breathing, and contemplated whether I should kill him. All I'd have to do is start the engine, put it into gear, and plow him down. He'd be out of my life forever. I now found him so repulsive it seemed impossible that I'd *ever* been attracted to him. It had been weeks since I'd had sex with him, despite the fact that he expected it at least every other day, and would throw temper tantrums if I didn't cooperate. For a while I complied simply to silence him, but it was becoming increasingly more painful, since I couldn't get aroused. He was always pathetic and self-serving in the sack, but now it was like being raped, only worse, because I *allowed* it, and not just once, but *repeatedly*. I couldn't change the past, but sure as hell could, and would, change the present. He would *never* touch me again. I'd chop off his testicles first.

"Move over!" he yelled, poking his mug into the driver's side window. "I'm driving!"

"Fuck you," I hissed, cutting through him with my eyes. "Get in or stay here, I really don't give a shit what you do, but you're not driving my car anymore."

He glared for a moment, then walked around to the passenger's side and got in. "Fine," he muttered, turning up the stereo, "I can eat my chow."

As I entered the freeway, I glanced over and noticed that he was spilling food all over my recently shampooed upholstery. "You're a fucking pig," I said angrily. "You're slopping shit all over my car. Cut it out."

"You mean, like this?" he laughed, removing the lid from his cup and dumping the cola on the floor.

"Motherfucker!" I yelled, knocking the cup out of his hand.

Then, without any warning, he smashed a cheeseburger into my face, leaving a mask of Thousand Island dressing, shredded lettuce, grilled onions, tomatoes, pickles, American cheese and medium rare ground beef. Worse yet, my nose ring, which I never wore anymore, had been torn out, resulting in a laceration, and subsequently, a visible scar. I was covered with slime, bleeding, and murderously enraged.

"You fucking cocksucker!" I screamed, smacking the back of his head.

He retaliated by smashing the strawberry milkshake against the ceiling above my head.

I shoved him as hard as I could, and delivered another smack to his head.

"Owwww!" he screamed, returning the smack. "You fuckin' bitch!"

Keep in mind that the car was traveling at seventy miles per hour on a crowded Southern California freeway, and as usual, I was loaded out of my mind.

Right when I thought it was going to wind down, he picked up the wooden crate that held a nice chunk of my music collection, rolled down the window, and tossed it. I was *livid*. After taking a couple of deep breaths to restrain my overpowering urge to defenestrate *him*, I grabbed the boxful of food and defenestrated *it* instead. Imagining it was him, of course.

There was a moment of silence, as I removed my shirt and began wiping my face clean. Then he launched into the expected masturbatory sulking fit, taking no responsibility for his part in what had just occurred. In his underdeveloped, twisted mind I was always entirely to blame.

When we arrived at Vince's, I did my best to pretend that all was fine, even though he could clearly see there had been a(nother) scuffle. My stubborn pride again. The incessant shit I was tolerating was humiliating enough. I didn't need others to know, especially since I'd always been so critical of "tempestuous, drug-fueled relationships that should have been over before they began." I was not only a failure, but a hypocrite as well.

In addition to that scuffle, there were some other black-letter moments that deserve mentioning…

Merely days after my birthday, I snorted the longest, fattest line of methamphetamine to ever occupy a mirror. On a dare. Hands down, one of the most suicidal stunts I'd ever performed, and within minutes, I was in full cardiac arrest. Or so I thought. At first I didn't care if I croaked, but it wasn't happening as quickly as I would have liked, and the excruciating discomfort was too much to ignore. It wasn't long before I made a mad dash for the emergency room. As I looked over the mandatory paperwork, I realized that coming to a hospital wasn't such a bright idea after all. What if they called the cops? I dropped the clipboard and made a madder dash for the exit.

The remainder of the day was spent sweating, trembling, and vomiting convulsively. The crushing sensation in my chest was ferocious, and my entire body – from my kidneys to my teeth – was aching so intensely I was certain Death had finally come to claim what was owed ten times over. I kept attempting to mitigate the torture with drugs and food, but couldn't even hold down saliva. Around midnight, the next door neighbor provided the cure with a lethal dose of morphine. I was out cold for seventeen hours, and despite what Wes claimed, my waking condition clearly indicated that he hadn't gone to any lengths to ensure that I was okay, let alone alive.

Despite the unprecedentedly horrific nature of the experience, I only waited two days before shoveling more strychnine into my nostrils.

Let's see, what else…

In June I attended my graduation and what would turn out to be my last Garth shindig. Wes hadn't come along that night and with good reason: I didn't want him there. I'd reached a point where I couldn't stomach being within ten miles of him. Besides, bringing him to Garth's would have been sacrilegious, it was one of the only places I could call my own. But Wes was a green-eyed bastard, and not in the way you'd assume. Believe it or not, as pathologically insecure and possessive as he was, he wasn't the least bit jealous of my numerous male friends. From the outset, I'd made it perfectly clear that they were family, giving Wes no choice but to accept them. He was, however, lividly jealous whenever I did drugs without him. How absurdly dysfunctional is that? What a sick fuck. And I was an even sicker fuck for remaining in the relationship.

I spent the night snorting myself into oblivion until my nose began to hemorrhage, which was the only reason I stopped. It was an utter drag. I was ready to go until dawn and beyond, but my nose was dripping like a faucet with a worn washer. I was "forced" to move on to the smack until I passed out.

The following afternoon, I returned home to find volumes of messages from Wes. I was frazzled, and in no condition to deal with him, even if I'd wanted to. I washed down a couple of sleeping pills Garth had given me, and drifted off.

That evening, my stepbrother knocked on my bedroom door. "Hey, Wes is on the phone, he says it's important."

Important, my ass, I thought, *I can just imagine*.

I didn't respond.

"Do you want me to tell him you're not here?" he laughed, being all too familiar with the drill.

It was tempting, but being the masochist I was, I decided to take the call. *Astronomical mistake*. Wes was consistently insufferable, but when it came to his twisted concept of "infidelity" he never failed to outdo himself, like a paranoid, jealous, clingy, nagging wife. Why couldn't I bring myself to leave him? In retrospect, I've realized that Wes was simply another drug, albeit the most irritating drug of all, but a drug nonetheless. I've also realized that my relationship with him was far more damaging to my spirit than all of the substance abuse combined. That said, the constant friction was key to my escape from that entire phase of my life, including the shackles of addiction. If there had been even a modicum of joy, I would have remained indefinitely.

And right when I thought it couldn't get any worse. On a whim, Wes adopted a Reticulated Python that was five yards long and weighed eighty pounds. The snake quickly outgrew the aquarium she'd arrived in, and Wes was too cheap to upgrade. His solution was to leave the lid wide open, allowing the creature to slither throughout the house. I frequently ran into her in the kitchen and bathroom, and there were far too many nights when I awoke to find her "snuggling up to me" in bed. A childhood trauma had sparked an intense aversion to snakes that's persisted throughout my life. If I hadn't been perpetually drugged out of my gourd, I wouldn't have lasted one day in that environment.

Wes soon realized that he could garner attention, praise, and above all, drugs from the biker neighbors by feeding the snake on the front lawn. It became a daily ritual, and before long, the meals – which had always consisted of mice and rats – became sacrificial offerings in the form of bunnies, baby chicks, and other cuddly critters. It was cruel, perverse, and completely at odds with my conscience. After tolerating it for longer than I should have, I returned to my mother's house for a much needed respite.

The following day, I was reading in my room, when I heard a cat crying. I followed the sound to the house across the street. There, cowering in the bushes, was a precious black short-haired kitten. It was emaciated, trembling, and bleeding from the mouth. I ran back to the house, and returned with some cheese, hoping to lure it out. Much to my vexation, it ate every chunk and quickly ducked back into the thicket before I could grab it. The tiny wounded creature was trying my patience, which was lacking to begin with, but I refused to give up. An hour later, it finally emerged. After learning it was a tom, I christened him Joe.

The next week was spent nursing Joe back to health, and as soon as he was well enough, he became my new sidekick. Unlike most cats, he enjoyed riding in a car. He'd sit contentedly in the passenger's seat, vigorously licking every crevice of his body with his pink tongue. He was the ideal companion: adorable, easygoing, meticulously clean, and a delightful listener. Unfortunately, my mother wasn't as crazy about him as I was, and insisted that I find him a new home right away.

As expected, it wasn't long before I returned to The Snake Pit for another helping of misery, bringing Joe along for the ride. The instant Wes' endearingly schizoid mother laid eyes on the cat, she fell head over heels. Joe had a new owner, someone who'd give him the love, care, and affection he so greatly deserved, after being dumped in the street like a used condom. He was happy, Wes' mother was happy, and I was happy. For a moment, at least.

When I returned from work the following night, there was no sign of Joe or Wes. I immediately asked Wes' teenage brother about Joe's whereabouts. Wes could have been in a Turkish prison for all I cared.

"Oh... um... oh," the kid said, fidgeting nervously, "that old lady down the street has him."

"And why is that?" I asked, staring directly into his shifty eyes.

"I dunno," he replied, looking up at the ceiling. "She just wanted him, so I gave him to her."

Lying was not one of the kid's strong suits. I wasn't buying it for a second.

"I know you're lying," I said, putting him in a headlock. "Now tell me where the cat is or I'll kick your ass."

When I heard the truth I nearly vomited. That sweet, innocent, helpless kitten, who'd already suffered the most unthinkable cruelty, had been fed to the snake! In my wrathful eyes, Wes was the leftover scrapings of an abortion. If I could have fed *him* to that snake, I would have done it in a heartbeat. I wanted to watch him shriek in terror and writhe in agony. I wanted to see his evil beady eyes explode as his beloved snake choked the life out of him. I wanted to watch his rotten carcass disappear forever, inch by inch, as she devoured him whole. At that moment I wanted him dead, and it's lucky I didn't have access to a gun, because I would have shot him on sight.

When he came walking through the door, I wasted no time in confronting him. He vehemently denied it at first, but soon broke into his "shifting the blame" dance. What ensued was the nastiest altercation we'd ever had. It's a miracle it didn't progress into a fist fight. To avoid redundancy, I'll let you fill in the blanks. And in spite of it all, I found myself lying next to him again that night.

Around three a.m. I was jolted awake by the snake, who was attempting to scale the wall directly beside me. Without giving it another thought, I got up, retrieved the Louisville Slugger from the kid brother's room, and returned to the bedroom to do what I should have done ages ago.

As I stood over Wes' dormant body, watching his respirations, I weighed the pros and cons of what I was about to do. A minute later, I hoisted the bat over my head, zeroed in on his cranium with my foggy eyes, and... crumbled into pieces.

Wes threw off the blanket and made some grumbling sounds, then rolled over onto his side.

Not wanting him to know what I'd nearly done, I stifled the sobbing and rushed out of the room, murder weapon in hand.

I don't know how I managed to stop myself. The feeling was indescribably horrible. There isn't a shred of gratification to be derived from truly wanting someone dead and coming frighteningly close to taking that person's life. My anguish, hatred, and rage had reached treacherous levels, driven by my inability (refusal?) to end a relationship that should have been over before it had begun. The cages one enters of one's own volition are often the most difficult to escape from. I felt trapped, and murder or suicide seemed to be the only way out.

EIGHTH CIRCUIT COURT OF APPEALS

Addiction is a war of attrition that inevitably ends in premature death, even if one is still breathing. On the longest day of the year, I floated across the threshold of Death's door with my pulse intact. My desperate and persistent attempts to seduce rock bottom were invariably met with merciless rejection. A life-threatening meth habit, combined with a masochistic fondness for angel dust, a handful of unprecedentedly traumatic acid trips, and a carcinogenic relationship had laid waste to my spirit. I was a wraith, meandering in search of eternal quietus.

The first half of the year had been a monotonous continuation of the perpetual self-imposed prison sentence: rotting away in The Snake Pit, enduring the torturous relationship that was saturating my mind with murderous thoughts, and forlornly pursuing emotional paralysis via self-anesthetization. I was caught up in a vicious rip current, and all attempts to swim out were in vain. The only option seemed to be floating along until my lifeless body washed ashore. Or, opening my lungs and inhaling the contaminated water until I drowned, which I nearly did at the onset of the second half.

There is no way to describe The Mortal Plunge without it sounding over the top, borderline redundant and parodic, which it was. I've likened it to zooming down a highway at a hundred miles per hour with my eyes closed. Similar to Aversion Therapy, it was a series of events that seemed to be driven by some cosmic intervention designed to override my staunch allegiance to self-annihilation.

The first event occurred early one morning, when Wes lost control of his vehicle while tearing around a corner. The result was a head-on collision with a parked car. I instinctively threw my hands forward, as if I were breaking a fall. Aside from being rattled and suffering minor wrist sprains, I climbed out unscathed. Wes walked away physically intact, but the hit-and-run accident would cost him his driver's license and a heap of money.

The second event occurred two days later, when I was struck by a car while jaywalking. I had just embarked on a PCP jag, making my visceral reaction beyond irrational. Seeing it as an affront rather than an accident *I* had caused, I impulsively climbed up onto the hood and attempted to kick in the windshield. Understandably, the driver panicked and gunned it. I fell to the ground and lay there for a moment, before getting up, dusting myself off, and stumbling back to The Snake Pit.

The following day I attempted to drive Wes' motorcycle into a lamppost. Contrary to what you may be thinking, it was not a suicidal act. Still under PCP's perverse influence, I'd convinced myself that I was immortal, and felt impelled to prove it. Luckily, the bike had different plans and took a tumble instead. I was banged up and disoriented, but otherwise no worse for wear.

Two nights later, while walking home from the local convenience store, a large and scary looking man jumped out from behind a building. I'll never know what his motives were – he may have only wanted some spare change – but as I mentioned, it was a crime infested neighborhood, and I certainly wasn't waiting around to find out. I was carrying a plastic grocery bag containing a can of mixed nuts, which I used to whack him across the skull as hard as I could. Then I bolted without looking back.

What occurred on the following night was by far the most traumatic. While riding out the tail end of what would turn out to be my ultimate acid trip, I accidently stumbled into a cerebral terra incognita, causing a metaphysical cataclysm of immeasurable proportions. What ensued was utterly harrowing. A torturous, horrifyingly *real* nightmare that ripped through my mind, shredding what remained of my sanity. Worst of all, there was no antidote. All efforts to claw my way out were in vain. I had no choice but to tumble down the hole, hoping the inevitable metamorphosis would be manageable, or at the very least, tolerable. *If* I found my way out, that is.

I was regurgitated the following afternoon, enervated, but overcome with relief, as though I'd just emptied my bladder for the first time in three days. After taking a moment to regain my bearings, I impulsively resumed my reckless consumption of controlling substances... but something had changed... there was no longer a payoff... no matter *what* or *how much* I consumed. The law of diminishing returns, which had already kicked in a couple of years prior, had completely taken over. It seemed impossible, but my tolerance had peaked, as though I'd been rendered physically immune. My compulsion to anesthetize was more overpowering than ever, so I continued to self-medicate, regardless of the futility.

The coup de grace came two days later. My stepbrother, who I consistently smoked pot with, had come down with Chickenpox when I was on that furlough from The Snake Pit. I'd never had them, and since my immune system was shot, I was counting the hours. The first blister appeared on my right thigh, and before long, others began to sprout. I shifted into denial mode the best I could and carried on with my self-loathing, self-annihilative business, but defeat was inevitable.

That Saturday night, Wes and I attended a party at a neighbor's house. My feverish state combined with the scorching heat made it impossible to ignore the blisters any longer. There was a stinging patch on my right deltoid, begging to be torched. While a rational person would have applied Calamine Lotion or even scratched, I impulsively yanked a lit cigarette from one of the biker's mouths and drove it directly into the pox. The resulting pain put an end to the merciless itch, but I was permanently branded with two Summer Triangles. By ten p.m. I was on the verge of collapsing. I dragged my perishing carcass back to The Snake Pit and zonked out.

Half a day later, I awoke to find every inch of my body covered with Chickenpox. It was *sheer torture*, and the nadir of my stint at The Snake Pit. I looked like a monster, and the discomfort was *agonizing*. If I'd had a surefire way to whack myself, I would have done so without hesitation. I instantly reverted to the state I'd been in whenever I was sick as a child, longing for my mother and the familiarity that house once had, fraught with its memories and former incarnations of myself. Operating entirely on auto-pilot, I sewed myself together enough to make the journey home. Under the circumstances, Wes didn't argue. Although it wasn't my intention when I left, I never returned to The Snake Pit or controlling substances again.

I've been asked on numerous occasions to reveal how I beat addiction, especially since I didn't return to rehab or the Twelve Steps. Well, I believe the answer lies in that ultimate acid trip. I didn't realize it at the time, but that nightmarish upheaval, which was tantamount to a near-death experience, permanently altered my mind, and in a positive way. The Chicken Pox took it one step further by making it impossible to get my hands on any drugs, forcing the physical dependence to give up the reins. Combined with the solitude and removal of *all* negative influences, I was able to exhaustively analyze the existence I'd condemned myself to. Even though I was bedridden and suffering, due to the illness and withdrawal, I was thinking more lucidly than I had in years. What I'd thought was overwhelming and invincible was, in fact, entirely conquerable, as soon as I disempowered it. The intravenous drip that had been anaesthetizing my soul could have been yanked out at any time. I'd only fooled myself into believing it had been permanently implanted. There was a choice to be made, and I possessed the ability to make that choice. I decided right then and there that I'd rather be dead than live one more moment as a junkie, even if that meant I had to take my own life, which I had no right to do, since that life was only beginning. Liberation would require abstinence from *all* controlling substances, and would come at a price in terms of releasing the people I saw as my true family. If I wanted to survive, I had to end my relationship not only with Wes, but my comrades as well. I hoped my getting clean would inspire them to follow suit, but apart from sporadic spells of sobriety they were more addicted than ever. The only option was to walk away, and considering how eventful our time together had been, my departure was as uneventful as could be. Aside from the breakup with Wes, which was surprisingly quick and amicable, there were no tearful goodbyes, or any other kind of goodbyes. I simply made myself increasingly scarcer and eventually vanished altogether.

HOW'S YOUR BACON?

What's up? I'm doing pretty good all considering. If you haven't heard I got arrested in Nevada for my 3rd D.U.I. It's a felony and they got me good, $3000 fine and 3 yrs in prison. Pretty harsh, huh. This state sucks. I can't believe the sentences they give out here. Pot is a felony and one guy here got 3 yrs for a roach. It ain't so bad. On a 3 year sentence I'll be eligible for parole after a year. If I don't make parole, which I should, I just do an extra 6-7 months and should be out by October of next year.

It's not so bad. I was at a camp, which is minimum security, live in trailers & go into Las Vegas & clean up parks & stuff. But then I got "rolled up" & sent to the "hole" at the main prison. The "write up" got dismissed. So now I'm at the main prison yard waiting to be transferred to another camp up north by Reno. Besides, the guards at the last camp were harassing me. I don't know why! Maybe it had something to do with the fact that I shaved my head, leaving a mohawk, and got a tattoo of a cross on the right side of my head.

So what have you been up to? Still going out with Wes? If so tell him "hi". If you want to write I'd love to hear from you. Even if they transfer me they'll forward my mail. I'll keep in touch. Take care of yourself.

LT

CODA

As you undoubtedly inferred from the Prelude, the story didn't end when I closed the door on controlling substances. Even though I'd removed the external toxins from my life, I was being internally poisoned by my own hand. I was physically drug-free, but my psyche had relapsed and fallen under the influence of long dormant insecurities. I truly believed that to survive in a world intolerant of anyone with an "abnormal" background, I had to erase my past and never speak of it again, which was not only wrong, but beyond the bounds of possibility. I'd seen the unseeable, and it could *never* be unseen. Rather than accepting what I'd been through, extracting the invaluable lessons, and forging ahead, I cast it all into the benthic zone and embraced regression in the form of forced adaptation to "normal" society. As expected, it felt completely unnatural and terribly uncomfortable, as though I were squeezing my feet into pointy-toed, five-inch stiletto-heeled shoes that were three sizes too small. The constant abrasion was bound to lead to disintegration.

By the late 90s I'd deteriorated into a dysphoric, stagnant, unmotivated, borderline shut-in zombie who would only leave her tomb for food, exercise, and the occasional mandatory social function. I'd lost both my drive and identity, and was immured in an impenetrable dungeon of despondency.

The deathblow came in the final year of the 20th century. With clean blood still coursing through my veins, I suffered another mental meltdown with the assistance of two Selective Serotonin Reuptake Inhibitors that were meant to provide salvation from the coma I'd fallen into. The first, Paroxetine, was taken for three days, followed by a three-week stint with its insidious cousin, Fluoxetine. Although I was only prescribed ten milligrams, the result was a serotonin overdose that ultimately dragged my battered soul even further into the abyss. It was worse than the worst acid trip, and physically torturous to boot, with an aftermath that was equally devastating. Twenty-three days of "legal dope" led to four years of debilitating anxiety that proved to be just as damaging as any of the traumas I'd endured during my adolescence. The despondency now took second place to the blue funk and panic attacks, which were incapacitating at times. Every single day was a struggle. I couldn't find solace *anywhere*, not even in the person who had become my rock. I was certain my life was over, that I was doomed to an eternity of existence deprivation, but thankfully, I was mistaken.

After crawling through the tenebrous, thorny passage for fifty months of Sundays, the mouth of the rabbit hole appeared, and I ascended to freedom.

Apophenia is an imprint of
www.paraphiliamagazine.com

For information and to purchase other titles:
http://www.paraphiliamagazine.com/books.html

24297192R00186

Made in the USA
Charleston, SC
19 November 2013